THE NEXT 500 YEARS

THE NEXT 500 YEARS

Scientific Predictions of Major Social Trends

by

Burnham Putnam Beckwith, Ph.D.

With a Foreword by Daniel Bell, Ph.D.

An Exposition – University Book

Exposition Press  New York

EXPOSITION PRESS INC.
386 Park Avenue South New York, N.Y. 10016

FIRST EDITION

Manufactured in the United States of America

LIBRARY OF CONGRESS CATALOGUE CARD No. 67-26390

EP 45791

Foreword

It must be quite startling to open a book with the title *The Next Five Hundred Years* which is not science fiction and which carries as its subtitle, "Scientific Predictions of Major Social Trends." Five hundred years from now is almost A.D. 2500. Five hundred years before was A.D. 1467, or before the discovery of America by Columbus. Would some court seer at that time dare make predictions about the next five hundred years, years which have been marked by the most quickened pace in human history?

Several things should be noted at once. Professor Beckwith is not a seer. He is a reputable social scientist who has taught at three universities and has published several serious studies, of particular interest, one on the economics of a socialist society. Moreover, Professor Beckwith is not dealing with events or discoveries; comparable to the discovery of America, there might be space colonies on the moon and even Mars by 2500. This we cannot foretell. What he is dealing with is *trends*—their durability, their rates, and their direction, combining history, logic and statistical method in a disciplined and imaginative way.

Once we understand that Professor Beckwith is dealing with trends, and with those which have a great likelihood of continuing over centuries, then his enterprise comes into a different perspective. While it still may be startling to think of looking ahead five hundred years, one realizes that the great historians have always taken periods of several hundred years to identify and explain the major social processes which lay behind the course of civilizations and empires. It took several hundred years for Christianity to become accepted in the Western world. Five hundred years is a period one takes, as Gibbon did, to deal with the decline of the Roman Empire. Five hundred years is a normal unit in the history of ancient Egypt and certainly of classical China. What Professor Beckwith is doing is writing *prospective* rather than *retrospective* history. This is his claim to novelty.

How well can this be done? It is clear that someone writing five hundred years ago might not have done very well. He could have predicted the spread of commerce, the enlargement of knowledge of the earth, the rise of cities, the decline of manorialism and possibly of feudalism, the clash of empires and the like. But clearly he was limited by the fact that the world as he knew it was segmented and walled in; and, more than that, he had no *techniques* for studying change other than the wisdom of the race itself about human nature and human aspirations. Today the world is one, bound together by rapid transportation and instant communication, in which the linked effects of change are quickly discernible in all parts of the social system. More than that, we have begun to gather data on specific trends, and in scientific observation and controls we have a method of checking our hypotheses.

Again, it should be noted that Professor Beckwith is not making a claim to a complete description of the future. He is arguing that he can specify *relevant* major trends, gauge their rates and extrapolate the future. The key point is that he is identifying *what* will come, not *how* something will come. To this extent he is doing rightly what S. C. Gilfallen points out is the relevant technique in technological forecasting. In the matter of inventions, one can predict what kind of inventions are likely (e.g., dispersal of fog) but not how it will be achieved. In this respect, surely he is right in arguing that the future will see a continuing spread of literacy, greater urbanization, the decline of agriculture, and the like.

Basically, Professor Beckwith's method rests on two assumptions. One is that what is present in the advanced nations of the world will, at some point, find their way into the less developed sections, and what is given or held as a privilege by the upper classes will spread throughout the rest of society. Here he is applying the classical dictum of Alexis de Tocqueville that what the few have today the many will clamor for tomorrow. The second assumption is that of the spread of *rationality*. The nature of science, for example, as applied in the field of economics, is to seek for those methods which give us greater output at least cost, which provide for a greater utilization of resources with less effort, and thus increase our productivity. Professor Beckwith is assuming that man will apply more and more rational methods to his control of nature, the environment, and himself. This is behind his adoption of the Comtean scheme of social evolution.

In certain human affairs he may be right. It is likely, for example, that marginal-cost analysis will take over from average-cost procedures as a means of determining the price of goods; and this is one of Professor Beckwith's "keys" in predicting changes in economic life. But given what we know of the extraordinary excesses of human behavior, the cruel and insensate forces that are released by impulses to power and domination, the irrationalities of war and concentration camps, one has to be a considerable optimist to take the spread of rationality as an axiom in one's geometry of prediction. It is true that Professor Beckwith posits the likelihood of a nuclear holocaust within the next fifty years, but argues that human civilization will recover from it to resume its upward stride. But there are many other, perhaps equally threatening clouds on the future horizon, such as war of color, and wars of new ideologies, as human frustrations and irrationalities chafe at the slow bonds of social change.

But all this is a small caveat. It is an act of rare intellectual courage to seek to deal with the next five hundred years, and it is a major intellectual effort to span as many fields as Professor Beckwith does in making, as he notes, more than a thousand specific predictions in more than eighty areas.

He has made one (he calls it "major") prediction which brings my own presence into this volume. Towards the beginning of his book, he predicts that in the future there will arise a new interdisciplinary field of "future studies." I think that this prediction will soon be realized and that a start has already been made. In October, 1965, the American Academy of Arts and Sciences, the oldest honorary learned society in America (going back to John Adams as its first president), set up the Commission on the Year 2000 to undertake exploratory studies about the "near" future. That Commission, of which I am chairman, consists of thirty individuals—biologists, economists, political scientists, physicists, sociologists—who are seeking to pool their competences in such an effort. The Commission has produced five volumes of "working papers," and out of these, a volume (to be published by Houghton, Mifflin) entitled *Toward the Year 2000: Work in Progress.* Spurred by the Commission, the British Social Science Research Council, an official government body, has set up The Comittee on the Next Thirty Years. In France, Bertrand de Jouvenel heads up a project entitled *Futuribles* which has published more than a hundred studies of future problems and now has a regular journal, *Analyse et Prévision.* In Vienna, Robert Jungk and Professor Winter have set up an *Institut für Zukünftsfragen.* And back in the United States, such research groups as Resources for the Future, and the Hudson Institute, among others, have now begun serious and systematic studies of social trends.

Thus Professor Beckwith is in the van of a large and gathering enterprise. The reader of this volume will have some exciting intellectual forays to make.

DANIEL BELL

Chairman
The Commission on the Year 2000
The American Academy of Arts and Science

Professor of Sociology
Columbia University

Chilmark, Massachusetts

Preface

For at least six thousand years, to our knowledge, men have persistently and ingeniously sought to foretell the future. The ancient Chinese tried to read their fate by studying cracks in dried turtle-shells. The Babylonians developed the art of astrology, still practiced widely today, even in the most advanced countries. The ancient Greeks visited the oracle of Apollo at Delphi and pondered her ambiguous answers. The Roman augurs examined the entrails of animals and birds in order to determine the future and advise the government. The Christians of medieval Europe relied on the Bible and its interpreters, as well as on soothsayers, astrologers, and prophets. Even today most of the world's people still rely on one or more of these prescientific methods of predicting the future. The hunger for foreknowledge is age-old and universal.

The theory that events and trends can be reliably predicted by scientific methods is relatively new and little known. The first significant efforts at scientific prediction of social events and trends were a product of the eighteenth-century French Enlightenment. The novel doctrine that natural events are governed by natural law suggested to some of the philosophes that historical events and trends are equally orderly and natural, and therefore predictable. And this conclusion was more plausible than in any previous age, because Europe had experienced more regular and obvious social change from 1500 to 1750 than ever before. The outstanding early product of such reasoning was Condorcet's brilliant outline of future social events and trends (which I shall summarize later).

In spite of a wide and growing popular and scientific interest in future social events and trends and in spite of the rapid development of social science since 1800, social scientists have grossly neglected the promising field of prediction. More and more of them have made individual predictions on specific trends within their specialties, but such predictions have usually been incidental and rarely treated as significant end products themselves. Few social scientists have tried to assemble, arrange, and fill out such specialized predictions into a comprehensive outline or summary of future history, and those few have achieved scant success. No social scientist has yet specialized in such comprehensive social prediction.

What are the reasons for this neglect? First, some modern social scientists cling to religious or philosophic dogmas concerning freedom of the will which assert or imply that human behavior is unpredictable. Second, many others believe that the causation of social evolution is so complex and so little understandable that social events and trends cannot be usefully predicted. Third, many men who have made plausible but unpopular predictions have been denounced or even punished as subversive. These reasons deserve individual discussion in Chapter 1.

In this book I shall set forth the most significant long-run historical trends which will continue or arise during the next five hundred years and which now are scientifically predictable. As a social scientist I shall concentrate on social change, leaving prediction of most specific inventions and technological advances to engineers and natural scientists. Though the scientific prediction of social trends is both easier and more important than the prediction of inventions, it has received much less attention.

Acknowledgments

MOST TRENDS cited in this book are supported by data in two well-known sources: *The Statistical Abstract of the United States* and *Historical Statistics of the United States, Colonial Times to 1957* (1960). Both books are published by the United States Bureau of the Census and are available in most public libraries. I have also used the 1962 *Statistical Yearbook of the United Nations* and official statistics published by the Soviet Union in *Naradnoye Khozaistvo SSSR v. 1960 Godu.* Most sociology texts include statistics and opinion surveys on social trends. I have used H. E. Barnes' excellent *Society in Transition* more than any other work on sociology. Finally I have used miscellaneous facts and statistics published in the 1964 to 1966 issues of the *Wall Street Journal, Time, Science,* the Los Angeles *Times,* Moscow *News,* and other periodicals.

Contents

THE NEXT 500 YEARS

"The Grand Dynamic of History"

"At bottom our troubled state of mind reflects an inability to see the future in an *historic* context. If current events strike us as all surprise and shock it is because we cannot see these events in a meaningful framework. . . .

"The problem, then, is to establish a sense of [historic] order and continuity . . . this does not mean that history is foreseeable in its infinite detail . . . those minutiae which spell the joy and sorrow of our individual lives. But the fact that the future is inscrutable for each of us individually does not mean that it is equally impenetrable for all of us collectively. . . . As a society we move into the future on the grand dynamic of history. It is this grandiose design which we must discover if we are to comprehend the meaning of the struggles of our time." Robert L. Heilbronner, *The Future as History* (New York: Harper and Row, 1960), pp. 15-16

CHAPTER I

The Nature of Scientific Prediction

Scientific Prediction and Freedom of the Will

Scientists assume that the phenomena they study, including human acts, are determined by observable causes. Although this assumption cannot be demonstrated to be absolutely or universally true—only religion and philosophy yield formally absolute factual conclusions—each success in achieving a scientific truth further justifies and verifies the basic assumption that all phenomena are determined.

Every scientific truth enables men to predict events. Indeed, the ultimate test of any scientific proposition is whether the predictions it suggests are verified by subsequent observation. A proposition from which no theoretically verifiable prediction can be inferred is senseless, non-factual, and unscientific. A proposition which implies predictions theoretically verifiable but as yet unverified is a mere hypothesis. It follows that all general truths of social science justify some predictions of social events.

Some scientists and philosophers have sought to use modern quantum mechanics, notably Heisenberg's indeterminacy principle, to support the thesis that human, and therefore social, behavior is unpredictable. A detailed discussion of their arguments would be inappropriate here. I consider them invalid, the product of wishful thinking. An able and lucid criticism of them is contained in Philipp Frank's *Modern Science and Its Philosophy*, (Harvard University Press, 1949).

It may seem that if social trends can be predicted, they cannot be altered or controlled by men. This conclusion is unjustified. When the social scientist successfully predicts a trend, he estimates and allows for probable human control over future events. This is possible because men are both hedonistic and rational; their basic wants or ends are known, and rational solutions to many future problems can be roughly outlined today.

If human behavior were largely unpredictable, no co-operative activity could be carried on. In his everyday life the average individual constantly predicts the behavior of other men. If he could not, he would be unable to function. He could not count on the arrival of the milkman, the postman, his bus driver, his co-workers, and so on. Of course, he cannot predict all the acts of his associates. Nor can social scientists predict all social trends. But prediction of many such trends is almost as easy as predicting the arrival of the milkman or the volume of next week's sales. In neither class of cases does prediction of human behavior imply that men cannot change their behavior when they wish to and are able and free to do so.

For instance, on the basis of observation a social scientist can predict with fair accuracy what percentage of the children of Christians, Buddhists, or Moslems will become Christians, Buddhists, and Moslems. This does not imply that men do not voluntarily choose their religion. It merely proves that some voluntary human choices can be scientifically predicted long in advance.

The fact that men control their own behavior, and therefore the course of events, does not support the religious or philosophic doctrine that men have freedom of the will. This doctrine is factually senseless, because it is impossible to conceive of any method of verification. It does not make any practical, and therefore observable, difference whether the theory is true or false. If it did, scientists would have tested it long ago.

The doctrine that some or all events are determined by so-called natural law was one of the most significant products of the Enlightenment. It still is accepted by many educated men. American scientists often assert that the course of natural events is determined by the laws of natural science; Russian Communists believe that the course of social events is determined by the laws of social science enunciated by Karl Marx.

The two beliefs are equally mistaken, and for the same reasons. As explained more fully in my *Religion, Philosophy, and Science,* (1957), the so-called laws of science are merely generalized descriptions of events. And descriptions do not determine the events described. Rather, the events determine which descriptions, or "laws," are correct.

All social events are caused by human actions. They are inevitable for the same reason they are predictable, namely because human actions en masse are predictable, not because social events are determined by known laws of social science.

Since the term *scientific law* suggests to most people that the so-called law governs events, the term should be abandoned. It is not enough to teach initiates that this obvious implication, the basis for the original adoption of the term *scientific law,* is now rejected by most scientists: the social trends discussed in this book should not be called scientific laws.

Is Scientific Prediction of Social Trends Possible?

The second plausible major objection to efforts at scientific prediction of social trends is the argument that social phenomena are so complex that one can rarely if ever learn enough about the numerous causal factors involved to predict their results. I shall offer two answers to this argument: first, that scientists often make predictions about equally complex phenomena, and second, that a few pioneers have achieved brilliant successes in predicting long-run social trends.

It is of course true that our knowledge of the numerous factors determining long-run social trends is imperfect and incomplete. But so is our knowledge of the factors affecting the weather. Weather predictions are usually vague or inaccurate, and often wrong. Yet advanced nations spend hundreds of millions of dollars annually on weather forecasting. Many, perhaps most, of the social predictions offered below are more reliable (and much more significant) than the average weather forecast.

In capitalist countries many economists now devote a large and ever-growing share of their time to predicting short-run trends in the stock market, wholesale and retail prices, employment, savings, investment, etc. Such short-run trends are far more difficult to predict—because of short-run business fluctuations—than major long-run social trends and when reliable are much less socially significant. Yet economists now devote ten times as much attention to the former—primarily because it pays better.

Perhaps the best way to prove that reliable prediction of major social trends is possible is to cite the success of an eminent pioneer in such forecasting.

The most gifted pioneer advocate and practitioner of scientific prediction of major social trends was the French encyclopedist and reformer, Condorcet (1743–94), who in 1794 wrote his *Sketch for a Historical Picture of the Progress of the Human Mind,* shortly before he died in prison. In this brilliant outline of future social progress he made many predictions, most of which have already been largely verified and some of which are likely still to be verified. He predicted, in the following order, that:

1. The political principles of the French revolution would spread and inspire reform or revolution in many nations.
2. All European colonies in the Americas would become politically independent.
3. European colonies in Africa and Asia would be freed from exploitation.
4. The nations of Europe would increasingly send doctors, teachers, and other experts, instead of adventurers and missionaries, to backward countries.
5. "Meanwhile everything forecasts the imminent decadence of the great religions of the East . . . ."
6. The laws and customs chiefly responsible for economic and political inequality among men would be radically reformed.

7. Public financial support or social insurance for the needy—especially the aged, widows, and orphans—would be introduced.

8. Education would become public and universal. (For Condorcet's detailed educational forecasts, see Chapter XIII.)

9. Scientific research would continue indefinitely to expand human knowledge.

10. More equal opportunities for education would enlarge the scientific community and the scope and number of the sciences.

11. Technology would improve and expand with the sciences.

12. Technological progress in agriculture and industry would support more people on an ever higher standard of living, with less work per person.

13. Women would be given the same legal rights and educational opportunities as men.

14. Wars would be regarded as disasters and would become less and less frequent.

15. "The progress of the sciences ensures the progress of the art of education, which in turn advances that of the sciences."

16. Improvements in medical care, food, housing, labor-saving machinery, and income distribution would lengthen life and improve health.

17. Advances in medical practice would eliminate infectious and hereditary diseases.

In other, mostly unpublished, works Condorcet "foretold the direction of scientific inquiry in many fields for the next 150 years," including the application of statistics and mathematics to the social sciences, and predicted an enormous increase in the volume of scientific research. He also clearly anticipated Malthus' main objection to prediction number twelve above and the answers to it. He thought that contraception would increase sexual gratification and reduce infidelity and perversion, as well as control population. But neither he nor his literary editor dared publish such irreligious predictions. Thus apparent success of the Malthusian criticism was due primarily to religious censorship of Malthus' opponents.

Opposition to Social Change

It is noteworthy that for centuries most major contemporary social trends have been unpopular, especially among laymen. Thus people have been moving from the farm to the city for ten generations, but popular opinion throughout this period held that life on the farm was morally or socially preferable to life in the city. Divorces have been increasing for a century, but both popular and learned opinion have consistently condemned this trend. The growth of birth control, the emancipation of women, the rise of trade unions, the advance of socialism, and most other important social trends have been similarly condemned by most lay and/or expert opinion throughout most or all of their development. It is therefore highly probable that many of the predictions made in this book will strike some readers as undesirable, immoral or even subversive.

If obvious current social trends are commonly condemned, predictions concerning even long-run trends are all the more likely to be condemned as radical or subversive. The rate of social progress has been rising for centuries and will continue to rise. This book covers a period of over 500 years. The mere continuance of contemporary trends will inevitably bring about many radical social changes in such a long period. And radical social changes are usually regarded as subversive before they have occurred.

While social change has by and large been considered harmful or immoral, popular opposition to it has been weakening for centuries and is likely to continue weakening indefinitely. This change in attitude is due to growing education, to the increasingly evident benefits of past social changes, and to experience of change. Men raised in a rapidly evolving society are less opposed to change than those raised in a more or less static society. Hence, sound scientific prediction of radical social change will encounter less and less criticism. But criticism is still a major reason why social scientists fear to predict the future.

Methods of Scientific Prediction

At least twelve methods of scientific prediction of social trends are available.

1. One can secure statistical or verbal data on continuing past trends and project them into the future. The older and more regular the trend, the more valid is a projection of it if there is no apparent obstacle or limit to its continuance. Among such well-established long-run social trends are the growth of knowledge, the growth of education, and the rise in real wage rates.

2. One can determine and study long-run trends in both public and expert opinion. Nearly all significant changes in social policy and practice are preceded by measurable long-run supporting trends in opinion. For instance, the abolition of Negro slavery in America was preceded by a long gradual growth of abolitionist sentiment. And opinion changes among experts precede those among the general public, often by decades. Unfortunately we lack reliable long-run data on nearly all opinion trends; but such data is now being accumulated more rapidly than ever before.

3. One can observe current differences in opinion between experts (social scientists) and laymen. If most experts now advocate social reforms which have not yet won public approval, one can safely say that these or similar reforms will eventually be adopted. For instance, because most American economists specializing in the field advocate a marked extension and simplification of social insurance, this is almost certain to be achieved within 100 years.

4. One can study the differences between backward and advanced countries and predict that the backward will steadily become more like the advanced. Since these differences are now great, this method permits many major long-run predictions, as

well as innumerable short-run predictions. Thus one may safely predict that birth control will eventually become as common in India as it now is in Europe.

5. One can study the differences in organization and behavior between more and less efficient similar social organizations—units of government, schools, corporations, churches—in an advanced country and then predict that the less efficient will gradually adopt policies now peculiar to the more efficient. Thus it is highly probable that more and more doctors will substitute group for individual medical practice, because medical groups like the Mayo Clinic now provide the best care.

6. One can determine stable differences in the consumption habits of the rich and the poor in any country, but preferably in the most advanced, and then forecast that as average real incomes rise, more and more men will adopt habits now peculiar to the rich. For instance, this method can be used to support the prediction that men will for centuries spend a larger share of their income on foreign pleasure trips. The larger the differences in income, the longer the duration of the trends which can be predicted in this way. One must of course first predict a long rise in real personal incomes, and this prediction must be supported by one or more other methods.

7. One can study differences in the consumption and living habits of the most intelligent (or best-educated) and the least intelligent (or least-educated) members of any social class in any advanced country, and then predict that over a long future period, more and more men will adopt the habits of the superior members of their own social class or of some higher social class. This method assumes a continuing increase in average intelligence (eugenic reform) and/or education, an assumption which must be justified by other methods.

8. One can discover successful pioneer social reforms in individual advanced states and predict that they will soon be adopted by other advanced states. Each such state is a leader in one or more social trends. For instance, the United States long led the way in developing free secondary and higher education and in allowing women to vote. Great Britain pioneered in

industrialization and in parliamentary government. France led the world in the adoption of voluntary birth control. In the last twenty years Japan has pioneered in effective state support of both birth control and free legal abortion. Germany was the first to introduce large-scale compulsory social insurance. Australia first experimented with compulsory arbitration of labor disputes. When such pioneer social reforms have proven successful and popular in the state which first tried them, there is good reason to predict that they will soon be adopted by other advanced countries.

9. One can safely predict that nearly all distinctive old customs and institutions, those peculiar to a single region and not justified by geography, will gradually be replaced by more universal ones. For example, the once almost universal custom of wearing a distinctive local or national dress has long been weakening everywhere and will continue to do so until all men in all countries with a similar climate wear similar clothes. And the same fate awaits most other peculiar local or national customs —religious, political, sexual, economic, etc. Of course, all social reforms are distinctive in the first country which adopts them. Hence this rule applies to old customs only.

10. One can study reports on major recent or prospective technological developments and anticipate their social consequences. Many social changes are the result of technological advances and become predictable as soon as these advances have been achieved or made possible. Moreover, the inevitable social effects of some major inventions continue for centuries. Thus study of the continuing effects of old inventions is often worthwhile. For instance, one can safely predict that the automobile, invented over a century ago, will continue to promote decentralization of metropolitan populations for another century or two.

11. One can read descriptions of utopias and science fiction, select the most plausible predictions contained in them, and see if they can be supported by one of the methods already discussed. Although the authors of such works have made many unrealistic, even fantastic, predictions, they have also made many predictions which have already been verified or which still are reasonable.

In the absence of more down-to-earth forecasters they were for centuries the experts on many future social trends. And they will undoubtedly continue to formulate their brilliant hypotheses.

12. Any qualified social scientist can engage in scientific social engineering and develop new predictions. For this the basic premises must be that men are partly rational and hedonistic and will therefore eventually adopt nearly all major social reforms which would enhance their welfare. Since few if any social scientists have tried to state most or all eventually advantageous social reforms, it is highly probable that any social scientist who undertakes any part of this task can easily predict important social changes which are likely to be generally adopted within 500 years.

Classical and neoclassical political economists developed an elaborate and useful body of scientific theory by observing that men are usually self-seeking, rational, and informed, and then deducing how men would behave in economic life. They may have exaggerated the rationality and knowledge of men, but their success in developing useful and verifiable economic theories proves that men are partly self-seeking, rational, and informed. And it is just as reasonable to develop scientific predictions of social trends upon such basic general premises as to base economic theory upon them. Indeed, many predictions of social trends are dynamic economic theories.

Condorcet predicted the general adoption of what we now call social insurance. He had no statistical trends, no recorded growth of public or expert opinion, no successful pioneer reforms, on which to base this brilliant prediction of a trend which did not even begin until almost a century after his death. He merely grasped the rational case for such insurance, assumed that men would behave more and more rationally, and concluded that his daring prediction was justified. The chief shortcoming of this sound method of predicting social trends is that it does not help one to predict *when* a particular rational reform will occur.

Before leaving the subject of methods of scientific predictions, I shall offer my first major original prediction, namely that a new inter-disciplinary science of predicting social trends will be created and rapidly developed during the next century. Professorships in this new science will be established at many universities during the twenty-first century, and more and more funds will be devoted to research in the field. The twelve methods of scientific prediction described above will be steadily improved, and new ones will be developed.

More and Less Reliable Predictions

Some kinds of scientific predictions concerning social change are easier to make or justify and/or more likely to be true than others.

It is much easier and safer to predict trends and totals than to predict individual acts or subtotals. This implies that it is often easier to predict a long-run trend than a component short-run trend. It also implies that in the short or long run, predictions concerning moving averages* are more reliable than predictions concerning annual totals. Finally it implies that it is safer to predict over-all trends for most or all similar countries than to predict the same trends for any one of these countries.

Nearly all social trends fluctuate unpredictably above and below a moving average. Such short-run fluctuations usually tend to cancel out over a sufficiently long period, so they are less likely to cause errors in long-run than in short-run predictions. Thus, since the weather is largely unpredictable for a year ahead, it is much safer to predict harvest trends for twenty years ahead. All specific numerical predictions in this study should therefore be understood as moving averages for suitable long-run periods, even when they refer specifically to a single year.

Second, the older an unlimited social trend, the safer it is to predict its continuance. An unlimited trend is one which has no natural limit, such as 100 percent. Moreover, the older a

---

* A moving average is a continuing average of data taken at regular intervals over an appropriate number of intervals (period of time), kept up by replacing data for the oldest interval with data for the newest. It is a method of delineating and measuring trends.—*Editor*

limited trend which is still far from its limit, the safer it is to predict its continuance. It follows that it is nearly always safer to predict the continuance of an established trend than to predict a change in it, or the appearance of any new trend.

Third, it is safer to project established trends which are more general or widespread among like groups or nations than to project established trends which are less so. On the other hand, it is much easier to determine local or national trends, because statistics are now collected locally or nationally.

Fourth, if a well-established trend has been scientifically determined and predicted for one society, it may also be predicted for similar societies. The more similar the societies, the safer the extension; but the additional, or extended, prediction is always less certain than the original one, unless further supported by other means.

Fifth, predictions for entire societies may be based upon past trends in the behavior of representative sections of them. The more homogeneous the society and the more representative the sample, the more reliable is the resulting prediction for the entire society; but it cannot be as reliable as the prediction for the sample.

Sixth, it is safer to predict that men will do things that are already desirable and feasible, such as wipe out most infectious diseases, than to predict that they will do desirable things which are not yet technically possible, such as wipe out cancer. But the rapid progress of science makes many predictions of the second class reasonable.

Seventh, if a given result, such as a 100 percent rise in real wages, can be achieved by two or more methods, it is safer to predict the result than to predict the method or combination of methods to achieve it. For instance, it is much safer to predict the formation of a strong world government than to predict the way in which it will be formed.

Significant social events and trends are usually much easier to predict than insignificant ones. They have more important and more easily observable causes, they affect more people, and they arouse earlier interest and study. As noted previously, results are easier to predict than specific methods, and results are more significant. Likewise, group or average behavior is much easier to predict than individual behavior, and it is much more significant. Even in the case of individuals, it is easier to predict major than minor acts. For instance, it is safer to predict that the son of a Moslem will become and remain a Moslem than to predict that he will perform most less significant acts.

Since there is now much less prejudice against technological change than against social change, books on future technological progress are more numerous than books on future social progress. In advanced states, however, major social trends are less difficult to predict than major technological advances. The latter resemble events more than trends. And they are not foreshadowed by gradual changes in public opinion or behavior. Thus, for a historian writing of the future in 1848, it would have been much easier to anticipate the growth of democracy and socialism than to predict the invention of nuclear bombs and electronic computers.

Causes of Error in Prediction

Those who engage in scientific prediction of social trends must strive constantly to minimize or avoid certain all-too-common kinds of error: wishful thinking; popular or conformist thinking; unverifiable, and therefore senseless, predictions; overreliance on short-run trends, especially reversals in long-run trends; overemphasis on local or trivial trends; overcertain conclusions; moralistic pessimism; and exaggeration or theatricalism to attract attention.

All scientists are occasionally tempted to arrive at certain conclusions partly because they wish they were true or because their employers or readers wish they were true. These temptations are much greater among social scientists than among natural scientists, and among social scientists they are especially strong for those few who try to predict scientifically. Indeed, it is impossible for any social scientist to free himself entirely from wishful thinking or to prevent it from affecting his conclusions. Such thinking is often unconscious; when conscious it may lead to undue hesitation to state desired but sound conclusions.

It is much easier to recognize external pressure to state popular or approved conclusions, but it often is inexpedient for social scientists to resist such pressure. Their books cannot be an influence unless they are published and bought. Hence they may be justified in avoiding or watering down unpopular predictions, and most social scientists do so.

Some predictions considered extremely significant by their makers are so vague that they are virtually or absolutely senseless. For instance, predictions that freedom, regimentation, democracy, religion, spirituality, materialism, culture, etc., will increase or decrease are often meaningless because their makers fail to explain what observable events or statistical trends could confirm them, and explicitly reject methods of confirmation proposed by others.

The rise of fascism and communism between 1920 and 1940 prompted some social scientists to predict a long-run expansion of dictatorship at the expense of representative or democratic government, which had been spreading for over 200 years. Subsequent events have confirmed the long-run democratic trend rather than the short-run reversal of it. Predictions based on such trend reversals are usually wrong and always dubious.

All predictions of social events and trends are uncertain because our knowledge of past trends is imperfect. It is easy and common for social scientists to imply or claim that their predictions are more certain than is warranted. On the other hand, the fact that such predictions are uncertain does not mean they are worthless. Any prediction concerning important events or trends which is at all probable is worth making.

Many pessimistic predictions of trends and events have been made only in order to warn men concerning possible future dangers. Such warnings become more effective in scientific and realistic guise. Hence moralists often try to present their dogmatic warnings as scientific predictions.

Finally, all who write about the future are tempted to attract attention by making exaggerated, fantastic, or shocking predictions. Moralists incline to shocking forecasts, and optimists to fantastic ones.

I have tried to minimize all these errors in this book. But since no author can reason perfectly, or recognize and allow for all his prejudices and other failings, let the reader keep the list of errors in mind to detect and allow for them in this and other efforts to see the future realistically.

Causes of Social Trends

The oldest influential scientific theory of social evolution is the Marxian theory that major social trends and revolutions are ultimately caused by fundamental changes in methods of production. This economic interpretation of history, in one form or another, is today the most widely accepted theory of social change. It is, however, incomplete and unsatisfactory, because it minimizes or ignores significant non-economic factors, such as the invention of opinion polls, contraceptive devices, and new methods of scientific research.

The ultimate causes of all human acts, including those which make up social trends, are human drives or instincts, the product of biological evolution. But human acts result in major social trends only when men create inventions (new ways of doing things) which have important and enduring effects on human behavior. *Invention* is used here in a broad sense. It denotes improvements (or a series of them) in thinking, writing, sexual relationships, medical care, education, government, etc., as well as new machines and methods of production. Inventions which most significantly affect the course of history, often for hundreds of years, may be called history-making inventions.

Among prehistoric history-making inventions the most significant were the domestication of fire, of plants, and of animals, pottery making, weaving, and the drying of food. Major ancient inventions included writing, the smelting of metals, the plow, paved roads, sailboats, city-states, empires. Among the most influential medieval inventions were guns and gunpowder, the compass, the burning of coal, paper, printing, double-entry bookkeeping.

In modern times, history-making inventions have been far too many to allow their enumeration in a brief space. The most important of all were the development of scientific methods of creating new truths and the application of these methods in organized continuous scientific research. Other major modern inventions were birth control, public education, civil service, democratic government, the steam engine, the electric motor, radio, television, the electronic computer, anesthesia, the germ theory, vaccines, and antibiotics.

It is noteworthy that many modern inventions have created or helped to create social trends which will continue for centuries. As explained earlier, one of the chief reasons it is now possible to predict social trends is that the full predictable effects of many history-making inventions have so far been incompletely achieved. For instance, medical inventions already made will continue for centuries to reduce death rates and prolong life. There is normally a long cultural lag between the creation of a history-making invention and full worldwide reaction to it.

While it is relatively difficult to predict most history-making inventions far ahead, both because they are individual events and because they are highly original and unique, it is safe to predict that most future inventions will have general effects similar to those of past inventions. They will reduce production, transport, and marketing costs, make communication at a distance easier and cheaper, reduce disease, increase foreign trade and travel, improve education and research, provide new means of recreation, and facilitate birth control and eugenics. To predict most major social trends, we need not be able to predict many individual inventions—only such general effects of past and future history-making inventions.

Other Preliminary Explanations

The recent invention of nuclear weapons has made a nuclear world war probable and destruction of all human life possible. Further improvement of these and other weapons is inevitable. But to justify long-run predictions concerning social evolution, one must assume or predict that there will be a long-run future. Furthermore, to justify use of the most promising method of prediction, the projection of secular trends, one must also assume or predict that future wars will not seriously alter the course and speed of social evolution. Fortunately, there are some reasons for treating these propositions as reasonable basic predictions rather than as purely arbitrary optimistic assumptions.

In the past advanced nations have recovered with surprising speed from terrible disasters, such as World Wars I and II. The earth is so grossly overpopulated that no loss of life less than 80 percent could long delay social progress in advanced countries. An equal loss of capital goods is more likely, and would be much more serious, but need not stop or long delay progress. Remaining plant and equipment could be operated two or three shifts a day instead of one or two. And the most productive capital in any country is the knowledge and skill of its people. Thus if any substantial part of the population of any advanced state survives future wars—and this seems likely—social evolution in now predictable directions will continue.

Although some or all advanced nations probably will be devastated by a nuclear war before 2100, I have largely ignored the possible effects of such a war in the main body of this book because I am trying to predict normal peacetime trends. In the conclusion, however, I shall briefly summarize the probable effects on numerous individual social trends.

As noted earlier, social changes occur first in the most advanced countries. And this book is written by a resident of such a country for readers in such countries. Hence most of the more specific predictions and dates here apply to such countries, especially to Great Britain and America. Similar changes will occur later, perhaps a century or two later on the average, in all undeveloped countries. In most cases, however, I have not thought it worthwhile to restate this obvious implication of individual predictions.

Many predictions stated here are in dollar terms. The value of the dollar probably will fall slowly for many decades. My monetary predictions are in terms of 1960 dollars, that is, their United States buying power in 1960.

In this book I have made over a thousand different predictions in some eighty different fields. Many of these predictions deserve and eventually will receive monographs. To justify in detail so many predictions would require many volumes, and I have had to minimize my discussion of the evidence supporting them. If time and space were available, all of them could be much more fully supported by relevant evidence—statistical trends in behavior or opinion, differences between advanced and backward countries, expert opinion, etc. Most could be supported by the use of four or more of the means discussed under "Methods of Scientific Prediction," above.

To predict social trends, one must ordinarily predict relative growth or decline. To make it clear that every such prediction in this book refers to relative as well as absolute growth would require monotonous repetition of this qualification. Hence the reader should assume that predicted increases refer to relative as well as absolute changes whenever they would otherwise imply no social trend or change.

All predictions in this book are probabilities, not certainties. But because constant repetition of *probable* and its synonyms would be tiresome as well as superfluous, I have usually omitted such qualifications.

The reader may wonder why this study covers 500 years (actually 500 plus) instead of 50 or 1,000. I chose 500 instead of 50 partly because often it is easier to predict very long-run trends than short-run trends. The latter are much more apt to be distorted by temporary factors, such as the cold war. Moreover, the cumulative changes of the next 500 years will be much greater and more significant than those of the next 50. And I am convinced that most predictable major long-run social trends will continue for centuries. In my final chapter I shall predict the continuance of many trends far beyond the year 2500. But it is of course possible to predict more accurately, more extensively, and more specifically for the next 100 or 200 years than for the next 500. That is why most of my more specific predictions apply to periods of less than 200 years.

The chief thesis of this book is that scientific prediction of many social trends is possible and desirable. As this thesis becomes more widely accepted, social scientists will devote more time and resources to such prediction. This will result in rapid improvement in all the predictions offered here. They are presented here as a tentative pioneer summary of future social development over the next 500 years.

This book has been written for educated laymen, not for specialists. I have tried to avoid the use of academic jargon and have provided almost no footnotes. I have also deliberately emphasized my discussion of those social trends—in population, communication, education, family life, crime, etc.—in which the general public is most likely to be interested.

CHAPTER II

Major General Social Trends

The history-making technological and social inventions of the past millennium have created, and future inventions will reinforce, major general social trends which will continue in all countries for centuries to come. This book could have been organized as a detailed discussion and illustration of each such general trend. Instead, I have chosen to organize it as a discussion of much more specific trends within, and grouped by, individual fields of social behavior—political, sexual, educational, etc.

A brief statement and discussion of the more important of these general trends is appropriate at this point. For over twenty-five hundred years philosophers, historians, and scientists have sought to discover enduring basic purposes or tendencies beneath the confusing variety of changing social phenomena. The major long-run social trends described below are the closest approach to this long-sought goal yet achieved by man. They are not absolute, unchanging, or eternal, but they are relatively enduring. As explained in the conclusion, most of them will continue much longer than 500 years, and some are already over 1,000 years old.

The major general social trends—those observed in or affecting many or all fields of social behavior—during most or all of the next 500 years will include:

1. The growth of population
2. The growth of knowledge
3. The relative growth of scientific research
4. The relative growth of education

5. Democratization of education
6. Decline of religion and superstition
7. Growth of social control over social trends
8. Rationalization of all social policies
9. Spread of birth control
10. Eugenic progress
11. Rise in real wage rates
12. Growth of leisure
13. Urbanization
14. Industrialization
15. Automation
16. Specialization
17. Professionalization
18. Increase in the scale of production
19. Growth of monopoly
20. Centralization of control
21. Collectivization
22. Rise of meritocracy
23. Advance of feminism
24. Decline in income differences
25. Relative growth of free distribution
26. Reduction of all personal economic risks
27. Increase in paternalism
28. Rise of humanitarianism
29. Growth of intergroup relations
30. Cultural homogenization
31. Growth of personal freedom

This list obviously is not definitive. Most social scientists will want to revise it. But I have been unable to find any other such list prepared by social scientists.

It is noteworthy that my list does not include the advance of political democracy (although this advance will continue for another century), the spread of economic planning (although some spread is implicit in the predicted growth of free distribution), the growth of industrial democracy (unlikely or short-run), more ethical social conduct (an unverifiable prediction), the decline of materialism (also unverifiable), the rise or decline of individualism (too vague), the rise or decline of militarism (too brief and irregular), the growth of international co-operation (soon to be replaced by world government), or the spread of nationalism (too short-run). The reasons for these and other omissions will be elaborated in later chapters.

Individual Trends

No one of these thirty-one social trends is independent of the others. Each reinforces, or is reinforced by, some, or even most, of the others. Thus, to explain why any individual trend is likely to continue, it is usually necessary to explain how it is promoted or reinforced by one or more other major social trends, or by some more specific trend within another social trend. A full explanation would make clear how it is affected by most or all of the other major trends and many minor ones. This would require more space than is available here; however, a brief explanation of each trend is given below.

1. The human population of the earth has grown fairly steadily for over 10,000 years and will continue to grow throughout most of the next 500. It may suddenly be reduced by one or more major nuclear wars, but it will grow steadily in peacetime. The chief causes of this trend have been technological progress in all industries, the advance of medical science, and the growth of law and order. These factors will continue to operate indefinitely but will increasingly be offset by rational individual and social control over reproduction.

2. The stock of human knowledge has been growing steadily for over 10,000 years and will continue to increase as long as mankind survives. This is the most basic and influential of all general social trends. It includes the creation of history-making inventions, as well as of all others. It is not dependent upon any other social trend, though other trends may accelerate the growth of knowledge. And most other trends are dependent upon it.

3. Since 1800 the growth of knowledge has been continuously accelerated by the rapid rise of private and especially public spending on organized, persistent scientific research and development (R and D). This trend is a result of the invention and improvement of scientific methods of investigation, increasing recognition of the great social gains from R and D, the steady rise in

real income per person, etc. All such factors will continue to promote the growth of R and D throughout the next 500 years.

4. Continued scientific research will steadily increase the stock of useful knowledge, and this will help to induce men to spend an ever-growing share of their lives in schools and private study. This in turn will make labor more productive and raise real wages, which will permit more spending on education. Moreover, as any society advances, it becomes more and more necessary that the individual be able to read and write and practice a trade or profession. Signs, instructions, blueprints, accounting records, labels, advertisements, become more numerous and more important. Employers increasingly discriminate against illiterate and unskilled workers. Finally all men are curious about the world around them and enjoy reading about it. Therefore they will demand and obtain more and more education.

5. Undemocratic education is proportioned to the wealth or power of the parent; democratic, to the intelligence and ability of the student. And education may expand greatly without becoming more democratic. Hence the trend toward more democratic education is a distinct trend. It is a major trend because it will gradually create a new ruling class in all countries and will greatly increase the productivity of labor in every field. It is two or three hundred years old in advanced countries, but fairly new in many backward countries. It is largely a result of the growth of knowledge and education. It will continue for centuries because men will become increasingly aware of the large personal and social gains it can yield.

6. Religious and superstitious belief and behavior have been declining for 500 years in most advanced countries and for shorter periods in all other countries. This trend is largely a result of the progress of science and education. Since this progress will continue indefinitely, for reasons already given, the decline of religion will continue throughout the next 500 years in all countries.

7. The steady growth of scientific knowledge, especially in the social sciences, makes government control over social trends ever

more feasible, and the growth of education makes such knowledge ever more widespread. In the past century or two the governments of all advanced states have steadily increased their efforts to control the course of social evolution, and they will continue to do so throughout the next 500 years. Much of this book will be devoted to illustrations of this highly significant trend.

8. The inevitable continuous future growth of knowledge and education would make social behavior and policies ever more rational or scientific, even without any improvement in innate human intelligence. Moreover, eugenic reform will greatly increase this intelligence and help to make social policies more and more intelligent. This trend will be obvious in every field of social behavior throughout all future time and is therefore extremely significant. It justifies predicting that men will eventually adopt any social policy or reform which can now be shown to be rational or scientific under probable future social conditions.

Some writers have asserted that since men are certain to adopt more and more rational technologies (both social and industrial), the future of mankind will largely be determined by an autonomous, impersonal force called "the machine," "technique," "science," or something else. This is a naive error! It is true, of course, that history-making inventions influence history, but such inventions are human artifacts, and their historical effects are therefore effects produced by their inventors and users.

The claim that human conduct is rational is often rejected on the ground that human conduct is emotional. But there is no necessary conflict between reason and emotion. All human conduct is both emotional (in motive or cause) and rational (in plan and method). When men are unusually excited emotionally, they may act less rationally than they normally do. But such individual aberrations have little effect upon long-run social trends because their effects normally cancel out.

9. The spread of birth control has been one of the most important causes of human progress in advanced countries since

1860. During the next century birth control will spread and grow throughout the world. It will continue to spread and increase for most of the next 500 years. It has been, and will long continue to be, due chiefly to improvements in birth-control methods, the spread of education, the growth of personal freedom, and the rise in real wages.

10. As yet there has been little if any eugenic progress due to social reforms designed to further it. But such reforms will soon begin to appear in the most advanced countries and will spread and improve steadily during the remainder of the next five centuries. This trend will result primarily from the inevitable future growth of popular education and eugenic science. It will affect all human societies and activities because it will change the people engaged in them.

11. Real income per person has been rising in some advanced countries for over 200 years and for varying shorter periods in many other countries. This trend will soon spread to all countries and will thereafter continue throughout the next 500 years. It has been largely due to the growth of political stability, the advance of technology, the expansion of education, and above all, to the spread and improvement of birth control. All these factors will continue to produce similar effects in the world as a whole for most or all of the next 500 years. Moreover, the major new factor of eugenic reform will help notably to raise average real incomes during the second half of this period, if not before.

12. For over 100 years the average amount of adult leisure in advanced countries has increased, due chiefly to a steady reduction in the hours of labor, the invention and use of labor-saving housekeeping utensils and machines, the gradual transfer of many domestic chores to commercial agencies, birth control, and the growth of public education and child care. All these factors will continue to increase the leisure of adults in advanced countries and will spread to or grow in all other countries. Hence the average amount of adult leisure will expand in all countries throughout the next 500 years.

13. Urbanization—the movement of people from rural to

urban areas—is a major social trend which has radically transformed life in all advanced states during the last two centuries. It has barely begun in most backward states but will transform them during the next 200 years. Moreover, it will continue in most advanced states until their population is over 95 percent urban.

Urbanization is primarily the result of an agricultural revolution which has steadily increased the productivity of farm labor in advanced countries since 1800. It is also partly due to cheaper transport and longer storage of farm products. These factors will continue to operate indefinitely.

14. Industrialization—the substitution of mass production for handicraft production in small shops or homes—is one of the most widely recognized and discussed general social trends. It is a result of the invention of the steam engine and other machines. It is already 200 years old and is likely to continue at least that much longer. In the future this trend will be most obvious and important in backward countries, but it will continue to affect incompletely industrialized industries, like dressmaking, in advanced states. Industrialization is especially significant as a major prerequisite of both capitalism and socialism.

15. Automation—the substitution of automatic for manually operated machines—is still in an early stage of development, even in the most advanced countries. It will become much more obvious there during the next century. Later, of course, it will spread to all other countries. Thus it will be important for centuries. It is a result of the invention of the assembly line, electric generators and motors, electronic controls, computers, automatic machine tools, and of all inventions which broaden markets and thus favor large-scale production and specialization.

16. Specialization—the ever-increasing restriction of workers, tools, machines, and factories to fewer and fewer functions—is another major general social trend which has been obvious for centuries and will continue to be significant for many more, in every industry and land. It is chiefly a result of the steady

growth of knowledge, industrialization, the cheapening of transport, the spread of monopoly, and population growth.

17. The proportion of the world labor force which has received a professional education and is occupied in professional work has long been increasing and will continue to increase throughout the next 500 years. This growth has been and will long continue to be due chiefly to the growth of applied science and the resulting rise in real personal incomes. It is much easier to invent and adopt labor-saving machines in agriculture and industry than in professional work. Moreover, the advance of knowledge and education makes professional work ever more common and productive. Finally every increase in real wages increases the relative demand for most professional services—educational, medical, musical, etc. Therefore most old professions will continue indefinitely to grow faster than world income, and many new professions will be created.

18. The scale of production—average output per plant or office—has been growing for centuries in advanced countries and will continue to grow for many more centuries in all countries. This trend is chiefly a result of the industrial revolution, the improvement in means of transport, the growth of population, and the rise of monopoly and socialism. The trend is obvious in education, medical care, scientific research, and other professional fields, as well as in business and industry.

19. The growth of monoply is a well-established worldwide social trend which is at least a century old in advanced states. It will continue and spread for most of the next 500 years. This trend is due to the many advantages of horizontal integration, the development of ever larger and costlier machines, the constant improvement of methods of large-scale management, and the fact that the creation of monopolies makes it much easier for governments to co-ordinate, regulate, rationalize, and stabilize economic activities.

20. Centralization of control—political, economic, educational, medical, etc.—is a well-established general social trend which will continue throughout most if not all of the next

500 years. It is a product of the numerous inventions which have cheapened and speeded transport and communication, facilitated military conquest, and improved the efficiency of bureaucracy. The invention of nuclear weapons has recently made world conquest and rule possible and a world government inevitable. The ever-growing specialization among firms and industries will steadily increase the need for central control to co-ordinate international economic activities.

21. Collectivization, or socialization, is the growing substitution of government ownership or control for private ownership or control. This trend is over a hundred years old in advanced countries and is likely to continue for several centuries. It is a product of the industrial revolution (which substitutes collective for individual work), ever-growing economic specialization and interdependence, the development of social science (most neoclassical economic theory is applicable only in a socialist economy), the rapid increase in the efficiency of large-scale management and government, and the near universal human desire for economic security and relative equality.

22. Continued progress toward meritocracy—rule and management by the most able—will be achieved in all fields in all countries throughout the next 500 years. Such progress will result from the growth of technological and professional knowledge (which will make ability easier to recognize and experts ever more influential), the inevitable democratization of professional education, the steady decline of private inheritance, the growth of general education (which will increase popular respect for all classes of experts), and the coming decline in personal-income differences.

23. Feminism is a highly significant modern social trend. By *feminism* I mean the steady increase in the influence and activities of women outside the home—in politics, business, the professions—and in their personal authority inside the home. This trend is over 200 years old in advanced countries and is only half complete there. It has barely begun in many backward countries, but will appear and continue for centuries in all of them.

Feminism is more difficult to explain than most other general trends. It is due in large part to the industrial revolution and urbanization. It has been furthered by, and has also furthered, the rise of birth control. The growth of internal peace and order, the spread of education, and the invention of many new or improved household machines and tools—stoves, refrigerators, vacuum cleaners—are also partly responsible.

24. Differences in real income per person among fellow citizens have declined radically in communist states and slightly in advanced capitalist states since 1900. This trend will continue and spread for centuries. The chief causes will be the common human dislike of large income differences, the growth of birth control, the expansion of free education, political democratization, eugenic progress, and the development of social science.

25. In all advanced countries the proportion of consumers' goods and services distributed free of charge has grown steadily for a century. Free distribution will continue to grow faster than national income for a century or two more in advanced countries, and for much longer in backward countries. In the world as a whole the share of free distribution will grow throughout most or all of the next 500 years. As a result differences in real income will decline faster than differences in personal money income in every country. The reasons why free distribution is growing vary from good to good and are too complex to summarize here. They will be stated in later chapters.

26. The average personal risk of losing property or income through any misfortune—unemployment, sickness, accident, flood, earthquake, crime—will be steadily reduced throughout the next 500 years in all countries. In other words, all personal property and income will become more and more secure. This trend is already centuries old in advanced countries. It has been due to the growth of peace and order, the rise of private and public insurance, improvement in medical care, the spread of monopoly, and the growth of free distribution.

27. Many writers have noted or complained that advanced societies are becoming more and more paternalistic. While the term is often too vague for scientific use, it can denote a very

well-established general social trend which will continue for centuries, namely an increase in legislation which protects relatively incompetent minorities against exploitation or their own poor judgment. Laws which restrict fraud and false advertising; prohibit or curtail the sale of harmful goods and services; make thrift, insurance, medical care, and education free and compulsory—are all paternalistic according to this definition. Such laws will increase in variety, coverage, and efficacy in all countries throughout the next 500 years.

Paternalism will grow indefinitely, for two major reasons. First, the inevitable progress of applied science will enable experts to give more and more valuable advice concerning many personal decisions now left to individuals. Vaccination became compulsory only after scientists discovered how beneficial it is. They will continue making such discoveries forever. Second, the inevitable growth of education will make all governments more and more responsive to expert advice; hence they will increasingly adopt paternalistic measures advocated by experts.

28. The rise and spread of humanitarianism has been a major social trend for over 500 years and will continue for another 500. It includes all phases of the movement from cruelty and brutality toward consideration and tenderness in the treatment of human beings. This general trend has been obvious in the ever more humane treatment of defeated nations, prisoners of war, heretics and dissenters, juvenile and adult delinquents, children, wives, the feeble-minded and insane, the poor, the sick, and all other potential victims of brutality. Over a hundred thousand witches, mostly helpless old women, were publicly burned at the stake in Germany in the sixteenth century, and such cold-blooded cruelty was typical of the age.

The rise of humanitarianism in Europe began about the same time as the decline of religion and the rise of science but is probably due more to the latter than the former. Another major cause was the growth of peace and order within, if not between, the new national states. War debases men by making them less sensitive to suffering. Finally the steady growth of wealth in all advanced countries since 1500 has promoted humanitarianism.

Poverty brutalizes the poor. Wealth has given rulers and managers the means to cover the often higher costs of humane treatment of the unfortunate. All these factors will continue to increase and spread more humanitarian personal and social behavior throughout the next 500 years, except in nuclear warfare. The Nazi horrors were a temporary local deviation from a long-run worldwide trend.

29. The growth of intergroup relations is a trend as old as civilization and will continue throughout the next 500 years. It includes the beginning, multiplication, and elaboration of social relations between families, clans, tribes, city-states, nations, and empires. In backward countries the growth of interclan and intertribal relations will long continue to be significant. Among the most advanced nations the growth of ever more numerous and complex international relations will continue to be important for more than 500 years. This is a general social trend, because it affects travel, trade, communications, government, education, crime, disease prevention, and most other major classes of social behavior.

30. Gradual but continuous cultural homogenization—the weakening and disappearance of cultural differences—will be a major general social trend throughout the next 500 years. Here *culture* is used in the anthropological sense; that is, way of life. Thus cultural homogenization includes standardization of all human beliefs and activities—political, economic, educational, sexual, artistic, scientific, recreational, etc.

This old trend has been and will continue to be a result of history-making inventions which cheapen and increase travel, migration, communication, and freight transportation. Distinctive customs arose when different human groups were isolated from one another, and tend to diminish whenever travel and communication become easier and more frequent. The mere fact that local customs are distinctive and not due to climate implies that they probably are non-utilitarian, and therefore they are almost certain to be eventually displaced by more useful and widespread customs. As men become more rational and scientific, social customs and policies will become more uniform.

The most significant homogenization trend will be the further Europeanization of all non-European countries, which will continue throughout the next 500 years. North America is of course a cultural colony of Europe, so Americanization is Europeanization. Backward Asiatic and African countries will adopt more and more European social customs and policies in order to improve their own standard of living. It is much easier to imitate successful methods than to devise new ones as good.

31. One of the most notable general social trends in advanced countries during the past 500 years has been the continuous growth of freedom, the opportunity to make and carry out uncoerced choices concerning one's own conduct. This trend will continue throughout the next 500 years.

This prediction does not imply that social or governmental regimentation or regulation of individuals will decline. The common belief that all regimentation restricts personal freedom is unjustified. Some regimentation does so, for instance blue laws, religious laws, sexual laws and customs. But most current regimentation increases personal freedom. For instance, the rule that cars must keep to the right when passing permits all drivers to travel more safely and freely. Such freedom-expanding regimentation will increase, and freedom-restricting regimentation will decline, throughout the next five centuries.

The chief causes of the growth of personal freedom have been and will long continue to be the continuous rise in average personal real income, the spread of education, the decline of religion, the rise of democratic government, and urbanization.

The period of transition from cold and hot wars to stable world government may involve one or more major wars, which always increase restrictive regimentation. Moreover, the nation or nations which establish the coming world government will probably restrict personal freedom in some subject countries. Personal freedom may therefore decline during the transition period, but it will certainly revive and expand indefinitely thereafter. The world of A.D. 2500 will not be ruled by brutal dictators who exploit and terrorize their subjects, as Orwell and Wells feared, but by benevolent and highly educated professional administrators.

This completes my brief discussion of the thirty-one major general social trends which I believe will continue through most or all of the next 500 years. In my concluding chapter I shall explain why most of them are likely to last well into or throughout the succeeding 500 years. All these trends will be illustrated in the intervening chapters by more specific trends and predictions.

The growth of interest in scientific prediction of social trends and events will result in a gradual but radical change in history books. Historians will devote less and less space to chronicling individual events, especially atypical events, and more and more to describing and emphasizing long-run social trends, notably those most apt to continue well into the future. The most honored historians of A.D. 2000 to 2500 will be those who have been most successful in determining and describing past and present general social trends and have thus provided the best foundations for scientific prediction of long-run social trends.

CHAPTER III

Government

In this chapter I shall predict some major trends in governmental structure and in the performance of the oldest and most basic general functions of government—administration, legislation, and adjudication. More recent and specific functions will be discussed in later chapters.

First, however, let us consider the possible effects of violent social revolutions on political and other social trends.

Evolution and Revolution

Successful violent revolutions may be divided into two classes: ordinary revolutions, which merely replace one government with a similar government; and social revolutions, which bring to power reformers, usually leaders of a different social class, who achieve major and enduring social changes. The former revolutions do not affect social trends significantly; the latter do.

One or more violent social revolutions are likely to occur during the next century. I shall not attempt to predict them individually, for three reasons. First, revolutions are single historical events and therefore far more difficult to predict than long-run social trends. Second, they usually affect directly only one country, and we are interested primarily in changes which are, or will eventually become, worldwide. Third, no violent social revolution has ever occurrred in an advanced democratic or semi-democratic state, and none are likely during the next 500 years. This book deals primarily with trends in such states. Finally, and most important of all, social revolutions do not create or seriously alter long-run worldwide social trends. Progressive social revolutions—like the English, French, and Russian—result from unreasoning conservative resistance to such inevitable trends and serve chiefly to remove political obstacles to their continuance. The trends they unblock or accelerate are usually much further advanced in other countries, some of which have achieved them by peaceful social evolution.

Even when a progressive social revolution accelerates some major social trends, there is often, perhaps usually, a subsequent conservative reaction which slows down the trends. Thus the successful English Revolution was followed by the Stuart restoration, and the French Revolution was followed by the Bourbon restoration.

Reactionary revolutions—like those of Hitler and Mussolini—merely delay temporarily the progress of some old social trends, which resume their course, often at a more rapid rate, after the revolutionists have been overthrown.

In sum, social trends result from major history-making inventions and the growth of knowledge and education, not from social revolutions. The latter may temporarily speed up or slow down such trends, but they do not start or stop or seriously alter them.

A few illustrations may strengthen this claim. The major achievement of the English Revolution (1644–60) was to increase the political power of the rising bourgeoisie, whose rise was basically due to economic evolution and would have continued inevitably whether or not Cromwell had defeated Charles I. No revolution was required to support the steady further increase of bourgeois political authority in Great Britain during the eighteenth and nineteenth centuries, or in Germany, which never had a successful bourgeois revolution. This discussion of the English Revolution applies equally to the French Revolution.

The chief achievement of the American Revolution was to make the thirteen colonies politically independent. But Canada, which opposed this revolution, is today as politically democratic and independent as the United States. It was not the revolution but the rapid growth in the population and wealth of the American colonies which assured their political freedom. And these basic trends would have continued even if there had been no revolution. Moreover, the destruction and disturbance caused by the revolution probably slowed rather than hastened these trends.

The Russian Revolution caused greater immediate social changes than any previous social revolution of modern times. But it occurred in a backward country, and its chief results so far have been to speed up general social trends long obvious in more advanced states, as well as in czarist Russia—industrialization, urbanization, the growth of education and research, socialization of industry, etc. In most such trends Soviet Russia is still behind one or more of the most advanced capitalist states. And the few trends which have gone farther in the Soviet Union may soon slow down, while other countries catch up. Some, indeed, may temporarily reverse themselves—for instance, centralization of output control and nationalization of private property.

Most of the social trends accelerated by the Russian Communists were well established in Russia before the Revolution and would probably have been accelerated by non-communist rulers. Certainly many of these trends have been actively promoted by non-communist governments in other European countries since 1917. There is little reason to believe that major social trends in a permanently Communist Russia would differ substantially during the next 500 years from those in other advanced countries, or from those which would occur in a non-communist Russia during this period.

While several violent social revolutions are likely to occur during the next century, they probably will all occur in backward countries, especially in Latin America and Asia. No democratic European nation will experience a spontaneous social revolution, because such revolutions are unnecessary, and have never taken place, in democratic countries. A violent social revolution is possible in an undemocratic European state, like Spain or Portugal, but even there it seems unlikely. A nationalistic conservative social revolution is possible in any East

European Soviet satellite. But the long-run effects of either class of revolution would be of little significance. To predict far ahead, one must study the more, not the less, advanced states.

Democratic Government

The major political trend of the past 300 years has been the democratization of government, a fairly steady increase in the proportion of the population allowed to participate in or approve the selection of legislators and chief executives. This trend arose and has gone furthest in the most advanced states. In general, the more advanced the country (measured by real wage rates), the more democratic it is. No advanced state is now fully democratic or even close to this goal, but all are moving slowly toward it and will continue to do so for another century or two. I shall follow popular usage and call democratic all countries which are largely or relatively democratic.

The mere holding of periodic elections which are regularly won by the party in power, as in Mexico and in the Soviet Union, does not make a country democratic. A country is predominantly democratic only if some recent major elections have been won by the opposition and most adult citizens are allowed to vote freely. The higher the proportion of adults allowed to vote and the less the direct and indirect control of voters by a ruling elite, the more democratic the country.

Democratic government is very new. America was in large part a slave state until 1865. Britain did not grant most workers the right to vote much before 1900. Sweden did not do so until after World War I. Only some 20 percent of the world's population now enjoys democratic government.

The growth of political democracy in advanced states has been largely due to the technological revolution in agriculture (which gradually weakened feudalism and slavery), to the industrial revolution (which steadily enlarged and enriched the urban middle classes), and to the spread of public education and birth control (which enlightened and strengthened the working class). These major social trends will persist and will continue to promote political democracy, especially in less advanced states, for another century or two.

All democratic countries are advanced countries, and all undemocratic advanced countries will soon become democratic. Democratic government is the normal and almost inevitable product of social progress. However, few if any backward African, Asiatic, and Latin-American states will become and remain democratic during the next 100 years.

In several newly independent countries, governments which were civilian and at least nominally democratic have already been overthrown by military officers. The same fate, or communist dictatorship, awaits India and nearly all other recently liberated colonies.

The countries most likely to achieve stable democratic government on their own during the next 50 years include the Soviet Union, Germany, Italy, Spain, Poland, Czechoslovakia, Austria, Hungary, Argentina, Chile, and Japan. Although the former Axis powers now are functioning democratically, they cannot be classed as stable or voluntary democracies, because their present form of government was recently imposed upon them by alien conquerors.

The communist dictatorships which govern Eastern Europe were established at a time when this area was too backward to allow the successful functioning of democratic governments. As the area develops socially, popular and expert support for more democratic government will grow steadily. Some cultural lag is normal in all social evolution, but it never stops or delays evolution for long. By 2050 all of Communist Europe will be democratic.

Capitalist democracy is a great advance over monarchy or dictatorship because capitalists are more able than aristocrats and generals and because peaceful persuasion is much preferable to arbitrary rule or repeated revolution, not because democratic government puts political power in the hands of the masses. Every society is ruled by a small elite, but the capitalist elite is more competent and progressive than previous elites and is steadily improving. Further democratization of government in advanced capitalist states will make these elites more and more responsive to popular wishes. Similar reasoning applies to communist countries.

In advanced capitalist states the chief obstacles to further political democratization are the grossly unequal distribution of wealth and partisan control of the press and other means of influencing public opinion. In a later chapter I shall predict a long-continuing decline in inequality of wealth and income. This will help greatly to further democratize capitalist governments. The future expansion of secondary and higher education (predicted in Chapter XIII) will have a similar effect in both communist and non-communist states.

The costs of campaigning for political office have been rising for many decades in all democratic countries and will continue to rise for many more. American campaign spending rose from $140 million in 1952 to $200 million in 1964. Such funds are largely supplied by a few wealthy men who usually expect personal favors from winning candidates and are much more conservative than the average voter. To reduce these evils, some democratic governments have already begun to assume part of the costs of political campaigns, and more will do so. By A.D. 2060 the costs of democratic political campaigns in advanced states will largely be met by governments. Methods used will include direct cash subsidies, income-tax benefits to small contributors, regulations requiring radio and television stations to provide more and more free broadcasting services to candidates, and similar regulations applicable to newspapers and magazines.

The political influence of very large campaign contributors will also be increasingly restricted in other ways. The amount which each person is allowed to give will be limited, and the limit will be steadily reduced. By 2060 it will be $1,000 or less per year in the United States. And the methods used to enforce public reporting of campaign expenditures will become more and more effective.

The 1964 decision of the Supreme Court on reapportionment of legislative districts, which requires that they be roughly equal in population, was a notable event in the advance of political democracy. In a perfectly democratic country all such districts would be perfectly equal. They will become more and more equal in democratic countries.

All remaining monarchial governments will become republics before 2100. Some monarchies will be eliminated by revolution (in Asia and Africa), and some by political reform, before a world government is created. A Soviet-dominated world government would soon retire any remaining monarchs. A United States–dominated world government would permit them to exist a while longer but not permanently. Monarchy is obviously obsolete in all advanced states, most of which have already retired their royal families.

While the governments of most countries, communist as well as non-communist, will become more and more democratic for a century or two, this trend will not continue throughout the next 500 years. It will first be supplemented, and then eventually replaced, by a trend toward government by experts, discussed later in this chapter.

Public Administration

One of the major trends in public administration during the next few centuries will be a continuous centralization of governmental activities. This trend will include the gradual shifting of many administrative functions now performed by local or regional units of government to regional or national units and ever-growing regional or central-government control over the performance of those functions remaining in local or regional hands. Such trends will be most marked in countries like the United States where government is still very decentralized.

In the United States local units of government now establish and operate schools, hospitals, jails, police departments, fire departments, public utilities. All such functions will be shifted to national agencies before A.D. 2200. Most will be shifted first to state governments and later to the national government. In the meantime state and national financing of and control over these functions will increase steadily. This trend is already old and obvious in the case of education, public relief, medical care, and certain other functions. Thus American state governments, with some federal aid, financed 33 percent of the 1962 cost of local school districts, which gave them considerable control over local education. This percentage will rise above 66 percent by A.D. 2050, and the national government will then provide over half of such state aid, compared with 11 percent in 1962.

The American system of public employment exchanges and the unemployment-insurance system are both now administered by the states. They will be among the first state functions taken over completely by the federal government, almost certainly before A.D. 2050.

The construction and maintenance of all city streets will be taken over by county governments in most American states before 2050. More and more county highways will be declared state highways and thereafter maintained by a state highway department. During the twenty-first century the United States federal government will assume the function of building and maintaining main interstate highways. By 2200 it will build and maintain all streets and highways.

The steady decline in the relative importance of local governments in the United States is clearly shown by the decline in their share of total federal tax revenues. In 1900 they collected about 50 percent of this total, but in 1960 only 15 percent. This share will continue to decline indefinitely, both in America and in all other advanced countries with local governments. In the United States it will fall below 10 percent by A.D. 2000 and below 5 percent by 2100.

The state share of total taxes rose from 13 percent in 1900 to 18 percent in 1964, due to the assumption of more and more local functions of government. It would have risen much faster if the federal government had not heavily subsidized state assumption of local functions. Since such federal subsidies will continue to grow for many years, the near-future trend in the state share of total federal tax revenues is uncertain. But this trend will probably turn down before A.D. 2050 and will decline to zero by 2200.

Many functions of local and state governments in America have been increasingly financed by federal grants in recent decades. Such grants were negligible in 1900 but rose to $0.9 billion in 1940, $2.4 billion in 1950, and $10.2 billion in 1964. They will continue to rise, both absolutely and relatively, for several decades. They will begin to decline only after most subsidized local functions have been assumed by the federal government, probably during the first half of the twenty-second century. In the meantime this growing federal financing of state and local functions will give the central government more and more control over their performance. Federal agencies will use this expanding control to improve, and especially to standardize, local methods of performing the subsidized functions.

The trend toward centralization of public administration will also include centralization of control over most now-independent administrative agencies of central governments, such as the BBC, the NCB, the FRB, the ICC, and the SEC. Before A.D. 2000 each new president of the United States will be authorized to appoint and remove a majority of the members of nearly all such boards and commissions. Before 2100 nearly all will be abolished and replaced by single executives appointed by the president. A committee cannot administer an army or a government agency as well as a single executive. And a chief executive ought to possess the authority needed to carry out his major policies and fulfill his responsibilities. Hence the proportion of political scientists who approve the changes predicted above has been growing for over 50 years.

A second major worldwide trend in public administration for the next two or three centuries will be a steady increase in the average size of all units of government—local, regional, and national. In the United States during the next century this trend will be especially obvious and significant among local units—cities and counties.

The geographical limits of most American cities have been

repeatedly extended but not fast enough to prevent the creation of numerous adjacent suburbs. For instance, Los Angeles is surrounded by over sixty independent city governments. This has greatly increased the costs of local government. However, the need for integration is being recognized by more and more political scientists and civic leaders. It seems almost certain, therefore, that by 2100 nearly all American metropolitan areas will be governed by new area-wide metropolitan city-county governments.

Most American metropolitan areas now have many government units other than city and county governments—sewer districts, flood-control districts, school districts, etc. The total runs to over three hundred in Los Angeles and over one thousand in New York. Nearly all these units will be merged with the coming metropolitan city-county governments. By 2200 there will be only one local government in each metropolitan area throughout most of the world.

More and more American county and township governments will also be consolidated or abolished. In small states they will be abolished; in large ones, consolidated. By 2100 the number of counties will have declined from 3,047 (1960) to 500 or less. And nearly all townships (17,198 in 1960) will have been abolished.

In order to achieve some of the economies of a larger scale of operation, hundreds of small American units of government have already contracted with larger neighbors to provide individual public services—library, health, police, tax collection, etc. Los Angeles County, the largest purveyor of such services, had over fifteen hundred contracts covering fifty different services in force in 1961. The number of such contracts will continue to expand for several decades, until the local-government consolidation trend has greatly reduced the need for such contracts.

The consolidation of local American government units will eventually be accompanied or followed by the consolidation of American states, now fifty in number, into fewer than twenty large states, or national administrative units, fairly equal in population. For instance, all six New England states will be consolidated into a single unit. By 2300 no new or surviving state will have fewer than 20 million people.

Similar consolidation or integration movements will prevail for a century or two in all foreign countries, in both local and regional administration units. The number of prefectures in France, states in Germany, provinces in Italy, etc., will be radically reduced by A.D. 2100, Indeed, the ninety French departments may be reduced to a dozen or so within a decade.

After the coming world government (predicted later in this chapter) has become firmly established, it will extend this consolidation trend to most national governments. In the beginning it will fear resistance from powerful, once rival, national governments and may subdivide some of them temporarily, but it will soon consolidate many small national governments into larger units to improve the efficiency and reduce the costs of national government. For instance, it will merge the forty-odd African states into fewer than ten states, and the twenty-one Latin-American states into fewer than six. Later, but before A.D. 2500, it will carry such political integration much further, probably creating a single national government for each continent or major subcontinent. These units will number less than twelve, and their boundaries will not follow old national boundaries, except where the latter coincide with continental limits. Every improvement in the means of communication and transportation, many more of which are coming, enlarges the optimum size of all units of government. Moreover, a single executive should not have more than twelve immediate subordinates.

In America it is now customary to elect several state officials in addition to governors and state legislators, and many local officials in addition to mayors and local legislators. The ratio of elected to appointed officials has, however, been declining for over 50 years, and this trend will continue until, by 2200, all officials except legislators and chief executives will be appointed by a higher executive or chosen by a professional association.

Bribery of public officials and legislators has been declining for centuries in all advanced states. It will continue to decline indefinitely for many reasons—increase in government salaries, the growth of education, centralization of control, improved police methods, and the decline of private profit seeking.

It is now difficult to demonstrate this generally recognized trend because the statistics required to verify it are largely lacking, and those available are unstandardized. In the future such statistics will become more and more complete and accurate. They will eventually, by A.D. 2100 in the United States, include full and uniform reports on all income and spending by key officials and legislators, all convictions for bribery, and all political campaign contributions and spending.

Increasing centralization of government functions will help to reduce bribery and corruption because it will establish ever more adequate supervision and control over thousands of local officials—mayors, police chiefs, sheriffs, judges—who are now virtually unsupervised. For instance, the growth of state and federal control over local police officials will greatly reduce police corruption in America.

Legislation

The fifty American states have up to fifty different laws on marriage, divorce, birth control, abortion, crime, automobile licensing and operation, highway speeds, civil contracts, etc. The function of legislating on such subjects will be gradually shifted to the national government. By 2100 the United States will have uniform national laws on marriage and divorce, crime, automobile licensing, and much else. These reforms are inevitable because they will make it far easier to learn what the law is, to obey it, and to enforce it. They will sharply reduce the number and costs of court trials and the costs of legislation. They will also improve the product of legislation—laws. Every increase in interstate migration, travel, business, and crime makes such reforms more desirable and inevitable, and nearly all such interstate activities will increase steadily and indefinitely.

Most legislators in all countries now function only part-time. They are practicing farmers, bankers, lawyers, businessmen, etc., who devote only part of their time, often a minor part, to their legislative duties. In the years ahead they will need to devote more and more time to legislation. Partly for this reason, and partly to minimize obvious conflicts of interest, many governments will soon require legislators to give up all other gainful activities. This rule will be applied to the members of most national legislatures and some large American states before 2050. To avoid undue hardships to legislators, governments will grant increasingly liberal pensions to all defeated and retired legislators.

The better the legislators, the better the legislation. Hence many reforms which will produce better legislators are inevitable. Educational requirements will be established and gradually raised as educational opportunities become more equal, and higher education more common. By 2100 most legislatures will admit only members with a university degree. Later a Ph.D. or its equivalent will be required. Moreover, retirement at a fairly early age (sixty to sixty-five) will be increasingly required. Modern legislatures contain far too many old men whose energy and intellectual ability have seriously declined. The seniority system of selecting legislative leaders is partly responsible for this. It will be abandoned in America within a few decades.

For centuries new laws have been growing longer, more comprehensive, and more detailed. They often run to many thousand words. They prescribe protective tariffs on each type of goods, provide funds for individual weapons and military camps, fix postal rates for each class of mail, etc. In other words, they include innumerable decisions which ought to be left to administrative agencies. The trend toward longer laws may continue for several more decades, but it will be reversed during the twenty-first century, if not before, in all advanced states. Thereafter the average length and detail of new laws will decline steadily for centuries. By 2500, new laws will merely state major general policies or total sums appropriated for major administrative units. Their average length will be less than five hundred words.

The coming gradual substitution of brief general policy statements for long detailed laws will result from, and be one evidence of, a more fundamental and significant political trend, the ever-increasing delegation of minor legislative functions to administrative agencies. The delegation of legislative functions to administrative agencies will continue indefinitely because the burden of legislative work will continue to grow faster than the abilities of legislators. All central governments will assume more and more legislative functions, and both new and old legislative problems will beome increasingly complex. To free more time for the consideration of major social policies, legislatures will gradually delegate more and more minor legislative functions to administrative agencies, which will employ experts much better qualified to perform these functions than elected legislators. Moreover, such delegation will grow because it will permit far more frequent review and more prompt revision of minor legislative rulings. Modern legislatures are rarely able to review and revise the details of old laws as often as they should.

Most national legislatures still consider hundreds of bills affecting only one person—special immigration visas, accident compensation, insurance benefits, pension awards, etc. Experts have increasingly recommended that jurisdiction over all such cases be assigned to administration agencies, so that legislatures can concentrate on more important problems. This recommendation will be adopted by nearly all national legislatures in advanced countries before 2100.

Legislatures now spend an inordinate amount of time considering annual appropriations and often fail to approve them before the fiscal year begins. This burden will soon be radically reduced by making many appropriations for two years instead of one. By 2300 most budgets and appropriations will cover three to four years; by 2500, five to ten years. Such reforms will enable administrators to plan their future operations more efficiently.

The substitution of one-chamber for two-chamber legislatures has already begun in both the United States and Great Britain and will continue until all legislatures have one chamber only. The United States Senate and the British House of Lords will both be abolished before 2200.

In the interim before the abolition of the Senate, the waste due to two-chamber legislation will be gradually reduced by the creation of more and more joint House-Senate committees and the conduct of more joint hearings by separate committees.

Legislators were originally divided into two or more houses to represent two or more classes of people. This division has been retained until now primarily because of cultural lag and because conservatives fear the speed-up in social reform which would result from making legislatures more democratic and efficient. But history shows clearly that in advanced countries conservatives nearly always lose out in such struggles against the growth of democracy and efficiency. And one-chamber legislatures are much more efficient because they attract able men and enable them to achieve results more quickly.

The history-making 1964 reapportionment decision of the Supreme Court requires that upper chambers of state legislatures be as democratic as the lower. This will sharply reduce conservative support for the preservation of two-chamber legislatures in America.

Several other artificial obstacles to efficient legislation by the United States Congress will be eliminated during the next 100 years. The right of senators to filibuster will be ended. The seniority system of selecting committee chairmen will be replaced by another, probably election by committee members. In the meantime the power of chairmen to delay approval of popular new laws will be reduced. These measures will make Congress more democratic as well as more efficient. They have received growing support among American political scientists for many years.

Adjudication

The United States now has a federal court system and fifty different state court systems, each with its own rules for selecting, supervising, paying, and removing judges. And within nearly all states there are county and city judicial systems. One of the major American judicial trends during the next century or two will be the gradual integration of these systems into a single national system with uniform methods of selection, supervision, payment, promotion, retirement, and removal of judges. This integration will begin at local levels with the integration of city and county courts (by A.D. 2050), will proceed to the integration of local and state courts (by 2100), will continue to the integration of all state courts into a single national system (by 2200), and will culminate in the integration of all national court systems into a single world judicial system (before 2500).

In advanced capitalist countries court trials are far too costly and slow to be suitable for the settling of most civil disputes and minor criminal cases. Many reforms to simplify and speed up court trials will be adopted during the next century or two; nevertheless, the proportion of civil disputes and criminal cases handled by lawyers and courts will decline steadily for centuries.

American businessmen have been settling more and more civil disputes among themselves by voluntary arbitration. This trend will continue to grow in most capitalist states for many decades, but it will eventually be reversed when court procedures become as efficient as voluntary arbitration.

In recent years the growth of social insurance and the rise of public regulatory boards (like the FTC, FCC, and SEC) has made possible administrative handling of more and more disputes which would otherwise have required legal services and court decisions. These trends are bound to continue for many more decades in non-communist states.

American states will soon begin to establish auto-accident compensation systems which will settle over 90 percent of all accident claims within a few months after accidents without any court trial or legal expense, as workmen-compensation boards now do. The question of accident responsibility will be largely ignored by these new compensation agencies because it is too difficult to determine and because those responsible for accidents usually need compensation. This new method of handling auto-accident claims will yield better results much more quickly and at far lower cost. It has been advocated by a growing number of experts and is opposed chiefly by lawyers who fear a loss of clients. It will be adopted by most American states and most advanced countries before A.D. 2100.

The gradual consolidation of other industries into giant monopolies will also eliminate many civil trials. Divisions of the same trust do not sue one another.

Reform of divorce laws will soon begin to reduce the need for legal services and court hearings. By A.D. 2100 all such cases will be handled by administrative agencies staffed with professional family counselors (see Chapter XV).

Many other social reforms, predicted in later chapters, will gradually reduce the use of lawyers and courts to settle business and personal disputes.

Civil cases now outnumber criminal cases in American courts by six to one. Opposition to the use of juries in civil cases has been growing in Anglo-Saxon countries for over 50 years. Most U.S. lawyers now favor dispensing with the civil jury. Great Britain began to curtail the use of civil juries in 1933, and by 1960 had virtually eliminated them. A similar development will occur in America during the next 100 years. The use of civil juries lengthens trials, greatly increases daily trial costs, induces lawyers to use emotional and illogical arguments, and results in decisions which are less sound than those rendered by professionally trained experts.

The proportion of United States judges who are appointed rather than elected has long been rising and will continue to rise steadily until all are appointed. Expert opinion strongly supports this trend.

Most judicial appointments in the United States are still made for political reasons, but the proportion of appointments made by means of a formal merit system has been rising, and will continue to rise, in all advanced countries until all judges are so selected, probably before 2100. Formal merit systems usually include a nominating committee of highly qualified lawyers, so their use is a step toward government by experts, which will be discussed later in this chapter.

Another major judicial trend during the next few centuries will be ever-increasing specialization among judges. A judge who is competent to decide an antitrust case is rarely competent to decide a case concerning the infringement of an electronic patent. Specialization among judges is as beneficial as specialization among engineers or physicians and will become more and more desirable as human knowledge expands. By 2200 all judicial systems will employ only judges specializing in one of many different fields, and all cases will be heard before judges who are specialists. Even national supreme courts will then have specialized divisions or panels which recommend verdicts to the full court.

The theory of jurisprudence will become less and less religious and ethical and more and more scientific. Lawyers, judges, and juries will gradually stop trying to achieve justice and instead will try to achieve socially expedient or utilitarian decisions. Criminal and civil laws will be revised to explicitly permit and encourage utilitarian decision. In the beginning this change will be concealed or obscured as a redefinition of the term *just* to mean expedient rather than moral or right, but before 2300 this radical change will be openly admitted in most law textbooks.

Increasing emphasis upon the utilitarian function of courts and lawyers will lead to ever-growing efforts to cut the costs of court procedures below the economic benefits from such procedures. Today minor court trials may cost several hundred thousand dollars, in part because "justice" is considered "priceless."

The size of the average law firm has been growing steadily for over a century in advanced non-communist countries, and this trend will long continue. It has already resulted in much specialization among the members of such firms, and specialization among independent lawyers has also grown steadily. But as yet, all American lawyers receive a similar general legal education, pass one bar examination in each state, and are authorized to handle all kinds of legal problems. Specialized education, degrees, legal functions, and licenses for lawyers will be introduced in all advanced countries before A.D. 2100. By 2200 nearly all lawyers in the world will be members of large legal staffs and will practice in only one of at least a dozen legal specialties.

Sale of the best legal advice to the highest bidder enables rich men to buy justice, to win court cases they ought not to win, and prevents many poor men from securing justice. Expert and lay recognition of these truths has long been growing and has led to the provision of more and more free legal aid to poor men accused of crime. The provision of free legal aid will increase steadily until by 2200 nearly all legal advice to individuals will be free. By then nearly all lawyers will be government employees, and the best lawyers will advise poor men far more often than rich men. In the meantime labor unions and consumer co-ops in advanced non-communist states will increasingly create legal staffs of specialists to advise their members on personal legal problems.

Nationalism

Most historians describe the rise of nationalism—the reorganization of national boundaries to coincide more closely with language and racial boundaries—as a major political trend of the last few centuries, and especially significant during the last century. In Europe this trend is nearing a natural limit, a separate nation for every major language group, but it still has far to go in Africa, Asia, and Latin America.

When Africa was divided among the colonial powers, little regard was given to language and tribal boundaries, and the new African states have yet done little to alter the former colonial boundaries. A complete redrawing of these boundaries along major language or tribal boundaries is inevitable, probably during the twenty-first century. Some of this redrawing will result from wars between African states, but most of it will be done by the United Nations, or by the coming world government, and enforced by international armed forces.

In Asia the breakup of both India and Pakistan into several national states with boundaries coinciding chiefly with language boundaries is highly probable. A successful communist revolution in India, also probable, would delay, but not permanently prevent, such a political reorganization. The coming world government will almost certainly divide India into semi-autonomous national states, each based chiefly on a common language and independent of Delhi, in order to weaken a potential center of resistance.

Since Belgium and Switzerland do not speak a single language, they will be broken up and divided among their neighbors along language boundaries before 2100.

In South and Central America there will be several mergers of independent Spanish-speaking states into larger and stronger nations. For instance, Uruguay, Argentina, and Chile will merge before 2100.

The white English-speaking nations, separated by the American Revolution and the granting of dominion status, will form a new federal union before 2100 unless the Soviet Union wins World War III and prevents this union. Americans, British, Canadians, and Australians have more in common than Bavarians and Prussians, White Russians and Great Russians, or Sicilians and Milanese. Moreover, the creation of such a union would yield notable economic and political advantages.

Two major social trends will increasingly limit the rise of nationalism, namely the trend toward political integration of the world (discussed in the following section) and the trend toward cultural homogenization.

In the past nationalists have created completely independent or sovereign nations. This will be impossible after a world government has been established. But such a government will favor the creation of subordinate states and, later, administrative units with boundaries based on language.

The chief driving force behind the rise of nationalism has been, and will continue to be, the almost universal human desire to associate with and be governed by men who speak the same language, belong to the same race, and have the same religion. As religion declines, language and race will become more and more important elements. For instance, the present division of the Indian subcontinent on the basis of religion will be replaced by one based on language before 2200.

World Government

I have assumed that mankind will survive and continue to progress in spite of probable heavy losses of wealth and population in future wars, but not that nuclear wars and heavy losses will be avoided. The long record of man's warlike past clearly suggests that one or more future major wars are inevitable. Since the United States and the Soviet Union are the only surviving great powers, and since the cold war has lasted so long, it is probable that World War III will be between these nations. It is far more difficult to predict the date of this war, which may occur at any time. It is likely to begin before A.D. 2060.

For ten thousand years men have been creating larger political states. Some great empires have broken up into smaller units, but this has never prevented the subsequent creation of much larger, more populous, and more homogenous states. Today the Soviet Union, the United States, and China are all much more extensive and populous than the Roman Empire ever was. This old trend toward larger political units is certain to continue until the world is ruled by a single government. The invention of nuclear and other modern weapons has made the rapid completion of this trend more desirable than ever before and has also made it feasible for perhaps the first time. Hence not only is creation of a world government now inevitable—it always was—but it is almost certain to occur before A.D. 2100.

Since only one nation (Japan) has thus far experienced the effect of nuclear bombs—two primitive ones—the American and Soviet governments are still willing to risk nuclear war for trivial reasons—for instance, to preserve face or to establish or protect friendly governments in minor foreign countries. But after the United States and the Soviet Union have experienced the horrors of nuclear war, they will be far more eager to prevent the recurrence of these horrors. One such experience will probably suffice to stimulate the creation of a world government strong enough to prevent nuclear warfare. But if one does not, two or three certainly will.

There are several ways in which the coming world government can be formed: by peaceful agreement among all or most nations; by world conquest by the United States or the Soviet Union; by creation of a Soviet-American condominium.

The ideal method, of course, would be peaceful international agreement, but such an agreement is most unlikely. Few nations are today willing to subordinate themselves to a strong world government, and the United States and the Soviet Union are much less willing than smaller states. World conquest by one of these great powers seems far more likely. Even a Soviet-American condominium is more likely than a multinational agreement, since it is much easier for two than for many powers to make agreements, and since such a condominium would leave much more power in the hands of the two powers.

While the first world government will in fact be an American, Soviet, or Soviet-American world empire, it will in name be a federal union of independent nations. Both the United States and the Soviet Union now are nominally federal unions, and this will facilitate annexation of some adjacent states, but the enlarged United States and/or Soviet Union will nominally become merely very large units in a new super federation, perhaps a reorganized United Nations. While some allies may be given significant auxiliary political roles in this new world federation, it will long be firmly controlled by its major founder or founders.

Whether American, Soviet, or Soviet-American, the coming world empire will initially permit almost complete national self-government outside annexed areas. But it will disarm all other national governments and will establish an effective system of worldwide inspection to keep them disarmed. The ruling state itself will not maintain large armed forces indefinitely. It will rely increasingly on the threat of nuclear bombing to ensure a free scope for its inspectors and obedience to its orders. By the year 2200 world military expenditures, which now exceed 10 percent of world income, will have fallen to less than 1 percent; by 2500, to less than 0.1 percent.

After the new world empire has become firmly established, it will gradually increase its control over national governments. Customs duties will slowly be lowered, a uniform international currency system created, a single world transportation system established, uniform civil and criminal laws enacted and enforced, a single world language (that of the world conqueror) promoted and eventually enforced. The process of world economic, cultural, and political integration will continue over many centuries, until all the peoples of the world are culturally and racially homogeneous.

Government by Experts

The first world government will not be even nominally democratic. It will be a world empire created by a semi-democratic capitalist America, a one-party communist Soviet Union, or a Soviet-American alliance. Neither the United States nor the Soviet Union will be willing to become a minor factor in a democratic or semi-democratic world parliament.

An American world empire would initially favor capitalist democracy within most or all foreign countries. By suitable encouragement and intervention it would make such government more and more widespread.

A Soviet world empire would initially create one-party

Communist governments in most or all subordinate nations. These one-party national governments, and the Soviet world government, would gradually become more and more internally democratic because such government is now, and will for centuries continue to be, more popular and efficient than dictatorships or one-party rule in stable advanced nations. Marx, Engels, and Lenin all looked forward to democratic government after socialism had become firmly established.

Whether established by an American, Soviet, or Soviet-American world empire, democratic national government will not be permanent. It will gradually be transformed everywhere into government by experts—by highly educated professional social scientists chosen by non-democratic means.

The gradual transition from rule by elected politicians or Communist-party leaders to rule by professional civil servants, often called the growth of bureaucracy, is already well under way. It will continue for centuries. Both capitalist and communist administrators will depend increasingly upon ever more highly educated experts and social scientists.

For over a century legislators in advanced countries have increasingly relied on expert consultants, employed by them or by administrative agencies, to propose, write, explain, and evaluate new laws. In the future they will employ ever larger staffs of expert consultants responsible solely to them and will rely more and more upon the professional advice of these and other experts.

The Legislative Reference Service of the Library of Congress was established in 1914 to give expert advice and information to members of Congress. Its staff grew slowly to 213 by 1963. It will rise above 1,500 by A.D. 2000 and above 10,000 by 2100. The professional staffs of congressional committees will also grow rapidly until they are merged with the Legislative Reference Service or its successor.

In capitalist countries the control of large corporations has long been shifting from heirs of the founders and other large stockholders to able professional managers. This trend will continue indefinitely, and it will steadily enlarge the political as well as the business influence of highly educated professional administrators. Such men will manage more and more state-owned as well as private enterprises.

America has made one significant contribution to the growth of government by experts in democratic countries, namely, the employment of professional city and county managers chosen by and subordinate to local legislative bodies. This system was first tried some fifty years ago and has since been adopted by a growing number of cities and counties in Canada and Ireland, as well as in the United States. By 1963 the number had risen to 1,891, including fifty-seven in Canada. By A.D. 2000 most of the larger British and American cities will have professional managers instead of politician managers. By 2100 all cities in advanced capitalist states will have highly educated professional managers.

Government by experts is government by the most able and is therefore incompatible with political democracy. In its early and middle stages the rise of government by experts is compatible with democracy, but achievement of full government by experts is possible only when ruling experts are selected by experts. No large mass of voters will ever be competent to choose its political leaders on the basis of ability alone. Only an expert can evaluate the performance of an expert.

During the transition period the proportion of public officials who have graduate professional degrees in their field of work will increase steadily. And the number of legislators who have Ph.D. degrees in social science will also increase continuously. By 2200 most members of Congress will have Ph.D. degrees in some social science.

Government by experts will be fully achieved when all world and national legislators and chief executives are professional men, mostly social scientists, chosen by their professional associations or by a legislature so chosen, not by the general public. Such full government by experts will be achieved before 2500.

These powerful professional associations and the educational system which creates their members will be equally open to all, that is, completely non-discriminatory. All superior children will be given a superior education. Thus government by experts will be a meritocracy—rule by the most able and best educated members of each generation.

These expert rulers will use scientific public-opinion polls to determine how much resistance there is to desirable social reforms. They will then minimize such resistance by education and propaganda. They will never yield permanently to uninformed prejudice but will always measure and allow for it in order to prevent riots, sabotage, revolution, and civil war.

Continued progress toward, and ultimate achievement of, some form of government by experts is certain because: political problems are becoming more and more numerous and complex; expert knowledge about such problems (social science) is growing steadily and rapidly; popular prejudice against inherited or undeserved political power is growing; and the public of every advanced country is becoming better educated, and therefore ever more willing to accept expert advice and leadership. All these trends will continue for centuries.

When the first advocates of democratic government began their campaign, about 200 years ago, the problems of government were relatively few and simple, and these advocates underestimated their complexity. Moreover, social science had barely begun to be thought of, and almost every educated man considered himself competent to deal with political problems. The democratic idealists believed that all men could and should be educated, and that this would make nearly all men competent to vote wisely.

Since 1800 world population has more than trebled, the industrial revolution has transformed and greatly complicated economic life, an ever-increasing division of labor has created many new competing or conflicting interests, the functions of government have become more and more numerous and complex, and new social sciences have appeared and begun to develop rapidly. By 2100 most adults in advanced states will have had some higher education, and this education will give them ever-increasing respect for the social sciences.

Although the social sciences have developed rapidly since

1760, they are still far from being sufficiently advanced to provide a basis for successful government by experts. The social sciences will, however, continue to advance at an ever faster rate during the next few centuries. Thus they will provide a firm basis for government by experts long before 2500.

Moreover, the growth of the political influence of social scientists will itself help to accelerate the growth of government expenditures on social research and social-science education. And the social sciences will become more and more prescriptive. For instance, welfare economics will receive ever more attention. Economics will again become political economy.

It has been argued that government by social scientists would create a slave world. But scientists do not tell men what ends they ought to pursue; they only help them to achieve what they already want to achieve. They are and will always be servants of mankind, not its masters. It is priests and other moralists who wish to alter normal human wants and goals, and the rise of science will steadily reduce the power of all moralists.

Public-Opinion Polls

Scientific public-opinion polling is less than fifty years old in the most advanced countries and has not even begun in many countries, but it is destined to become a major social institution in all countries within a century or two. As predicted in Chapter I, public-opinion polls will become an increasingly valuable source of data for social scientists and historians, especially those who predict scientifically. Moreover, such polls will be used more and more widely by business firms to discover market preferences, by religious organizations to determine religious opinion and the results of religious propaganda, by medical organizations to determine prevailing health habits and opinion, by educators to discover the effects of educational broadcasts and articles.

The most significant use of public-opinion polls, however, will be in political and governmental activities. American politicians have already begun to use private public-opinion polls to determine what political views and policies are most popular. This practice will grow steadily in America and will soon spread to and grow in all other democratic lands.

It is noteworthy that public-opinion polls can reveal political opinion far more accurately than any election. In an election one votes for a man or a party with many different political opinions, most of which have been deliberately concealed or ambiguously expressed. In well-designed political-opinion polls men can express their opinion on each major issue separately, and each issue can be clearly stated.

The chief function of a politician in a democratic country is to determine what his constituents want, and then advocate the most popular policies. Public-opinion polls are the ideal means of determining such wants, and they will therefore be improved and increasingly used as long as democratic government survives.

As democratic government is gradually transformed into government by experts, opinion polling will become an ever more vital means of communication between the public and the government. While elections are imperfect means of such communication, their elimination will make opinion polls even more necessary. When government by experts is fully achieved, opinion polls will replace elections as a means of political communication and pressure, and will function much more effectively.

The United States has already begun to conduct polls in some foreign countries in order to ascertain public opinion concerning American foreign policies and the effects of American foreign aid and propaganda. This use of polls will also expand steadily. The coming world government, which will initially be undemocratic, will find it essential to measure public opinion throughout the world on all new political policies affecting subordinate countries.

For all of these reasons the proportion of gross national product (GNP) spent on public-opinion polls will increase much more than tenfold in the United States during the next 500 years and will grow even faster in other countries.

CHAPTER IV

Population

The greatest threat to mankind is the danger of unlimited nuclear war. This danger will be eliminated by the creation of a world government. The second greatest threat is excessive population growth. World population was less than 10 million when men turned from hunting and fishing to agriculture, around 6000 B.C. It reached 200 million by A.D. 200 and 550 million in 1800. In the 160 years from 1800 to 1960 it skyrocketed to 3,000 million, and it is now growing faster than ever. Throughout this period most men have been illiterate, diseased, hungry, miserably housed, and short-lived, primarily because of gross overpopulation. Only during the past 200 years in a few advanced countries has the advance of technology and birth control been rapid enough to raise the masses to a tolerable, but still inadequate, standard of living.

Birth Control

In the absence of birth control, technological progress (broadly defined as all improvements in techniques and practices) merely results in an increase in population. Thus the rise of birth control in the West is largely if not entirely responsible for the fact that the people of the West live far better than the poverty-stricken masses of Asia, and therefore for the fact that the entire world will be rapidly westernized during the next few centuries. The growth of birth control was the most beneficial and significant historical trend of the past 200 years in Europe, and it will be the most significant trend during the next 200 years in Asia, Africa, and Latin America.

Crude and largely ineffective methods of birth control have been used since ancient times, but the significant and steadily growing use of more effective methods is only 200 years old. Like most other major contemporary social trends it began in Northwestern Europe, specifically in France, and then spread to Eastern and Southern Europe and North America. In 1750 the English birth rate was about 37 per 1,000. It fell only to 34 by 1850, but to 18 by 1960. In both North America and Europe the birth rate fell over 40 percent between 1850 and 1960. Since 1930, birth rates in Eastern and Southern Europe have fallen especially fast, and they are now little above the English rates. In one brief decade after World War II, Japan cut its birth rate 50 percent and thus caught up with Europe. And the rest of the world will soon follow this European path. In Latin America, mainland Asia, and Africa birth rates are still above 40. They will fall below 30 before A.D. 2050 and below 20 by 2100.

Voluntary birth control spread rapidly in advanced countries because infant-mortality rates had fallen earlier, because birth control permits parents to reduce the burden of child bearing and rearing, and because it permits them to give each child more care, a better education, and a larger inheritance. It also allows more frequent and more satisfying sexual intercourse among parents who desire to limit or space their families. In advanced countries public attitudes toward sexual intercourse have long been changing from disapproval to approval. Public demand for unworried sexual satisfaction will continue to grow for centuries, which will produce ever-growing opposition to laws that restrict such satisfaction, including laws against effective methods of birth control.

The Gallup Poll surveyed American public opinion on the dissemination of "birth control information" ten times during the years 1936–64. The proportion in favor of legalizing such dissemination rose from 64 percent in 1936 to 81 percent in 1964, and that opposed fell from 27 percent to 11 percent. In 1964 the higher the education, the greater was the support.

The number of public birth-control clinics in the United

States rose from none in 1920 to about 550 in 1950, and to over 1,000 in 1964, of which over 680 were tax-supported. But all clinics together still served fewer than 300,000 women in 1964. By A.D. 2000 American tax-supported clinics will number over 4,000 and will serve over 20 million persons free of charge each year. By 2100 all American medical clinics and general hospitals will supply birth-control information and contraceptives free of charge, and no separate birth-control clinics will remain.

The governments of several advanced countries and of some American states still penalize or obstruct the teaching and use of birth control. They will gradually stop doing so during the next few decades, and soon thereafter will begin to teach and subsidize the best methods of birth control. These changes, together with technical progress, will notably increase the use of birth control among the poorest and least-educated classes, who now produce an unduly large share of the next generation in every advanced country. By 2100 birth rates among the least-educated and least-able classes in such countries will be lower than the national average, instead of far above it.

During the next century or two the most rapid growth of birth control will occur in backward areas—Latin America, Asia, and Africa—not in advanced countries, because birth control is little used and is desperately needed in the poorest countries. For instance, in both China and India, which together contain over one third of mankind, population grows by over 10 million a year, which makes a rise in real wages extremely difficult, if not impossible, to achieve. Hence the governments of both countries are certain to make increasingly energetic and effective efforts to increase birth control. And the growth of public education will make Indians and Chinese ever more responsive to such government measures.

Since 1945 the Japanese have demonstrated for the first time that a strong government can quickly reduce the birth rate in a grossly overpopulated Asiatic state to the European level, chiefly by means of cheap legal abortion. The communist governments of China and other Asiatic states are strong governments and will soon become aware of their need for birth control to ensure rapid economic progress. They will adopt radical birth-control measures before non-communist Asiatic states do so and before a strong world government requires them to do so.

The continued uncontrolled growth of population in poor countries is a threat to world health—it creates epidemics—and to world peace—it results in revolutions and wars. Hence the governments of advanced countries will increasingly promote the spread of birth control in poor countries. The coming world government will be dominated by one or more advanced states and will use persuasive methods first, and coercive measures later, to induce the population of backward countries to practice enough birth control to slow their rapid population growth.

Abortion is now, and will long continue to be, a widely used method of birth control, even in the most advanced states. It is estimated that over a million illegal abortions are performed annually in the United States, where the best means of contraception are widely available. In Latin America the illegal abortion rate may be higher than the very high birth rate, and the resulting loss of life and health is large.

While abortion is not an ideal means of birth control, it is effective, and usually beneficial both to the individual and to the community. Public support for legalization of birth-control abortion has been growing steadily in all advanced and many backward states, especially among doctors and social scientists. Hence it is certain that such abortion will be legalized, and later subsidized, in more and more countries. By 2050 it will be legal, in most advanced states. By 2100 it will be legal, and probably also subsidized, in nearly all countries.

Legalization and subsidization of abortion will temporarily increase the number of abortions, especially in backward countries. But this effect will last less than 50 years in most states. The steady advance of education, real wages, and contraceptive techniques will cause a gradual substitution of more advanced methods of birth control for legal abortion.

Abortion for a few causes is now legal in nearly all states of the United States. In most of them it will be further legalized by increasing the number of legal causes and the discretion of doctors, not by suddenly declaring all abortions legal. Only some 8,000 legal abortions were performed in the United States in 1960. As doctors are given more discretion, this number will rise rapidly. It will exceed 200,000 a year by A.D. 2000, and 400,000 by 2060.

It has been said that the Roman Catholic church will never approve of abortion, because it is murder. But in fact it did approve of timely abortion (during the first eighty days) for many centuries before it changed its doctrine in 1869 (about the time it also condemned liberalism and socialism). Hence it should find it relatively easy to return to and liberalize its traditional doctrine.

It is noteworthy that Anglo-Saxon laws against abortion before quickening are almost equally recent (1803 in England and 1829 in New York State). This suggests again that there is no obvious case or strong tradition against abortion in Christian nations.

The cheapest, most convenient, and most effective method of birth control is sterilization. For males this is now a fifteen-minute operation requiring no hospitalization, and later desterilization is usually possible. It does not affect sexual activities except by reducing worry.

Statistics on the growth of sterilization, as on many other vital social trends, are scarce and imperfect, but it is estimated that about 1.5 million Americans had been sterilized by 1960, which implies that about 7 percent of all married couples of childbearing age used sterilization for birth control. A century earlier the rate was less than 0.1 percent. By A.D. 2100 most fathers of two children in all advanced countries will be voluntarily sterilized. And many men will be sterilized for eugenic reasons before the birth of any children.

During the next century the use of sterilization will grow much more rapidly in poor than in rich countries, because it is much cheaper and much more feasible than continuous use of contraceptive devices and pills and involves less cost and suffering than abortion. By 2200 the great majority of Latin-American and Asiatic fathers of two children will be sterilized.

World Population

Experts have made more demonstrable large errors in predicting population totals than in predicting almost any other social trends. For instance, in the 1930's population experts predicted that United States population would be less than 150 million in 1970. It reached 192 million in 1964. The chief reason why it grew so much faster than expected was World War II, which heavily penalized childless married men and single men by drafting them, and which also ended the great depression and began more than twenty years of unprecedented prosperity. The Korean War had similar, but lesser, effects. Such individual events are far harder to predict than social trends. In 1958 the century-old prewar decline in the United States birth rate reappeared. It will continue for many more decades.

Experts now predict that United States population will rise to about 300 million by the year 2000, assuming no major war losses. But prospective advances in birth-control methods and changes in immigration laws make this estimate unreliable.

Most population experts predict that world population (3 billion in 1960) will be 6 to 7 billion in A.D. 2000. These estimates do not make sufficient allowance for rapid improvement in the means of birth control and for coming changes in public opinion and government policies. The recent Japanese achievements in birth control have proven that any advanced nation can reduce its population growth quickly and sharply. The Chinese Communists may adopt similar measures within a decade or two. And other governments may greatly expand their birth-control programs at almost any time. It is, however, extremely difficult to predict how soon and how far any government will do so. In this field short-run predictions are much less reliable than long-run predictions. And long-run predictions concerning population totals are much less reliable than those concerning birth-control trends because such trends are only one of several major factors affecting population. Hence the following rough estimates of future world and United States populations are among the least reliable in this book.

Year	World (billions)	U.S. (1960 boundaries) (millions)
2000	5.5	280
2100	7.0	450
2200	8.6	600
2300	9.0	800
2400	10.0	1000
2500	11.0	1200

Most of the predicted increase in world population during the years 1960–2100 will occur in backward countries, and most of the increase after 2200 in advanced countries. The population of China and India will be less in A.D. 2500 than in 2100. The resulting changes in the distribution of world population will help to reduce international differences in real wages. That is a major reason why the world government and the people of backward nations will favor them.

These estimates imply that the world population growth rate is now near its all-time peak, about 2 percent a year. It will soon begin to decline and will thereafter decline steadily for centuries. The United States population growth rate reached its all-time peak early in the nineteenth century, and it will soon resume its long-run decline and continue it indefinitely. But the share of United States population in total world population will increase steadily throughout most of the next 500 years.

Migration

Human migration may be international or internal, and each may be due to economic or climatic factors. Economic factors have been dominant in the past, but climatic factors are destined to become increasingly important, and eventually dominant, first in the most advanced countries and later in other countries.

European migration to Siberia, Australia, and the Americas will continue for a long time, primarily for economic reasons. An American world empire would encourage and subsidize such migration for political and military reasons, and the Soviet Union is already subsidizing European migration to Central Asia and Siberia. But population is growing so rapidly in once little-settled areas—North and South America, Australia, Africa—that international migration to these areas will decline steadily throughout most of the next 500 years. And the international migration that continues will be increasingly for climatic rather than economic reasons.

In most advanced countries migration from areas with less desirable climates to those with more desirable climates has been going on for many decades. In England and France hundreds of thousands of families have moved from the north to the south. In North America millions have moved from the East and Middle West to the Pacific Coast, the Southwest, and Florida. These trends will continue for centuries, and similar trends will appear and continue indefinitely in all large countries. The cumulative result will be a radical redistribution of population—first within each country, and then between countries—from less to more pleasant climatic zones.

Every increase in average real income facilitates and stimulates migration to areas with a similar culture and a more pleasant climate. And personal real incomes will continue to rise indefinitely (see Chapter V). Moreover, it will become more and more easy for migrants to obtain suitable jobs in all areas.

Within the United States there are great differences in climate, and the people have the highest real incomes in the world. Hence internal migration to better climates will long continue to be much larger in America than in other countries. In 1900, California had only 2 percent of United States population. By 1960 its share had risen to 9 percent. It should rise above 20 percent by 2100 and above 30 percent by 2500. The populations of Florida, Oregon, Washington, Arizona, and New Mexico should also grow much faster than total United States population, largely for climatic reasons.

In Canada the substantial migration to British Columbia will continue indefinitely. In 1960, British Columbia had only 9 percent of Canadian population. This share will rise to 30 percent by

2100 and to 60 percent by 2500. Furthermore, a great many Canadians will move to milder climatic areas below the border, especially to Florida and California.

In Mexico also there will be heavy migration to more agreeable climates, which include the central plateau and the Pacific coast of Lower California. In 1960, Lower California had less than 2 percent of Mexican population. By 2100 it will have 10 percent and by 2500, 20 percent.

The migration of North Americans from harsh to mild climates will continue throughout the next 500 years. As real incomes rise and transport costs decline (see Chapter X), it will become less and less economically advantageous to live and work near the sources of raw materials. Moreover, the share of the United States labor force employed in agriculture will soon fall below 2 percent (see Chapter VIII). As a result the population of New England, the Middle West, the inland South, and other areas with unpleasant climates will begin a long decline before 2100. By 2500 many large American cities with the worst climates —Washington, D.C., Memphis, Houston, Dallas, Birmingham, Richmond—will have been largely abandoned. Most states in the fertile Mississippi Valley will retain only the small population needed to operate and service highly mechanized farms, mines, and transport facilities.

In Europe population movements are still largely determined by non-climatic factors, especially by a search for jobs, but this situation will soon change. During and after the twenty-first century Northern Europeans will move in ever-growing numbers to Southern Europe and North Africa in order to enjoy a milder climate. Political unification of Europe and the world will greatly facilitate such movements. In Russia, where northern climates are especially severe, cities like Leningrad and Moscow will be virtually abandoned long before A.D. 2500. The Russian Black Sea coast will then have over 50 percent of the population of European Russia.

In Africa there will be a vast migration of population from Central to South Africa, the Rhodesias, and the highlands of East Africa. In South America most of the population of northern

Brazil will migrate to the south. And in many other areas of the world urban populations will migrate from hot, humid lowlands to cool, dry uplands or from cold uplands to cool sea coasts. In the most desirable climatic areas—the European Riviera, central Mexico, the California coast, etc.—the population will be so dense that nearly all people will live in tall apartment buildings, and little if any land will be farmed.

Racial Minorities

Nearly all nations not ruled by racial minorities mistreat these minorities, and those ruled by such minorities mistreat their racial majorities and/or other minorities. The greater the difference in race, the worse the mistreatment. Thus Negro minorities suffer the most from racial discrimination. The treatment of non-ruling racial minorities has, however, been slowly improving in all advanced countries for centuries and will continue to improve indefinitely. The cruel Nazi anti-Jewish campaign was too brief and isolated to demonstrate a reversal of this trend.

The most significant and easily measurable evidences of racial discrimination are the differences in average income per person. These differences will continue to diminish until they have almost vanished, before 2500 in most countries.

The real incomes of American Negroes have risen faster than average incomes for over 100 years. Chiefly because of World War II, Negro family median income jumped from 37 percent to 54 percent of the white figure between 1940 and 1960. This ratio will rise above 65 percent by A.D. 2000 and above 90 percent by 2200.

This trend has been and will continue to be due chiefly to a gradual reduction in educational, medical, and employment discrimination against Negroes. By 2200 the proportions of American Negroes who finish secondary and higher schools will be as high as the proportions of whites who do so. Negro doctors, scientists, carpenters, plumbers, will become relatively almost as numerous as white ones.

The segregation of American Negroes in separate, usually inferior, schools has been declining slowly for a century. The 1953 decision of the Supreme Court, the gradual economic advance of American Negroes, the growth of higher education among whites, and increasing foreign criticism of American racial discrimination ensure a continual decline in school segregation and in most other forms of public discrimination. By A.D. 2100 the great majority of American Negroes will attend truly (not merely nominally) desegregated schools. All other forms of racial discrimination will also continue to decline for centuries.

In every country where two or more races or racial strains live side by side, miscegenation is inevitable, and the number of persons of mixed blood tends to increase steadily. Most of the Jews killed by the Nazis were more Aryan than Jewish biologically, and 70 percent of American-census Negroes are mulattoes. Many mulattoes have "passed over" into the white population, most notably President Warren G. Harding. Some experts estimate that 20 percent of American "whites" are partly Negro.

As late as 1900 the great majority of American states still prohibited marriages between Negroes and whites. By 1964 the number had fallen to nineteen. Moreover, the enforcement of these laws had become less and less strict. In 1964 the Supreme Court finally declared such laws unconstitutional, and southern states will eventually accept this decision. Yet for many years longer most American miscegenation will be unintended or illegitimate. The popular prejudice against deliberate miscegenation will remain strong throughout the next century. But as American Negroes become more prosperous, better educated, and lighter in color, this white prejudice will continue to weaken until it has completely vanished.

Within a few decades it will be possible to determine by physiological tests which persons have one or more Negro ancestors. Such tests will show a steady and indefinite increase in this proportion. If it was 18 percent in 1960 (estimates range from 10 to 27 percent), it will be over 30 percent by 2100, over 50 percent by 2300, and over 90 percent by A.D. 2500. The official census figures will, however, rise much less rapidly, for the proportion of mulattoes able to pass over will increase steadily as they become better educated and lighter in color.

In countries like Brazil, Cuba, and Puerto Rico, where the proportion of Negroes and mulattoes is higher than in the United States, miscegenation will proceed more rapidly. Such countries will all have a homogeneous mulatto population well before 2500. In Mexico, Peru, Colombia, South Africa, and other countries where Europeans are a small minority, they will be almost entirely absorbed by the mulatto or mestizo population within two or three centuries.

The Soviet Union has many racial minorities, some of them quite large, but they will be almost completely absorbed in a new homogeneous Russian population by A.D. 2500.

The migration of natives of backward countries (mostly negroid, yellow, or dark-skinned) to advanced countries inhabited chiefly by Europeans will long continue to be strictly limited, but some migration and travel both ways will occur and will increase miscegenation. As miscegenation in advanced countries progresses, as living standards in backward countries rise, as the world adopts a single language, limitations on international migration will gradually be relaxed, and this will increase migration and miscegenation. Miscegenation will not, however, eliminate international racial differences during the next 500 years. The creation of a racially homogeneous world population will take over 1,000 years.

Eugenics

The most important of all social trends during the next millennium will be the introduction, extension, and constant improvement of compulsory eugenic measures. These measures will radically improve man himself, bringing the average for all men up to at least the level of the best 1 percent in 1960. At present the average man is far inferior to the best in health, appearance, longevity, native intelligence, disease resistance, emotional adjustment, human sympathy, and all other desirable traits. Moreover, the men who now excel in one or two of these respects rarely excel notably in all the others. By the year 2500 most men in all countries will be as handsome as today's movie stars, as intelligent as today's eminent professors, as energetic and healthy as today's athletes, emotionally well adjusted, kindhearted, and physically active until age ninety.

It is easier to predict the results of eugenic trends during the next 500 years than during the next 100 years, because eugenic reform is still a program, not yet a trend, and it is uncertain how soon the trend will become obvious and how fast it will develop. The world has more pressing major problems—war, hunger, poverty, disease—and probably will devote little attention and effort to important eugenic measures until these more pressing problems have been largely solved. As predicted in other chapters, these major problems will be largely solved before 2200; thereafter eugenic progress should speed up rapidly and become the most significant social trend, long before 2500.

The first major eugenic reform will be sterilization of the least fit—feeble-minded, insane, hemophiliacs, etc. A few thousand such persons are already being sterilized each year, and public support for such a program is growing in advanced countries. The proportion of defective persons sterilized will rise slowly but steadily. By A.D. 2100 over 3 percent, and by 2200 over 10 percent, of all children in the world will be sterilized before they become sexually mature.

Another important early eugenic program will first legalize, and later advocate and subsidize, voluntary artifical insemination with sperm from superior males. Small but growing numbers of childless couples in advanced countries are already resorting to artificial insemination, in spite of religious and legal obstacles. The sperm is now usually taken from superior males (mostly medical students, because they are more accessible to doctors). The eugenic effects of such practices will be gradually increased by more careful selection of donors, and artificial insemination will become far more popular when it is publicized as an inexpensive or free means by which parents can be almost sure to have superior children.

Eventually the use of artificial insemination will be increased by compulsion. Cocrcion will first be applied to couples with the least fit husbands. By 2300 most husbands will be sterilized before marriage, and couples will rely on artificial insemination.

Large-scale artificial insemination is now the ideal means of human eugenic progress because it permits rapid genetic improvement without interfering with normal family and sex life. After the entire human race has been raised to the level of the best year-1960 men, eugenic improvement will become much less needed, men will be far more intelligent, and eugenic coercion will be radically reduced or ended. But that is unlikely to happen before A.D. 2500.

In the meantime many grossly deformed and otherwise handicapped children will be born. As a means of reducing the costs and misery due to such births, eugenic infanticide will be widely adopted before the year 2200 and will become universal before 2400.

These and other eugenic measures will raise the average intelligence quotient of mankind above 130 before 2500. They will have equally remarkable effects on creativity quotients, disease susceptibility, insanity, juvenile delinquency, crime rates, longevity, and other measures of human performance. They will vastly increase the productivity of expenditures on scientific research and development because they will produce far more able scientists and more scientific geniuses. Eugenic measures will more than double the productivity of labor in most other occupations. By raising average intelligence, they will make government by experts and all other beneficial social reforms more and more politically acceptable.

The creation and indefinite continuance of an effective worldwide eugenic trend is inevitable because all parents want superior children, because all taxpayers dislike paying for the support of defective people, and because an ever-growing proportion of mankind desires social progress. Moreover, once international war has been eliminated, international competition will become largely economic and eugenic. The powerful desire for national distinction will promote economic and eugenic reform as effectively as it now promotes the armaments race.

The chief current argument against compulsory eugenic measures is that we do not know which persons are biologically inferior and which superior. The only element of truth in this argument is that our knowledge is far from complete, and always will be. We do know roughly which men are more healthy, intelligent, handsome, popular, industrious, and that children take after their parents. Our knowledge of eugenics will increase forever, but we already know enough to improve mankind radically within a few centuries.

In this section I have predicted some eugenic trends which will improve the entire population of the world. In the next I shall predict those which will increase the proportion of highly gifted persons in the world population and raise the ability of the most gifted.

The Creation and Use of Geniuses

Much, perhaps most, scientific and social progress is a result of the creative thought and work of less than 0.1 percent of mankind—geniuses and near geniuses (I.Q. of 160+). Their achievements will be more and more essential and significant in the future because scientific research and social problems will become ever more complex.

All the eugenic policies predicted in the preceding section will eventually increase the proportion of geniuses. Moreover, a current educational trend is already increasing this proportion.

The rapid growth of coeducational higher education has caused a marked but unplanned increase in the incidence of geniuses in both the United States and the Soviet Union. On many coeducational university campuses, the most intelligent 1 to 10 percent of young men and women are now thrown together at the ages when they are most susceptible to romance and marriage. Large university faculties and research towns provide similar contacts. The genetic result has been, and will long continue to be, a notable increase in the proportion of geniuses and near geniuses. Marriages between superior university graduates produce five to ten times the normal proportion of geniuses. As a result of their pioneering in mass coeducational higher education the United States and the Soviet Union will soon have relatively over twice as many geniuses as most other advanced states.

In a later chapter on education I shall predict continually growing segregation of gifted students, in both secondary and higher schools. This trend will notably accelerate the rise in the marriage rate between superior students, and therefore in the number of geniuses they produce, in all countries.

Nearly all American women's and men's colleges will become coeducational by 2060. The number of women students at Harvard, Yale, Princeton, etc., will rise steadily until it equals the number of men. And most of the students will then marry before they finish their university studies. When their gifted children also attend schools and universities for superior students and intermarry, they will produce twenty to fifty times the normal proportion of geniuses, and so on.

Artificial insemination of all women with semen from gifted men is of course the ideal method of achieving a maximum output of geniuses, as well as the ideal method of general eugenic progress. As previously predicted it will be widely used long before 2500. But during the next century it will do much less than coeducational universities to increase the number of gifted children.

Throughout the next 500 years all governments will adopt more and more effective measures to ensure that geniuses and near geniuses are given suitable encouragement, education, and employment. At present the great majority of gifted people fail to receive these benefits and are employed in entirely unsuitable work. Even in advanced states most male geniuses from poor families receive no professional education. And those from well-to-do families are often ignored or grossly neglected, merely because they are not sufficiently charming, self-confident, aggressive, or conformist. Nearly all female geniuses are denied suitable education or employment simply because they are female. Einstein was advised by his high-school teachers to leave school before graduation, and did so. He later returned to school and graduated from college, but he was not given suitable employment for ten years after his graduation.

To avoid such common discouragement and waste of highly gifted persons, most governments will increasingly give suitable intelligence tests to all children (see Chapter XIII) and provide suitable specialized segregated education for the gifted, along with immediate opportunities for highly creative work when they leave school. The proportion of world geniuses now so treated is less than 1 percent; even in advanced countries it is less than 10 percent. It will rise above 50 percent in all countries by A.D. 2200 and above 90 percent by 2500.

National Personnel Records and Symbols

The more information experts have on the heredity of individuals, the better they can plan eugenic measures and control reproduction. Hence advanced states will soon begin to collect and preserve an ever-expanding range of data useful for eugenic control—medical records, school grades, vocational tests, crime reports. By the year 2200 all such records will be duplicated and sent to regional, national, and world record offices, where they will be preserved at least for several hundred years. These central personnel records will be gradually enlarged, until by 2500 they will contain all personal data of probable interest to future biographers, historians, social scientists, and descendants, as well as all data of current interest to police, employment agencies, health statisticians, and other research workers.

At birth each person will be assigned a number to be used throughout his life for identification—as a social-security number, a bank-account number, a passport number, a property-identification number, an army serial number, a police-record number, a medical-record number, an automobile-license number. By 2100 this number will be indelibly tattooed on the body of each infant shortly after birth.

The use of such numbers and the recording in suitable form of ever-increasing information about each person will, by 2500, enable scientists to correlate the incidence of any disease, crime, accident, divorce, religious affiliation, etc., with any other significant personal fact, such as month of birth, age of father, education, color of eyes, number of cigarettes smoked, amount of coffee consumed, occupation, and income.

Long numbers are much harder to recognize, remember, repeat, and copy than short numbers. That is why automobile license plates now use letters of the alphabet as well as arabic numerals. By using 100 symbols in each symbol place, officials will be able to assign every person in the world a different identification number containing no more than five symbols. The 100 symbols will include all small and capital letters of an enlarged future alphabet (predicted in Chapter XII) as well as all arabic numerals.

CHAPTER V

WORK AND WAGES

ECONOMIC ACTIVITIES still occupy most of the waking hours of the vast majority of mankind, and relative success in these activities greatly influences all other personal and social conduct. It is therefore fitting that a book on major social trends should devote many pages to economic trends. This is the first of seven chapters on such trends.

Economic trends directly affecting the work and wages of workers are of widest interest and significance.

Occupational and Job Choice

Two hundred years ago most Europeans and Americans inherited both an occupation and a job, usually on their fathers' farms. Today the great majority must choose an occupation and seek employment from strangers, who seldom offer enough jobs for all. Moreover, since it is expensive, most workers receive insufficient or unsuitable vocational education. Two hundred years from now nearly all children will receive an adequate and suitable vocational education and will be assured of immediate suitable employment, both upon the completion of their education and whenever they later desire a change in employment. These results will be achieved by a gradual increase in government control over economic activities. I shall discuss education later; here I wish to predict only full and suitable employment.

When an unemployed worker is put to work, his wages permit him to add to total demand about as much as he adds to total supply. His employer's additional profit or loss makes up the balance. But the additional demand serves chiefly to increase the sales of other firms, not those of his new employer. Hence it is often unprofitable for a firm to hire such a worker. However, it is always socially desirable for some firm to hire him. To achieve full employment in a capitalist state, it is necessary to offer public employment to the unemployed or to induce private firms to do what is socially desirable by offering them financial inducements. Competition with communist and socialist states and ever-increasing public demand for full employment will compel all capitalist states to gradually reduce and eventually abolish unemployment, probably before A.D. 2100.

In the next few decades the United States will establish a new Civilian Conservation Corps and gradually expand its functions and enrollment until it provides jobs for most unemployed single men between sixteen and twenty-six. It will also introduce and gradually expand a flexible federal public-works construction program which will offer part-time work at regular wages or full-time work at lower wages to most unemployed married men.

All capitalist states will continue to increase their control over the formation and loan of private investment funds in order to achieve a more stable economic growth rate and fuller employment. They will also gradually adopt the practice of varying public investment, taxation, and spending in such a way as to achieve and preserve fuller employment. Since capitalist legislators cannot exercise such controls promptly and wisely, they will increasingly authorize some public official to quickly raise or lower public investment, taxation, or spending by up to 5 or 10 percent whenever he considers such action necessary to reduce unemployment or prevent inflation. The president of the United States or some special federal agency will be authorized to take all these steps before A.D. 2000.

Since 1945, unemployment rates in most advanced capitalist states have been well below normal prewar rates. They will continue to decline irregularly for many decades. The most marked decline will be that in the official United States rate, still relatively high (about 6 percent) in 1960. It will fall below 3 percent by A.D. 2000 and below 1 percent by 2100, in spite of the further growth of mechanization and automation and the future revision of this rate to cover more of the unemployed.

The Soviet Union now admits no unemployment. It will begin to admit some unemployment and publish unemployment rates by regions before A.D. 2000. By 2100 official unemployment rates will be about the same as in the United States.

The publication of official government estimates of unemployment is a recent historical development, one of many evidences of growing government interest in public welfare. All such statistics are now grossly inadequate and misleading. For instance, the United States figures for 1960 probably understated unemployment by at least 50 percent, and failed to state how many unemployed were feeble-minded, blind, crippled, illiterate, colored, etc. They will be gradually revised to include more and more of the hidden unemployed, persons not actively seeking work who would work if offered suitable employment near home at union wage rates. The revised figures will include and list separately all classes of handicapped persons, housewives, aged workers, part-time workers, Negroes, etc., seeking work in each local area and each trade.

In a capitaist state where unemployment is chronic, employers rarely find it profitable to hire the least productive workers—the old, the blind, the crippled, the illiterate, dropouts—but this does not prove that such persons are unemployable. Many experiments have demonstrated that when special efforts are made to create suitable jobs for such persons, they can become productive and happy workers. All advanced societies will steadily increase their efforts to provide such jobs. The mere elimination of unemployment among more productive workers will help greatly. But growing efforts will be made to design special jobs for the most handicapped. As a result nearly all "unemployable" persons will be employed before A.D. 2100.

By that year every school leaver in an advanced country will be offered a choice among many suitable jobs. Vocational education and economic activities will be so closely co-ordinated that the annual supply of each kind of graduate will almost fit the demand for that kind. Losses due to imperfect co-ordination will be borne by the nation, not by unfortunate individuals. And if any person wishes to move or change jobs, he will be offered suitable employment wherever it is available. There will be no job seekers, only job choosers. Finding suitable work will be as easy as buying any retail good. If too many apply for work in any occupation or plant department, supply and demand will be equalized by altering wage rates, not by turning down any job applicant or discharging any worker. And when sales drop and staff must be reduced, this too will be achieved by wage cuts, not by firing workers.

The mere achievement of full employment will permit far more workers to choose work for which they are best suited and which they most enjoy or least dislike. Moreover, schools and employers will spend more and more money on vocational guidance.

The applied science of vocational guidance is still in an early stage of development, but it will steadily improve. For instance, vocational testing will be expanded to include careful observation of students performing several different kinds of work under normal working conditions. And students will be given more and more vocational guidance by professionally educated experts.

In the decade 1950 to 1960, American parents and schools probably spent less than $20 per school leaver on scientific vocational testing and guidance. This amount will rise above $2,000 by A.D. 2100 (which will be less than 0.2 percent of average lifetime earnings) and above $10,000 by 2500 (still less than 0.2 percent). The increases in lifetime earnings and work satisfaction due to such expansion of vocational testing and guidance will fully justify the additional investment.

Hours of Labor

The average hours of paid labor have been declining slowly but steadily for at least a century. In 1860 the United States average for full-time workers was about 66 hours; it had declined to 42 hours (including overtime) by 1964. In the Soviet Union it also fell to 42 hours in 1964. These averages will continue to fall slowly, at an ever-decreasing rate, throughout the next 500 years.

Thus far the decline in working hours has not reduced output per worker; indeed, it has helped to raise both daily and lifetime output. But a continued decline will eventually reduce real output and wages per worker. Thereafter the chief reason for further curtailing working hours will be a growing marginal preference for leisure over income. As real incomes rise men will demand more and more time for recreation, hobbies, travel, and family life.

The hours of labor per year will be cut by reducing work hours per day, days per week, and weeks per year. All three methods will be repeatedly employed. In advanced countries the five-day week will be general in A.D. 2000. The hours of labor per workday will fall to 6 by 2100 and to 5 by 2200. Long before 2500 they should fall to 4. Less advanced countries will achieve these reforms much more slowly.

The proportion of workers who enjoy paid vacations has been rising for over 100 years in advanced countries. Most American industrial workers now receive two weeks of paid vacation. Both the proportion of workers and the average length of vacations will continue to grow, the latter indefinitely. By 2100 the average American employee will enjoy four weeks of paid vacation each year; by 2500, ten weeks.

These predictions concerning specific methods of reducing average working hours per year are of course much less certain than the more significant and general prediction that all methods will together reduce the average annual hours of labor in advanced countries by over 40 percent before A.D. 2200 and by over 60 percent before 2500.

As factories, stores, offices, become ever more mechanized and automated, multi-shift operation will become more advantageous and common. Gradual reduction of the hours of labor will have the same effect. By 2100 most American factories and computer-equipped offices will operate twenty-four hours a day. This will help to justify similar operation of many retail stores; and sound retail pricing in highly mechanized stores will greatly stimulate nighttime shopping by all customers (see Chapter VI).

Night shifts will become much shorter than day shifts, and day-shift lengths will be increasingly varied in order to attract the desired number of workers to the less popular shifts without raising their annual earnings unduly. Thus four and five shifts of different lengths will become customary in most factories and other highly mechanized places of employment before 2100. Such multi-shift operation will become or remain much more common in backward countries because they will always have much less machinery per worker than advanced countries.

Many persons now prefer regular part-time work to full-time—for instance, married women, elderly workers, and handicapped persons—and are unable to get it. Moreover, men differ widely in the desire for leisure, and every future increase in real wages should enable those who enjoy leisure most to buy and enjoy more of it by working fewer hours for lower pay. Hence business managers and governmental officials will steadily increase the variety of workers' choices concerning their regular hours of labor. Long before A.D. 2500 nearly all firms will operate different-length shifts simultaneously or offer part-time work to all who desire it. Most wives with children and most elderly persons will then work less than full time. It is just as desirable to design jobs to fit workers as to design products to please consumers. And workers differ as much as consumers.

To make retirement of elderly workers less painful, more and more firms will introduce gradual retirement programs. These will permit most workers over some minimum age, perhaps fifty at first, to reduce their weekly or annual hours of work every few years until they stop working altogether. Only 2 percent of American firms now have such a program. This rate will rise above 10 percent by A.D. 2000 and above 60 percent by 2100.

The growth of gradual retirement will permit most elderly workers to postpone their full retirement by five to ten years. Medical progress, eugenic reform, and reductions in full-time hours will have similar effects. By 2500 nearly all men and women will work full-time (three to four hours a day) to age seventy-five and part-time to ninety.

While the annual hours of labor per worker will decline by

over 50 percent in the next 500 years, the years of paid labor per worker in each country will increase by 40 to 100 percent, due to the elimination of unemployment, the reduction in accidents and sickness, and the postponement of retirement. Thus the average hours of labor per worker's life will fall by only some 30 percent in advanced countries and far less in backward countries.

Free Distribution

Free goods are those distributed free of charge; price goods, those sold for a price. The share of free goods in real wages has been rising steadily in advanced countries for over a century, and now averages 20 to 25 percent. In many backward countries it is still below 5 percent. This share will rise gradually in all countries until it exceeds 50 percent of world consumption, or 100 percent of spendable money wages.

Military protection is now the chief free good, but the creation of a strong world government will reduce world military spending by 80 percent before 2200. However, world expenditures on free education, free scientific information, free health services, free legal aid, free child care, free parks and gardens, free urban passenger transport, free television and radio broadcasting, free books and magazines, free zoos and museums, free streets and highways, free mail service, etc., will increase steadily for centuries. By 2500 free education, child care, research, and health care will together make up over 30 percent of world GNP.

While a great and long-continuing expansion of free distribution is certain, free distribution will never long exceed 70 percent of consumers' goods, because this would unduly weaken monetary incentives to optimum personal output. Piece rates and other monetary rewards are ineffective in increasing output unless money income can be spent on price goods. Moreover, price distribution is the ideal way to distribute most tangible goods among consumers.

It is noteworthy that free distribution is not socialism. Capitalist states provide many free goods and will provide many more.

Free goods can be produced by private firms, and socialist trusts can sell their output for profitable prices.

More specific predictions concerning the free distribution of individual goods will be made in several later chapters. The reasons for the growth of free distribution vary from good to good and will therefore be discussed with these individual predictions.

Real Income per Person

Real income per person is the best available measure, or index, of economic welfare per person, and its rise or fall is therefore extraordinarily significant. It equals real consumption plus real saving per person, and real consumption includes the consumption of free goods as well as price goods. In all such terms *real* means adjusted for price-level fluctuations.

In nearly all advanced countries real income per person has been rising fairly steadily for over 300 years. This trend will continue throughout the next 500 years. It has been briefly interrupted by major wars and will probably be interrupted by one or more additional major wars. Moreover, since future, nuclear wars will be more devastating than recent world wars, they will cause more serious breaks in this trend. But the establishment of a strong world government will end such breaks and assure a steady and indefinite further rise in real income per person and therefore in the standard of living. This is one of the most significant and certain predictions one can make.

Real income per person in nearly all countries will continue to rise steadily in peacetime throughout the next 500 years, chiefly because: (1) men will improve their methods of production in every field of activity, largely through scientific research; (2) men will continue, or begin to practice, enough birth control to permit technological progress to raise personal real incomes; (3) educational investment per person will rise steadily; (4) the organization of government, industry, education, etc., will be continuously rationalized; (5) after A.D. 2100, if not before, eugenic measures will bring about a steady increase in labor productivity; and (6) medical progress will have a similar effect throughout the next 500 years. These predictions are discussed in other chapters.

In advanced countries the only serious threats to an indefinite increase in real income per person are possible nuclear annihilation and the exhaustion of natural resources. The first threat will be ended by the creation of a strong world government, the second by the development of substitute materials and products and by continuous improvement in the methods used to extract scarce materials from sea water, air, and low-grade ores.

In backward countries the chief factor delaying or restricting the rise in average real income is the rapid growth of population. The gradual adoption of birth control will reduce this population growth by 50 to 90 percent within 100 years.

While it is safe to predict that real income per person will continue to rise throughout the next 500 years, it would be far more difficult and also highly misleading to predict rates of increase and average real incomes for several hundred years ahead. Income data is meaningful only to those familiar with relevant prices and products. These will change so radically in coming centuries that estimates of real income for more and more remote centuries quickly become largely meaningless or misleading. They are misleading to anyone who assumes that prices and consumers' goods will remain the same or little changed, and meaningless to anyone who does not know what goods will be consumed and what prices will be paid centuries hence.

In the United States average real income per person—$2,500 for the year 1960—has roughly doubled every 50 years for a century or two, and because of the cold war will probably rise even faster in the next 100 years. But if we project this well-established trend a few centuries ahead, we get results—such as $20 million per year in 2500—which are not only apparently absurd but which, even if accurate, are grossly misleading. Thus, a person with an income of $20 million in 2500 could not afford to hire a single full-time servant, would pay taxes exceeding half his income, and would pay fantastic prices for personal services rendered by persons earning wages about equal to his own. Therefore I do not think it worthwhile to predict average real incomes more than 100 years ahead.

If American average real income continues to double every 50 years, the average four-person family will enjoy a real income of about $40,000 in 2060. Almost half of this will consist of personal services which will cost over four times as much as in 1960 and be less than twice as productive.

While it does not appear useful to predict real wages more than a century ahead, they will continue to rise indefinitely, and this rise will be largely responsible for many social trends discussed in this book. The discussion of these other trends should make this long future rise in real wages more meaningful than any projection of money income.

International and Regional Income Differences

Since 1945, personal and national real incomes have grown much faster in Japan and most of Europe than in the United States, but large differences in growth rates among advanced countries are quite temporary. Any advanced country is free to adopt the growth-rate stimulants proven effective in other countries. And Soviet-American rivalry will soon prompt Britain and the United States to adopt effective means of achieving and maintaining economic growth rates as high and stable as those of the Soviet Union. These high competitive GNP growth rates, over 5 percent a year, will become more common and more uniform among advanced countries and will remain so indefinitely.

It is much more difficult to predict growth rates in backward than in advanced states, especially for the next 50 years. No stable secular trends have been established. Overpopulation, conservatism, and superstition still are serious obstacles to economic growth, and while they are sure to diminish, the rates of decline are uncertain. The governments and political institutions of backward countries are now unstable and subject to sudden radical change.

Since 1860, Japan and Russia have both proven that a strong

government can sharply increase the rate of economic development in a backward land. Other backward states will achieve similar successes during the next century or two. But it is much easier for an advanced state to speed up its economic growth, and most advanced countries have done so since 1945.

The difference between average real incomes in advanced and backward countries has been widening steadily for over 200 years and will continue to widen for another century or two, most rapidly during the next 50 years, because the population of backward countries will grow faster; their annual savings per person will remain much lower; their school systems will long continue to be inferior; their annual investment in research and development will be much smaller and less productive; their governments will be less stable and efficient; and their people will remain less receptive to technological advances and social reforms.

This income gap will begin to narrow only after backward countries have reduced their population-growth rates well below those of advanced states and have increased their investment rates above those of advanced countries.

Some readers may believe that foreign aid from advanced states will enable most backward states to raise their per-person economic growth rates above the average for advanced states. This is most unlikely during the next few centuries.

The cold war has already increased the amount of such foreign aid far above any previous level, but much of this aid has been wasted on military forces, uneconomic prestige projects, and simple graft. Moreover, public support for American foreign aid has been declining for fifteen years. Further relaxation of the cold war will lead to further curtailment of such aid. And creation of a strong world government will end the cold war, the chief current reason for foreign aid.

Until the establishment of a world government able and willing to prevent local confiscation of foreign investments in backward countries, such investment will expand slowly. During the next 100 years most such investments will be confiscated. After the coming world government has ended this threat, investment by advanced countries in backward countries will grow steadily, but it will enrich advanced as well as backward countries. Hence it will do little to close the real income gap.

Large-scale migration from poor to rich countries could, of course, gradually reduce this income gap. But such migration is most unlikely because it would slow down the rise of real incomes and create racial and other social problems in advanced countries.

All comparisons between real incomes in backward and advanced countries are crude because consumption habits and the buying power of money differ widely, and statistics in backward countries are poor. Available data suggest, however, that real incomes per person in the United States average ten to twenty times as high as those in Asia. I predict that they will still be over four times as high in the year 2500. On the other hand, the poorest countries will then have an average real income over ten times the United States 1960 level, and the marginal utility of further income increments will be relatively small.

While these international income differences will grow for another century or two, regional income differences within countries will continue to diminish and will become negligible long before 2500. All governments will adopt more and more measures to reduce such differences. They will improve education in low-wage regions and will increasingly encourage and subsidize the relocation of plants and workers. Such measures will be effective because workers are, or will soon become, free to migrate within their own country.

Within the United States average real income still varies widely from region to region. In the South, 1960 real income was 20 percent below the national average and over 30 percent below the California average. By 2200, it will be about equal to the national level and well above the California level. California incomes, now 15 percent above the national level, will fall well below this level by 2200, because when workers are free to live and work where they please, they refuse to work in less agreeable climatic regions unless wages are higher there. And by 2200, United States workers will be assured suitable and immediate employment wherever they wish to live.

Interpersonal Income Differences

The long-continuing growth and spread of Fabian socialism and communism have been due in large part to increasing resentment and criticism of great differences in personal income. Moreover, an ever-growing proportion of capitalist social scientists and liberal voters in advanced countries have come to approve measures designed to reduce differences in income, and many such measures—progressive income taxes, inheritance taxes, etc.—have been adopted. In communist countries the range of personal income is far narrower than it was in 1900. It may also be slightly narrower in advanced capitalist states, including the United States, although expert opinion on this point is divided. In any case it will narrow in all countries throughout most or all of the next 500 years.

The basic psychological or emotional reasons for growing criticism of gross differences in personal income will continue indefinitely. And economists are increasingly accepting and steadily improving the scientific arguments against wide income differentials—for instance, that these differences are unearned personal rents, or monopoly gains, or due to inherited social status or undeserved educational advantages, etc. Hence the continued growth of expert and public opinion favoring the gradual reduction of current wide differences in personal and family income is inevitable. It will result in the adoption of many widely differing methods of reducing such income differences. Most of these methods are predicted in other chapters.

The further growth of public ownership of land and capital goods (see Chapter VI) will turn more and more private profit and rent into government revenue, most of which will be used for public purposes. The growth of compulsory saving (Chapter VII) will increasingly equalize private interest income. Since the unequal distribution of private profit, rent, and interest income is now a major cause of inequality in capitalist states, these trends will do much to make personal incomes less and less unequal.

All insurance tends to make personal incomes less unequal, and a vast further expansion in income and property insurance is inevitable (see Chapter VII). Furthermore, every reform which makes vocational education more available or less costly to students tends to make subsequent earned incomes less unequal, and more and more free or liberally financed vocational and professional education will be provided in all countries throughout the next 500 years (Chapter XIII). Finally every increase in free medical care for children also makes subsequent productivity and earnings less unequal, and a vast expansion of such free medical care is certain (Chapter XIV).

During the past century wage rates in agriculture and in small country towns have remained substantially below wage rates in cities because population growth and a prolonged technological revolution have produced a continuous surplus of farm laborers, most of whom first seek new jobs in nearby towns. The total farm labor force in advanced states will soon be so small that further emigration from the farm will have little depressing effect on nearby small-town wages. Hence farm and small-town wage rates will rise faster than city wage rates in all advanced countries throughout most of the next century or two for this reason alone.

By A.D. 2300 average net money wages will be almost equal in all occupations within each country. The least skilled occupations will pay about as much (after amortization of investment in education) as the most skilled occupations. Executives will receive little if any more pay than their subordinates. The major remaining intra-country wage differentials will be between more and less productive workers in the same occupation and plant. And the most productive workers will earn less than twice as much as the least productive. Moreover, as noted earlier, by 2300 most consumer goods will be free goods, so that differences in consumption will be far less than differences in money income.

In order to make personal money incomes less unequal, some

countries now grant family allowances or child subsidies to families with three or more children. This practice will soon spread to all advanced countries, including the United States, which will introduce such subsidies before A.D. 2060. Even before this the United States will extend its current AID (aid to dependent children) program to children of unemployed workers not on relief. And many other such minor reforms to reduce differences in income per person, as well as those in income per worker, will be adopted in advanced states during the next century.

As a result of such income-equalization measures and the steady rise in average real incomes predicted earlier, there will be no families with real incomes below $20,000 (1960 dollars) in the United States or below $9,000 in any other advanced state, in A.D. 2100. Unemployment benefits, relief payments, pensions, etc., will be high enough to ensure minimum incomes above these levels throughout Europe and North America. All other countries will achieve such minimum incomes before 2300.

Labor Unions and Strikes

For over 100 years labor unions have been growing in membership and in economic and political influence. These trends are almost certain to continue for another century or two in all non-communist states.

In the United States most white-collar and professional employees—teachers, accountants, engineers—will be unionized before A.D. 2050. And American unions will become more and more active in politics. They will either gain control over the Democratic party or organize a new union-controlled labor party by 2050. In other words, American union activity and achievements in politics during the next 60 years will resemble those of the British unions during the past 60 years.

Throughout non-communist Europe most unions will continue their long-time support of socialist political parties but will become less and less revolutionary as real wages rise, and less and less Marxist as socialist economic theory advances. The large communist parties in France and Italy will gradually turn into or merge with democratic Fabian-socialist parties.

During the next century capitalist governments will adopt numerous laws and regulations designed to make union elections more frequent and democratic, ensure more honest handling of union funds, reduce bribery of union officials by employers, curtail racketeering by union officials, protect union members against arbitrary acts by union officials, enable workers to enter unions and unionized trades more freely, and otherwise improve the management of unions. Such new laws will be especially numerous and significant in America, where many unions are now badly managed. By 2020, American union leaders will be as democratic, honest, and politically advanced as English and Swedish union leaders were in 1960.

In recent decades the governments of most democratic states have used more and more public pressure to compel the arbitration of major labor disputes. This trend will continue. By A.D. 2100 strikes will be prohibited, and all otherwise unsettled union-management disputes will be settled by special labor courts or arbitrators. Strikers will be fined, and the fines will be deducted from their post-strike wages.

The recent West German experiment with labor co-determination is significant. The boards of most large capitalist corporations will include one or more union representatives before 2100.

Because unemployment has existed continuously in all capitalist countries, labor unions have adopted and enforced hundreds of union rules designed to make labor less productive and thus make a given job last longer. They have required railroads to employ superfluous firemen on diesel engines, forbidden painters to use sprayers, required contractors to hire extra specialists for a full day to do ten minutes' work other workers could do, and restricted prefabrication of buildings. During the next century most such uneconomic union rules and state laws will be gradually repealed or outlawed, for several reasons: unemployment will decline, and unemployment insurance benefits will rise. Workers will therefore become less and less fearful of unemployment.

Furthermore, the growth of public ownership will gradually make labor-management disputes less numerous and less bitter because it will ensure that more profits accrue to the public, not to rich employers. And the gradual future reduction of differences in wage rates, predicted earlier, will have a similar effect. Finally methods of wage determination will become more and more scientific and less and less arbitrary, which will reduce disputes.

In order to permit more scientific methods of wage determination, all governments will eventually (before 2200) prohibit labor or union participation in wage determination. Wage rates, like other prices, will then be fixed so as to balance supply and demand. Union efforts to raise wages above such levels will be illegal.

In recent years American labor unions have accumulated enormous insurance funds to finance retirement pensions, unemployment insurance, medical care, and other fringe benefits for their members. They have performed a useful function in pioneering and increasing such benefits, but they have not managed the insurance monies efficiently or honestly. Moreover, they cannot provide insurance as economically or universally as a national social-insurance system. Hence the insurance functions now performed by American unions and employers will gradually be shifted to an enlarged national insurance system. This shift will largely be completed by 2060. In the meantime union insurance functions may continue to expand for another decade or two.

In communist countries labor unions are now essentially organs of government administration and propaganda. Their leaders are appointed from above, not freely elected by the members. During the next 50 to 100 years these unions will become steadily more independent and democratic. They may never be allowed to call strikes, but they will represent more and more honestly the opinions and complaints of their members. Increased consideration of such complaints will improve business management and worker morale. In this as in other respects communist and capitalist unions will become more and more alike in their organization and functions, until there are no significant differences between them.

In the world of A.D. 2500 the chief functions of labor unions will be to determine or formulate worker complaints and present them to management, to discuss and co-determine some working conditions—hours of labor, rest periods, etc.—and to arrange social events. They will not negotiate wage contracts, manage insurance funds, help plan output, construct housing, etc. And no full-time union officials, if there are any, will be paid much more than he had previously earned as an employee.

CHAPTER VI

Production Control

THE PREVIOUS CHAPTER dealt with those social trends which will affect workers most directly and widely. This chapter contains predictions concerning those social trends which will affect managers most directly and generally.

The basic common problems of managers are problems of production control—what goods and services should be produced, where should they be produced, how should they be produced, and how much of each should be produced. The way such questions are answered depends in large part on who chooses the managers or owns the means of production. Hence I shall begin with some predictions concerning the growth of professional management and public ownership.

Corporation Managers

During the past 100 years corporation stockholders have become less and less able to elect managers and determine policies. When one man or a few friends own most of the stock in a corporation, they can easily become or choose its managers, but as stock becomes more and more widely distributed, this becomes ever more difficult. By the time a corporation has thousands of stockholders scattered throughout the nation or the world, few if any of whom own more than 0.1 percent of its stock, they no longer have any significant control over its management. When a stockholder becomes dissatisfied, he sells his stock. The management is independent and self-perpetuating.

A self-perpetuating corporation management does not stop

going through the legal formality of allowing stockholders to elect the board of directors. It periodically sends printed ballots (proxies) to all common-stock holders. But these ballots usually show only the names of the old management or its agents. Stockholders who dislike the management cannot vote effectively against it without organizing a costly and difficult proxy fight. And the old management can use corporation records, reports, lawyers, and funds to win such a fight. Hence less than 0.1 percent of all elections in large corporations are contested, and such contests are usually won by the management.

Since most large corporations have long been growing and will long continue to do so, and since more and more investors like to diversify their investments, the stock of most old corporations becomes ever more widely distributed. Among the two hundred largest United States non-financial corporations, the proportion of firms with independent self-perpetuating managements grew from 44 to 84 percent between 1929 and 1963. The number and proportion of corporations with such managements will increase in all capitalist countries throughout the next 100 years.

This trend will result in growing public criticism of corporation managers as irresponsible, that is, responsible to no one. And this criticism will help to bring about ever-increasing government regulation of private corporations, appointment of public representatives on boards of directors, and eventual nationalization.

The gradual transfer of corporate control from stockholders to managers has already greatly increased the proportion of self-made and professionally educated managers. In 1900 almost half of top executives in some six hundred very large United States non-financial corporations came from wealthy families. By 1964 this share had fallen to 11 percent. Moreover, the proportion of executives with some higher education doubled during these years, and the proportion of those with science or engineering degrees increased fivefold. In 1964, 33 percent of the younger top executives had attended graduate school, compared with 10 percent in 1900. In 1964, of the top executives from poor families, 40 percent had higher technical education, as against 20 percent of those from wealthy families. All these trends except the growth of technical education among top executives will continue in the United States and other capitalist nations. Technical and other professional education of top executives will gradually be replaced by training in business administration.

In recent decades corporation managers have become more and more like professionally trained lawyers, doctors, and military officers. The number of graduate schools devoted to the training of business executives has grown, and the quality of their work has improved steadily. Large corporations have become more eager to hire and promote the graduates of such schools. The decline of stockholder influence over large corporations has more and more allowed experienced managers to select their successors. They increasingly prefer professionally trained people because they, the managers, are more intelligent than most stockholders, because the increasing size of corporations makes managerial problems ever more complex, and because the new applied science of management is advancing rapidly. By 2100 nearly all top executives of large American private and public corporations will be Harvard Business School graduates or the equivalent and will periodically return to such professional schools for further graduate work, as American military officers now do.

In the future as in the past the growth of professional education of business executives will be both a cause and an effect of increasing specialization in managerial work. Every increase in the scale of management justifies a further division of labor among managers, which promotes the development of specialized theories of scientific management, which increases the need for professional training. By 2500 few business managers will be professionally trained and experienced in more than one small field of management. General or over-all management of a firm will itself become a specialty requiring a special postgraduate professional education, one given to less than 10 percent of all professional managers. In other words, more and more executives will spend their entire professional lives as managers in accounting, sales, research, personnel, maintenance, production, or some other department and will be trained for such specialized work only.

Public Ownership

The share of real property which is publicly owned has been increasing fairly steadily in most non-communist states for a century or two and is certain to continue growing for another century or two. In most advanced states this share is already well above the United States level. The current United States figure, about 15 percent, will rise above 25 percent by A.D. 2000, 50 percent by 2100, and 90 percent by 2200. Communist countries, of course, have already nationalized most real estate, so public ownership cannot grow as much there; rather, it is likely to decline during the next few decades, and then grow again later.

The growth of public ownership in advanced non-communist countries during the past century has been due chiefly to three causes: public demand for more and more free goods—education, health services, social insurance, police and fire protection, etc.; public demand for the elimination of monopoly profits earned by private public utilities; and government efforts to ensure ample supplies of superior munitions, especially airplanes, rockets, and nuclear weapons. These factors will continue to be very influential during the next century, but several others—growing public demand for the reduction of unearned income, for full employment, for elimination of the wastes of competition, for more economic democracy, for more rapid economic growth—will become much more influential than they have been.

It is true, of course, that most of the purposes advanced as reasons for nationalization of private firms could be largely achieved by suitable public regulation of private business. But in the absence of such regulation, the argument that such purposes can be achieved by nationalization will continue to be influential. Moreover, suitable regulation will often be more difficult to achieve and less effective than public ownership and management. A further increase in public regulation of private firms is inevitable in all advanced non-communist states, but growing recognition of the high costs and inadequate achievements of such regulation will steadily increase the demand for nationalization of closely regulated industries.

In America outright public ownership will advance most

rapidly during the next few decades among public utilities, hospitals and clinics, insurance firms, transport agencies, banks, and child-care facilities. In Europe the next socialization measures are likely to affect banks, insurance companies, urban housing, the refining and distribution of petroleum products, and highway transport.

It is noteworthy that those industries which now are largely publicly owned—education, highways, public utilities, research, air transport—are rapid-growth industries. Investment in them is growing faster than investment in other industries and will long continue to do so.

One of the principal methods of expanding public ownership in advanced capitalist states during the next 100 years will be government purchase of shares in large privately owned firms like I. G. Farben and General Motors. For instance, social-insurance funds will be increasingly invested in such stocks. This will leave management in the hands of professional non-political managers but will enable governments to share in profits, co-ordinate and stabilize private investments, reduce private inheritance, curtail advertising, etc. By 2100, capitalist states will own a majority of the common stock in nearly all the largest private corporations.

Another important new method of nationalization will be large-scale government purchase of farm land, especially that near old cities and where new cities are to be built. This will shift much unearned increment in land values from private to public hands.

It is politically much easier to nationalize foreign enterprises than to nationalize domestic enterprises. That is why so many backward countries have already nationalized so much foreign property and will nationalize more and more. By A.D. 2060 over 50 percent, by 2100 over 90 percent, of all investments by advanced countries in backward countries will have been nationalized, usually at a heavy loss to investors.

Plans and Profits

The only methods of production control now widely used in advanced countries are production according to profits and production according to plan. The former permits and works best with highly decentralized output control. The manager of each producing unit measures his profit on each good, increases output when profit rises and decreases it when profit falls. By contrast, economic planning is usually highly centralized. An economic plan determines in advance (it does not merely suggest or predict) how much of each good should be produced in each office, school, or plant, and managers strive to fulfill the plan, whether or not fulfillment is profitable.

The production of free goods cannot be controlled according to profits. Their outputs must be planned. Since the production of free goods has long grown much faster than that of price goods, economic planning has steadily become more extensive and significant, even in capitalist states. As predicted earlier, the share of free goods in total national output will continue to rise indefinitely. It follows that production according to plan will long continue to replace production according to profit in non-communist states. This cause alone should eventually make plans more important than profits in determining outputs of consumer goods in all countries.

In communist countries most price goods, as well as all free goods, are still produced according to plan. And many democratic socialists in non-communist countries have argued that all price goods should and eventually will be produced according to national plans. I am confident that this prediction is unsound. The arguments in favor of producing most price goods according to profits are so strong that both communists and democratic socialists are certain to understand and accept them increasingly. Indeed, there is much evidence that this change of opinion is already well under way in the Soviet Union.

I predict, therefore, that production of price goods (which include nearly all tangible goods) according to profits will be gradually restored in all communist states. The restoration will begin with some consumer goods but will eventually also cover all producers' goods. It is difficult to tell how long this process will take, but it should be largely completed by A.D. 2000. Thereafter the growth of free distribution will again make centralized economic planning more and more significant.

One of the chief reasons why so many communists and socialists came to believe that price-good outputs should be based on plans rather than profits and losses is that capitalist profits and losses are imperfect signals for output control. For instance, widespread capitalist losses often result in business depressions and mass unemployment; and high average profits, in inflation. Such general distortion of profits and losses can and will be greatly reduced by suitable monetary and fiscal policies, which will stabilize some key price level. But many other reforms are needed and will gradually be adopted to make profits and losses better signals for use in controlling price-good outputs. The most important will be reforms in methods of individual price determination. The following discussion of these coming reforms in price determination is relatively technical, and should be skipped by readers little interested in price theory.

Price Policies

During the past 100 years the governments of all advanced capitalist countries have continuously expanded and elaborated their control over the prices and pricing policies of public utilities, chiefly in order to reduce monopoly profits and price discrimination. During the next 100 years they will steadily expand and elaborate their price control over other private industries, chiefly in order to reduce unemployment and speed up and stabilize economic growth by limiting price inflation. The fiscal, monetary, and investment policies which will be increasingly used to achieve full employment will tend to cause continual inflation in so-called competitive industries (because they are not fully competitive) unless their prices are properly controlled.

The first steps toward government control over the prices charged by private competitive industries is normally informal.

High government officials advise the top executives of great capitalist corporations to delay or refrain from inflationary price advances. The United States is now in this early stage of price control and may remain there for a decade or two more. But such informal price control is certain to prove unsatisfactory and to be followed by gradual extension of formal price control to most competitive industries. Nearly all advanced capitalist states, including the United States, will create formal systems of price control over some competitive industries before the year 2000 and will extend and perfect such control throughout the twenty-first century.

It is far easier for a capitalist state to regulate the pricing policies of a few large firms than of many small ones. Hence the well established trend toward concentration of production in fewer and larger firms will continue to reduce the difficulties of government price control. It has already resulted in widespread voluntary price leadership, which can easily be replaced by compulsory price leadership. Moreover, this concentration reduces competition and makes price control ever more necessary as a means of preventing undue profits and inflation.

My second major prediction concerning price policies is that all advanced countries, both capitalist and socialist, will soon begin to adopt and enforce a radical new pricing policy: marginal-cost pricing. At present both capitalist and communist firms try to fix their prices so that they equal average costs (including a desired profit). Since all allocation of overhead costs to individual units of output is arbitrary, average costs are indeterminable. Indeed, the term *average cost* is literally meaningless because it does not designate an agreed unique referent. Hence all efforts to make prices equal average costs have been fruitless. But both capitalist and communist firms usually have succeeded in fixing their prices high enough to yield large marginal profits. This policy is uneconomic and will gradually be abandoned.

If any price is above marginal cost (defined as direct cost at the margin, not increment in total cost), the production of one more unit normally yields a marginal profit (profit on the marginal unit, not increment in total profit) which measures a social-welfare gain from production of the marginal unit. A marginal profit normally measures a social-welfare loss on this unit. Hence the prices of most reproducible goods will eventually be made almost equal to marginal costs by means of price or output control.

In increasing-cost industries (largely extractive), marginal-cost pricing yields continuing surpluses or rents, and it therefore has long been practiced by capitalist firms. In decreasing-cost industries, however, such pricing would yield deficits, and it therefore has never been practiced by capitalist firms.

For instance, the marginal cost of seating one more patron in an unfilled theater is negligible. Hence theater ticket prices should be raised above this negligible cost only in order to restrict supply to demand. This policy would greatly increase patronage and want-satisfaction at no extra cost to society, but it would result in large deficits whenever demand for tickets is insufficient to justify profitable prices.

The marginal cost of printing and selling one more copy of a book includes no writing, editing, and publishing charges. Hence book prices equal to marginal costs will yield large deficits. The same logic applies to all reproductions of works of art or other articles with significant design or development costs.

Marginal-cost price-output control will not be widely adopted in this century but will be widely used in all advanced states by A.D. 2100. It will be applied first to those industries in which prices are now most often the farthest above marginal costs—theaters, publishing, public utilities, air and rail transport, etc. Railroads may be the first industry affected, because railroads require costly facilities, which in most capitalist states are now operated far below their ideal level.

Since marginal-cost price or output control in non-extractive industries would result in large deficits, it will be adopted more quickly and more widely by socialist and communist governments and by public enterprises in capitalist states than by private firms. Capitalist governments will, however, begin during the twenty-first century to subsidize marginal-cost pricing by many large private firms. Furthermore, even without such subsidies, private utilities can and increasingly will reduce their use rates toward or to marginal costs without incurring losses because they can raise their monthly service charges enough to cover all non-marginal costs. Some private utilities have already begun to apply this method of approximating marginal-cost pricing, and more and more will do so.

Non-marginal expenses—rent, interest, research, depreciation and maintenance not due to marginal output, executive salaries, fringe benefits, advertising, and other overhead costs—have long grown faster than marginal or direct costs. They will continue to do so throughout the next 500 years because of growing mechanization, automation, research and development, and vocational training. Thus the difference between prices nominally based on average costs (however calculated) and those based on marginal costs of the same goods will continue to widen for centuries. By A.D. 2500, 80 percent of all production costs of price goods will be non-marginal and non-price-determining.

At present less than 1 percent of university economics texts in either communist or capitalist states teach that prices should equal marginal costs (defined as direct costs at the margin). By 2060 the great majority of such texts will teach this new price theory.

The third major pricing trend will be growing acceptance and application of the old but widely ignored rule that prices should balance supply and demand. This trend will be especially marked and significant in communist countries, where rationing, waiting lists, and queues have often been due to fixing retail prices unduly low. But capitalist price fixers also will gradually abandon the practice of setting prices which do not balance short-run demand and supply.

Prices which fail to achieve such a balance result in profits or losses which are poor guides to output control because they do not measure well how much consumers want marginal output. Since such prices often result in great inconvenience to customers and always yield profits or losses unsuitable for use in regulating output, they will gradually be replaced by prices which come ever closer to balancing current demand and supply.

Fourth, in both capitalist and communist countries more and more marginal money costs which now measure no marginal real costs will be abolished in order to make marginal costs per unit of output, and prices based upon them, measure the relevant real costs more accurately. For instance, by A.D. 2100, patent royalties will be abolished or paid by the state rather than by producers because they measure no real cost of marginal output. And all taxes which now enter marginal cost but measure no real cost of marginal production will gradually be reduced or abolished, as explained in Chapter VII.

Finally in all countries many cost prices will be created or raised by governments because money costs now fail to measure certain relevant marginal real costs, so-called external costs. For instance, the price of soft coal is now too low because it does not measure the damage to persons and property caused by the soot and smoke resulting from its use. Soft coal, gasoline, noisy trucks and planes, tobacco products, alcoholic beverages, etc., will all be taxed more heavily in order to raise their prices until they measure the full real costs, external as well as internal, of their marginal production and use.

Properly determined prices are today and will remain indefinitely the best available measures of the real costs and benefits of most tangible goods. They are indispensable means of rational economic calculation, which will always be socially useful. Hence the process of increasing the accuracy with which prices measure pain and pleasure will continue throughout the next 500 years—indeed, as long as civilized men survive.

Liquor, Tobacco, and Drugs

Nearly all advanced nations have long been intensifying their efforts to restrict the sale and use of habit-forming drugs, alcoholic beverages, and tobacco products. And scientific research has made the need for such restriction more and more evident.

It would require too much space to summarize the scientific case for these restrictions, but one little-known fact suggests how strong the case against cigarette smoking is. In 1900 in the United States the age-adjusted male death rate was only 13 percent above the female rate. Owing chiefly to the growth of cigarette smoking among males, this difference rose gradually above 60 percent between 1900 and 1960. In 1900, United States women could expect to live two years longer than men; by 1960, six and one-half years longer. And the female death rate itself was significantly higher than it would have been if many women had not taken up cigarette smoking. On the average, cigarette smoking in the United States shortens life by more than five years.

Since more and more women have taken up cigarette smoking since 1930, and since men will soon begin to reduce cigarette smoking, the wide difference between male and female death rates noted above will shortly begin a long decline. By 2100 it will be back down near the 1900 level.

Thus far the chief methods of restricting drug, liquor, and tobacco consumption have been prohibition, which has rarely worked well, and discriminatory taxation, which has produced large revenues but has not greatly restricted consumption. Such taxes will continue to rise. By the year 2000, additional taxes will have raised United States cigarette prices more than 100 percent above their 1960 level and liquor prices more than 50 percent.

The manufacture or sale of tobacco products has already been nationalized in several capitalist states, primarily in order to increase public revenues from the industry. The recent discovery of the harmful effects of smoking will help to induce other capitalist states to nationalize the industry. A state monopoly can curtail or abolish advertising and aggressive selling much more easily than a competitive private industry can be made to do so. Britain and the United States will nationalize their tobacco-manufacturing industry before 2100.

Many capitalist states will soon begin to curtail and censor advertising by private producers and distributors of tobacco products and alcoholic beverages or will continually strengthen old programs of this sort. Nearly all such advertising will be prohibited before 2050, and much of the additional sales-tax revenue from these industries will be used to cure addicts and persuade young people not to start smoking or drinking.

In 1960 no government required that cigarette packages bear a statement of the harmful results of smoking. By A.D. 2000 most governments will require such labeling, and these requirements will become more and more strict and widespread until all governments require a clear and full warning.

Similar regulation of labels on bottles containing alcoholic beverages will be adopted by more and more nations during the twenty-first century. The new labels will eventually summarize the effects of overindulgence on auto accidents, sickness (including alcoholism), and death rates.

Such increasingly effective discouragement and restriction of consumption will be followed, before 2200, by almost complete prohibition of the non-medical consumption of harmful tobacco products and of beverages containing more than perhaps 4 percent alcohol. Public support for such prohibitions will increase steadily as men become better-educated and more intelligent and as daily life becomes more complex and more satisfying. Moreover, most of the factors responsible for the failure of the premature prohibition of alcoholic beverages in America—police corruption and inefficiency, poverty, unemployment, etc.—will weaken continuously through coming centuries.

While government programs to restrict the consumption of most harmful goods will become more numerous and effective for centuries, current American restrictions on the sale and consumption of habit-forming drugs will soon be relaxed to permit doctors to provide cheap or free maintenance doses for all drug addicts able and willing to live a normal life as addicts or to reduce their drug consumption under medical guidance. This reform will immediately reduce the demand for high-priced illegal narcotics, and resultant crime, by 50 to 80 percent.

Drug addiction is little if any more harmful than heavy cigarette smoking. In the long run, therefore, drug addicts and cigarette addicts will be handled in much the same way: they will be treated by physicians and psychiatrists.

Investment Control

Production control includes investment control. Most output increases are achieved by more intensive use of existing facilities, but sooner or later such output increases raise marginal costs high enough to justify additional investment. The total volume of new investment largely determines the growth rate of national income in all states and the total volume of employment in capitalist states. Hence centralized government control over total investment is certain to continue in communist states and to increase in capitalist states.

The relative stability of growth rates and the high levels of employment in advanced capitalist countries since 1945 have been due largely to increased central control over the total volume of investment. France and Germany have made such control more complete and effective than England and America, which is probably the chief reason their growth and employment rates have been so much higher. Their success will soon persuade England and America to follow.

Capitalist countries will continue to expand their control over total annual national investment by collecting more complete and current data on investment plans and acts, by expanding and centralizing control over all banks, by regulating installment credit more closely, by increasingly adopting tax policies which help to expand investment at desired growth rates, and by directly influencing the investment plans of large private and public firms. By 2060 nearly all capitalist governments will have succeeded in stabilizing these growth rates at desired levels.

It is impossible for a national legislature or a group of independent government agencies to act promptly and efficiently enough to achieve stable investment growth. Hence more and more capitalist governments will delegate to a single state agency all the price-control, financial, and fiscal powers needed to achieve stable investment growth. These agencies will collect weekly statistics on interest rates, retail sales, housing starts, construction contracts, machinery and equipment orders, etc., and will reconsider their controls at least once a month. By 2060 they will be able to reverse almost immediately any undesired trend in total national investment without calling for any new legislation. The theory needed for such control is already available, though not yet widely known and accepted by capitalist politicians.

While all capitalist governments will gradually assume, and communist governments will preserve, centralized state control over the volume and growth rate of total national investment, the former will not adopt, and the latter will not long continue, centralized planning of individual investments in industries producing price goods. State planning of individual investments in industries producing free goods will continue because such investments cannot be based on profits, but economic planning of individual investments in firms producing price goods is uneconomic for the same reasons that economic planning of their outputs is uneconomic. Communist leaders will therefore abandon economic planning of most individual investments before 2000. Public and formal admission of this radical change in communist investment control will, however, be long delayed. The new national investment budgets or estimates, which will replace coercive plans, will continue to be called investment plans.

The gradual increase of central government control over the collection and investment of capital funds by private firms will be accompanied or followed by the gradual nationalization and centralization of these functions. This trend, which is already well established, will continue until by 2200 all capital funds in each country will be assembled and lent out by a single national agency. This agency will then lend such funds to the highest bidders, all of whom will pay the same current rate of interest for all loans, old as well as new.

Insurance companies now collect and invest large amounts of capital funds, as well as provide insurance. Eventually, probably during the twenty-first century, they will be restricted to insurance, the pooling of losses, in order to permit the concentration of loan-fund collection and distribution in the hands of a single national agency. Division of responsibility for performing any social function is uneconomic.

Moreover, commercial banks in all countries, communist as

well as capitalist, will be deprived of the power to lend capital funds before 2100. As explained in the following chapter, they will be restricted to the functions of permitting and recording payment by bank credits and debits. And one major reason for this reform will be the desire to concentrate the allocation of all loan funds in a single national or world loan agency.

For the same reason, all capitalist savings banks will eventually be denied the right to lend their funds to individual borrowers. They will be required to transfer all savings to the single national loan agency for investment by it.

The gradual nationalization and centralization of all financial investment will increasingly limit the number and functions of private investment bankers, brokers, and stock exchanges. By 2200 most saving will be done by governments, and private savers will deposit all their savings in savings banks. Men will no longer invest in securities, either private or public, because none will be issued. All capital funds will be borrowed from a single national investment agency.

By 2200 all enterprises in advanced states will be so large and financially secure (most will be state monopolies) that no loans will involve any risk of loss to the lender. And the central loan agency will never have any good reason to charge more or less for long-term than for short-term loans. Hence at any given time all loans will bear the same rate of interest, which fact will be evidence of a near-ideal allocation of funds. Indeed, centralization of the assembly and investment of loan funds is inevitable, chiefly because it is a prerequisite for the achievement of a uniform interest rate and a near ideal allocation of loan funds. As long as two or more independent loan agencies exist in one nation, two or more interest rates may be charged, and misallocation of investment funds will be common.

In both capitalist and communist countries nearly all investment loans are now made for specified periods of time. This is necessary in capitalist countries because individual lenders may need their capital funds for other uses. But it is illogical and uneconomic in a socialist state which has centralized the allocation of all investment funds, because it should increase its total investment every year and should regulate the use of investment funds only by controlling the uniform national interest rate and by general rules prescribing sound investment policies. Hence socialist states will gradually abandon the practice of lending investment funds to state enterprises for specified periods of time. By 2100 all such loans will be for unlimited periods at uniform but fluctuating short-run interest rates. Executives who misuse or misinvest borrowed money will be demoted, but competent managers will never be required to repay any borrowed funds for whose use they are willing to pay the current uniform rate of interest. And the total capital investment of almost any socialist trust should increase indefinitely.

In capitalist countries private firms are still allowed to determine many of their accounting practices. As a result such practices differ widely, and reported costs and profits are usually incomparable. This makes it impossible for governments to regulate prices properly and for investors to learn which proposed investments are most profitable. It is inevitable, therefore, that as capitalist governments expand price and credit control, they will regulate accounting by private firms more and more closely. They have long been increasing their regulation of cost accounting by privately owned public utilities and banks. And they have regulated some accounting practices of all firms subject to income taxes. They will continue to extend such regulations until, by 2100, all private and public firms within each advanced country use uniform accounting methods.

After the investment of capital funds has been centralized in each advanced country, the coming world government will begin to centralize such investment on a world basis. The reasons for this eventual world centralization will be similar to those for the previous centralization within individual states. Of course, they cannot become compelling until a world government has been established and become strong enough to enforce such centralization. Nevertheless, the complete centralization of world investment will bring about standardization of accounting practices, a uniform interest rate, and a near ideal allocation of capital funds throughout the world before the year 2500.

CHAPTER VII

Finance

In this chapter I shall predict some important long-run trends in the methods used to finance the provision of free goods, family allowances, economic subsidies, and net new investment. Since nearly all financial transactions require the use of money, commercial banks, stockbrokers, or stock exchanges, I shall predict their trends also.

Revenue Taxes

The tax systems of advanced capitalist states differ widely, but all are incredibly complex and very uneconomic. They are, and will long continue to be, based chiefly on old customs and political bargains between numerous pressure groups rather than upon economic principles. Hence it is especially difficult to make short-run predictions concerning future tax trends. But major long-run trends can be anticipated, for voters and rulers will steadily become better educated, more intelligent, and more responsive to expert advice.

Taxes may be divided into two classes: revenue taxes, those used chiefly or solely to raise revenue; and special-purpose taxes, those used to help achieve special purposes—restriction of the consumption of harmful goods, income redistribution, cost correction (measurement of external costs), etc. Many new special-purpose taxes, especially cost-correction taxes, will be introduced during the next 500 years. Some are predicted in other chapters. Here prediction will be limited to major trends or changes in revenue taxation.

The number of different revenue taxes has long been increasing in all advanced countries, because politicians believe that taxpayers feel and resent many small taxes less than a few large ones. This increase will continue for a few decades, but the trend will reverse itself during the twenty-first century. As men become wealthier and better educated, governments will find it less and less necessary to hide or fragment revenue taxes. And only one pure revenue tax can be the best. By 2500 no country will have more than one such tax.

The share of the national income taken by taxation has risen steadily in peacetime in all advanced states for over 100 years, due to the continuous relative growth of free government services. In general, the richer the country, the higher the taxes. Their share of national income will continue indefinitely to rise in all countries, because free distribution will continue to expand faster than price distribution.

In the United States this tax share rose from about 6 percent of national income in 1900 to about 27 percent in 1960. It should reach 36 percent by 2000, and 50 percent by A.D. 2100.

While the share of taxes in national income will rise for centuries in all countries, in non-communist countries it will not rise as fast as government spending. Non-tax revenues—land rent, interest, new money, etc.—will grow steadily and will finance an ever larger part of government expenditures for two or three centuries.

It is noteworthy that the predicted further rise in the ratio of taxes to national income will result largely from the continued growth of free distribution, not from the growth of socialism. In the long run the latter will substantially restrict the growth of taxation by providing more and more income from government property and by reducing the need for income redistribution. In capitalist countries most of the coming relative increase in taxation will come under capitalism.

Perhaps the most significant revenue-tax trend during the last century has been the growing use of personal income taxes. In the United States such taxes, negligible in 1900, now raise about one third of all tax revenue. During the next century they will continue to grow, at a slower rate, in the United States and Great Britain, but they will grow much more rapidly in backward non-communist countries, where they still are a relatively minor source of revenue.

Another major capitalist tax trend since 1900 has been the rapid growth of corporation income taxes, which now raise about 17 percent of total United States tax revenues. Such taxes probably fall more on consumers than on capitalists, but they are popular with workers unaware of this. They are highly uneconomic, because they discourage saving and investment and affect different retail prices very unequally. During the next century, therefore, they will gradually be replaced by more economic taxes, chiefly by higher sales and personal-income taxes.

In most advanced capitalist states, revenues from inheritance and gift taxes have risen for several decades. During the next century they will rise much more rapidly than any other major tax revenue. In 1960 such taxes raised about 2 percent of all United States tax revenue; by 2060 they will raise over 10 percent.

Property taxes, by far the most important a century ago, have been providing an ever smaller share of total tax revenue in advanced countries for many decades, due chiefly to the rapid growth of income and sales taxes. In 1940 property taxes yielded over 30 percent of United States tax revenue, but by 1960 this share had fallen to 12 percent. It will continue to decline, more slowly, indefinitely. Moreover, this tax will gradually be converted from a tax on property to a tax on land, that is, on land rent, largely because taxes on buildings and improvements discourage investment and distort retail prices. The eventual nationalization of land will of course convert this land tax into government rent income.

The most important tax reform during the next 500 years will be the gradual substitution of poll taxes for all other explicit revenue taxes. Poll taxes are now unpopular because they are universal and regressive. But they will become ideal taxes in the far richer and more equalitarian societies of the future because they do not reduce the rewards for marginal work or saving and do not affect the costs of production. It is now difficult to predict how soon any country will be rich enough, equalitarian enough, and wise enough to use a poll tax as the chief revenue tax, but some advanced state may do so before A.D. 2100, and all will do so before 2300. These future poll taxes will eventually take 20 to 40 percent of personal income; they will be deducted monthly by the state bank from personal checking accounts.

The tax systems of communist states now differ radically from those of capitalist states. The Soviet Union relies largely on heavy and unequal turnover taxes and on the widely varying profits of state enterprises to finance investment and free goods. Both methods are highly uneconomic and therefore sure to be modified or abandoned. In the short run, turnover taxes will be gradually equalized and converted into uniform retail sales taxes, which will make all prices more useful to those who control current output and investment. And Soviet retail and wholesale prices will gradually be reduced until state trusts yield no substantial net pure profits (they will, however, earn large interest and rent incomes). In the long run, the turnover or sales tax will be completely replaced by a heavy and universal poll tax, for the reasons previously given.

The centralization of government predicted in Chapter III will of course bring about a gradual centralization of the functions of tax collection and tax determination in all countries, especially in countries like the United States which are now the most decentralized. This trend will continue throughout the next 500 years.

In 1960 the United States had over 80,000 units of local government (including 35,000 school districts) empowered to levy taxes. The continued consolidation of towns, cities, and school districts will reduce this total below 50,000 by A.D. 2000, below 10,000 by 2100, and below 1,000 by 2500. The parallel decline in the number of tax-collecting units of government will go much further. By 2500 there will be only one remaining tax-collecting agency in the United States. This centralization will reduce tax-collection and tax-payment costs per dollar by over 80 percent, saving billions of dollars each year.

Saving

All capital funds must be created or saved before they can be invested. Advanced capitalist countries now save and invest in capital goods, housing, and public works 6 to 16 percent of their national income. This estimate excludes operating (non-capital) expenditures on education, research and development, and health, most of which eventually will be treated as investment but are not now so treated. The predictions offered here deal with saving and investment as traditionally defined, unless otherwise noted.

Two centuries ago, nearly all net saving in advanced countries was done voluntarily by private persons, chiefly by landlords and merchants. Ever since then the share of such saving has been declining, and the shares done by non-financial corporations, banks, and governments have been rising. In 1860 less than 10 percent of all United States saving was done by these organizations, but their share had risen to above 70 percent (nearly all corporate) by 1965. The corporate component of this share will continue to rise for several decades. The share of voluntary personal saving will continue to decline for centuries. It will fall below 15 percent by A.D. 2060, and below 10 percent by 2200. Moreover, throughout this period, saving by private corporations, already involuntary for most stockholders, will become less and less voluntary as stockholders continue to lose control over corporation managements.

Compulsory social saving enforced by governments—through the use of taxes, new means of payments, and the profits of state enterprises to finance investment—which now produces less than 20 percent of all savings in advanced non-communist states, will continue to grow for centuries. By the year 2100 it will provide over 50 percent of all such savings, and by 2300, over 90 percent. The balance will then come from voluntary personal saving. These results will be achieved in Western Europe several decades before they are achieved in the United States.

Most private and public firms now finance part or all of their new investments out of profits. Such self-financing has been growing for over 100 years and may continue to grow for a few more decades. It is, however, uneconomic, because it prevents capital funds from flowing freely into the most profitable uses and because it raises most market prices still further above marginal costs. The power to finance investments out of monopoly profits is the power to tax the public, and this power should not be delegated to individual firms. Centralization of the collection and distribution of capital funds is inevitable because it alone could achieve both uniform forced saving by all persons and uniform interest charges to all borrowers. Local plant managers cannot determine whether any proposed investment is socially desirable unless the interest rate they must pay is the same as that other borrowers must pay. Hence all governments will gradually restrict and eventually end self-financing, largely during the twenty-first century.

After all non-personal wealth has been socialized and compulsory social saving has largely replaced voluntary personal saving, national governments will pay off all government debts except those which represent personal savings by still-living persons. This will be done in order to eliminate some unearned personal interest income, to reduce the amount of inheritable private property, to free government income for uses other than interest payment, and to reduce taxes. By A.D. 2300 all government debts other than non-inherited savings accounts in government-owned banks will have been repaid. Inheritance taxes and occasional capital levies, as well as compulsory social savings, will be used to pay off these debts.

Insurance

Insurance has long been and will long remain a rapid-growth industry. The major insurance trends during the next 500 years will include a steady increase in the proportion of the world population insured against each risk for which insurance is now available; the provision of insurance against more and more risks for which insurance is not now available; an indefinite further substitution of social for private insurance; growing use of non-uniform sales taxes to finance and properly allocate the costs of social insurance; gradual integration of all social-insurance systems; discontinuance of social-insurance premium-payment records for individuals; and a steady increase in the proportion of insurance claims settled without resort to the courts.

In advanced countries the proportion of the population protected by each traditional form of insurance—life, fire, accident, etc.—has been rising for centuries and will continue to rise for another century or two. And this trend will be much more rapid and long-continued in backward countries, because the present coverage is far smaller there. Every increase in average real income tends to increase the proportion of the population able and willing to buy private insurance and vote and pay for social insurance. And real incomes will rise indefinitely in all countries.

The variety of risks against which insurance is available has been growing for several hundred years and will continue to grow for several hundred more. In 2300 most people in the world will be insured against all possible major property or income losses, including many which are now uninsurable. For instance, few Americans can now obtain economical insurance against losses and costs due to floods, earthquakes, droughts, hailstorms, sand storms, tornadoes, hurricanes, tidal waves, earth slippages, violent crimes, birth defects, paralysis, insanity. By 2100 most Americans will be insured against all substantial losses due to these causes; by 2200 nearly all will be so insured.

Since it began a century ago, social (compulsory state) insurance has grown much faster than private insurance, even in capitalist states. This trend will continue, until by 2500 everyone in the world will be insured against all major risks by social insurance.

All well-designed insurance—that which does not unduly increase fraud and waste—is socially as well as individually beneficial. It lightens both the individual burden of personal misfortunes and the social tax burden of welfare aid, and it makes consumption per person more equal. But the private competitive sale of insurance policies is costly and can never achieve ideal or full coverage. Those who need insurance the most are the least likely to buy it voluntarily. Hence more and more experts and voters have come to favor and will increasingly favor the extension of compulsory social insurance. The shift from voluntary private insurance to compulsory social insurance will be the major social trend in the insurance field during the next 200 years.

Private insurance firms have performed a most beneficial social service by permitting individuals to purchase an ever wider range of insurance, but the methods they have had to use as competitive profit-seeking firms are entirely unsuited to social insurance. For instance, a private insurance firm must incur heavy selling costs, sell a separate policy to each insurance buyer, and record separately the premiums paid by each buyer. Moreover, each insurance customer must buy many different personal insurance policies (each a complicated legal agreement) to obtain the most complete protection. Social insurance permits the elimination of all these costly procedures and has already ended many of them. It will end many more during the next century. By 2200 every advanced state will have a simplified, rationalized social-insurance system which insures all persons against nearly all substantial undeserved losses and costs without requiring any voluntary payments by individuals and without maintaining individual premium-payment records. By 2500 all persons in all countries will be thus insured against all such losses. Insured persons may be required to pay a small part of all losses, in order to minimize insurance frauds, and to pay all losses below some minimum, in order to eliminate claims whose handling costs make them uneconomic.

In the United States the next big expansion of social insurance will be the gradual adoption of universal health insurance. This will occur in several stages—first, limited health insurance for most of the aged, then perhaps for children, later for most wage workers, and eventually for the entire population. Once each system of health insurance has been adopted, its loss coverage will be steadily widened.

Automobile accident insurance will also be socialized in most advanced countries before 2050. It will largely be financed by special sales taxes on gasoline and tires, because such taxes can be designed to vary closely with risk and are easy to collect.

The latest and least-known extension of social insurance is the provision of insurance against personal injuries inflicted by criminal acts. In 1964, New Zealand and Great Britain both began to provide this insurance, and public support for such insurance is growing in other advanced countries. By 2100 most such countries will provide social insurance against nearly all losses—property losses as well as injuries—due to criminal acts.

Payments to beneficiaries by American social-insurance systems rose from 0.6 percent of GNP in 1935 to about 4.0 percent in 1960. They will rise above 8 percent by 2000 and above 16 percent by 2100, but will decline slowly thereafter as free distribution continues to grow and diminish the need for monetary insurance benefits, and as more effective accident, fire, and disease prevention reduces losses.

The further expansion of social insurance and free distribution will steadily reduce the need for private life insurance. Life-insurance sales, now growing rapidly, will begin a long decline in all advanced countries during the twenty-first century. By 2200 nearly all countries will prohibit the sale of life-insurance policies in excess of some low maximum in order to limit private inheritance.

The fourth major long-run trend in insurance will be the growing use of sales taxes to finance insurance. As noted earlier, auto accident insurance will be socialized and financed by sales taxes on gasoline and tires. Several other new kinds of social insurance will eventually be financed by appropriate sales taxes. For instance, fire insurance will be increasingly financed by taxes on tobacco products, matches, gas-burning domestic equipment, combustible building materials, etc., in order to allocate the costs of fires to those persons and practices responsible for them. All costs of social insurance against accidents, industrial illness, and property losses will be thus allocated by sales taxes before 2200. And the fact that social insurance makes possible such allocation will become an influential argument for replacing private with social insurance against such losses.

The fifth major insurance trend will be ever-growing integration and centralization of social insurance. Most advanced capitalist states have several independent social-insurance systems —for different classes of risks, regions, industries, etc. The United States has several hundred such systems. These will be gradually integrated into national systems for each type of insurance, then into national systems handling all kinds of insurance, and eventually, before 2500, into a single world social-security system providing uniform insurance against all risks to all persons in the world.

The preparation and maintenance of records of social-insurance tax payments by each person for each risk is extremely costly and will become unnecessary in any region as soon as all persons are uniformly insured by a single system. Therefore the preparation of such accounting records will cease soon after such universal uniform coverage is achieved, before 2100 in all advanced countries.

Finally the common United States practice of using court trials to determine insurance awards will be gradually curtailed, and completely abolished before 2100. The growth of social insurance and public ownership will help to limit this practice. Government agencies rarely sue each other. Social-insurance awards will be increasingly determined by social-insurance administrators, because court trials are an inefficient and unduly expensive means of fixing insurance payments. Moreover, the interpretation of uniform national social-insurance policies will be much easier than the interpretation of thousands of different and constantly changing insurance policies issued by competing private firms.

Commercial Banks

Commercial banks perform two major distinctive functions: they create and invest most new money (bank notes) and money substitutes (demand deposits and checks); and they enable men to substitute payment by bank debit for payment with cash. Both functions will suffer radical changes in the next 200 years in all countries.

The function of creating new purchasing power will be taken from banks, whether private or public, and will be entrusted to a single new non-banking agency which will become the sole agency permitted to create money or money substitutes. As long as the function of creating purchasing power is in the hands of banks, they will be tempted to create it in order to make profitable loans, but new money and substitutes should be created solely in order to stabilize prices or to reduce unemployment. No agency should be entrusted with two partially conflicting functions.

It is noteworthy that communist as well as capitalist banks are still allowed to create new purchasing power and lend it to business firms. The price inflation which occurred in the Soviet Union during the first three five-year plans was due largely to the excessive creation of new bank money in order to finance bank loans. Communists as well as capitalists still share the naive illusion that banks should put "idle money," that is, reserves behind demand deposits, to work.

The best way to prevent the creation and loan of new money and money substitutes by banks is to require them to keep a 100 percent cash reserve behind all bank notes and demand deposits. Other less effective methods may be tried in the next few decades, but by 2100 all capitalist and communist banks in advanced countries will be required to maintain such cash reserves.

The application of this policy, usually called 100 percent money, will eliminate two major functions of central banks, that of replenishing the reserves of member banks and that of printing bank notes. Other minor functions—the purchase and sale of government securities, stabilization of foreign-exchange rates, the clearing of checks, etc.—will be abolished or taken over by other agencies. The purchase and sale of securities will be taken over by a new price-level-stabilization agency, and later, when all government securities have been retired, will be ended. The policy of stabilizing foreign exchange rates will be replaced by a free market policy. The clearing of checks will be handled by the new commercial banking monopoly itself. No functions will remain for central banks to perform, and all central banks will stop operating before A.D. 2200.

In addition to losing the functions of creating and investing new money and demand deposits, commercial banks will gradually lose other less significant functions. The coming centralization and rationalization of investment, predicted in the previous chapter, will eventually end all investment and loan functions of commercial banks. The growth of public ownership will eliminate their trust and property-management functions, and so on. By 2300 all commercial banks in the world will be restricted to the single major function of making possible payment by bank debit and reporting such payments in the most useful form and detail. They will also continue to cash small checks for deposit and to accept cash deposits.

The substitution of bank checks for currency in business transactions has been growing steadily for centuries and will continue until all payments of more than some small sum (perhaps five or ten dollars) are made by check or check substitute. This change is inevitable, chiefly because payment by bank debit is often more convenient and economical and because it creates records useful to private parties, to police, to tax officials, etc. Moreover, it makes theft of money more difficult and bribery more detectable, eliminates much counting and recounting of money, and facilitates payment by mail.

The use of checks is far more common in America, where most workers now have checking accounts, than in other countries. Hence the greatest expansion of check use in the next few decades will occur in Europe, especially in the Soviet Union. By 2050 most European workers, and all Soviet adults, will have personal checking accounts. The use of checks to pay wages will increase rapidly for a few decades but will later be replaced by an even more economical method of wage payment.

The growing use of personal checking accounts will soon permit employers to pay wages and salaries by instructing their banks to credit the checking accounts of their employees. This method of wage payment will save the substantial costs of preparing, distributing, and depositing payroll checks. It will also eliminate loss and theft of such checks. Hence most United States wages and salaries will be paid by such direct bank credits before 2050. To obtain more business and to share the large savings from this method of wage payments, some American banks will soon begin to offer free checking accounts to all employees of firms which adopt and pay for such bank payment of wages and salaries.

The growing use of personal bank accounts will also eventually permit retail stores, landlords, and other firms to collect more and more debts by sending bills directly to local banks, eventually by wire to computers. By 2200 all debts will be so collected in the United States. Monthly bank statements for individuals will then include all personal income and all personal expenditures over a small minimum sum. They will be designed and prepared as family budgets in order to facilitate comparison of each class of expenditures for different months and families.

The growing use of checks and check substitutes by business firms will provide commercial banks with data on ever more financial transactions of their business depositors. To reduce the resulting duplication of financial accounting records and increase their revenues, commercial banks will gradually take over more and more accounting tasks of business firms and perform them as instructed by their depositors. The Bank of America, the largest in the world, already uses its expensive computers to prepare and record payroll checks for business firms. By 2200 commercial banks will make all payments, keep all financial records, and prepare all financial reports for their business depositors in both capitalist and communist countries. Cost accounting will of course continue to be done by each firm, but the determination of marginal costs requires only data on material prices, wage rates, quantities used, etc. It does not require accurate records of total payments for any purpose.

To facilitate their performance of financial accounting services for depositors, banks will soon print checks with different expense-account numbers on them. Computers will classify all checks by firm and expense-account number and turn out complete daily or weekly financial reports for each business firm in the form desired by that firm. Later, when bank checks for paying wages and debts have been replaced by direct bank debits, all debits will be similarly classified and reported.

The costs of handling checks will be steadily reduced by growing mechanization of banks and by the gradual consolidation of banks. Chain banking has been expanding its share of activities in all advanced countries for many decades, and this trend will continue until each country, and later the entire world, has a single chain-banking system. This consolidation process will greatly reduce the relative number of bank buildings, bring about the use of more and larger office machines and computers, simplify ever-increasing government control over bank loans and investments (as long as they are permitted), and facilitate bank performance of financial accounting for all depositors. All United States commercial banks will be merged into a single national chain-banking system before 2100.

The American banking system now includes both national banks (private banks regulated by the federal government), and state banks (regulated by fifty different states). Moreover, all banks are regulated by several different federal agencies—FDIC, SEC, Treasury, Federal Reserve system, etc. This complex system will be greatly simplified during the next century. All state control over banking will be ended, and all federal control will be concentrated in a single federal agency, before 2100. Later, federal control itself will become superfluous, and the single remaining United States commercial bank will be freed from outside control of its banking methods and policies before 2200.

Government ownership of commercial banks in capitalist countries has grown for over 100 years and will continue to grow slowly until all such banks have been nationalized. This process will be largely complete in Europe by 2050 and in the United States by 2100. The chief reason for this trend has been and will continue to be growing recognition of the need to increase public control over the amount and allocation of private investments and over the creation of bank money and demand deposits.

In the United States and many other advanced countries, some or all banks are required to maintain reserves of gold or silver or both. During the next few decades one country after another will reduce or abolish such requirements. By 2060 the United States and most other countries will have substituted paper money or government bonds for all precious metals in bank reserves. They will continue to maintain national stocks of precious metals for use in settling international debts, but the entire national stock will be available for such use without causing any reduction in bank loans. The coming world government will of course eventually eliminate this last financial use of precious metals, probably before 2200.

Money

As explained previously, payment by check has been displacing payment with money and will long continue to do so. By 2500 less than 1 percent of all retail payments in the world will be made with money.

The relative use of gold and silver coins has been declining for centuries and will continue to decline until they disappear. Gold coins already have virtually disappeared in most advanced countries. Silver coins will soon follow. They will be replaced by checks, paper money, and coins of non-precious metals.

In many capitalist states paper money is now printed and issued by local or central banks. This function will be transferred from banks to the national governments in one country after another during the next century. By 2100 all paper money will be issued by governments. They will control their issue of new money in such a way as to stabilize some wholesale or retail price index. Since every country needs some additional means of payment every year—usually a 2 to 6 percent annual increase—the creation of new means of payment will provide every government with a substantial permanent revenue. As predicted earlier, all capitalist and communist banks will soon be required to maintain 100 percent government paper-money reserves behind their demand deposits, which will prevent them from creating any additional means of payment.

Since it is much easier to count and calculate in decimal than in non-decimal money, all countries which have not yet adopted a decimal currency will soon do so. The British will probably do so before 1980. They will adopt new coins made like American coins in order to facilitate the sale of British coin-operated machines in America, and vice versa.

The coming world government will eventually establish a uniform world monetary system. It will not do so immediately after its creation but will certainly do so long before 2500, probably before 2300. Thereafter all nations will use the same money and the same commercial banking system.

The coming requirement that all payments over some small maximum be made by check or bank debit will eventually make most paper money superfluous. If no payment over five dollars can be made in cash, the government will print only one-dollar bills. And counterfeiters have rarely tried to counterfeit one-dollar bills; hence both counterfeiting and printing and coinage costs will decline sharply after the use of cash has been radically restricted.

Stock Exchanges

Stock exchanges are important and characteristic capitalist institutions, and they will continue to function as long as private ownership of securities survives. They will, however, experience many predictable reforms during this period.

All advanced capitalist governments will continue to expand and intensify their regulation of stock exchanges in order to reduce fraud and uneconomic fluctuations in individual and average security prices. For instance, they will further restrict the use of credit and margin accounts until all buyers are required to pay in full for all securities. Moreover, most advanced capitalist states will prohibit short sales of securities before A.D. 2060.

Most stock exchanges are exclusive private clubs run for the benefit of the members, so far as capitalist governments allow this. But they perform a vital economic function, and their continued malfunctioning is one of many preventable threats to the future of capitalism. Hence capitalist governments will soon reorganize these private clubs and turn them into closely regulated public utilities or government enterprises. Club members will lose all special trading privileges.

When this is done, if not before, the member floor traders and their staffs will be replaced by computers, and all stock-exchange floor operations will be mechanized and automated. This is already quite feasible, and member opposition to it is a perfect example of featherbedding.

Among the major costs and inconveniences of buying, owning, and selling securities are the obtaining, storing, finding, delivering, transferring, and redepositing of the certificates. These costs and nuisances will be sharply reduced by two major successive reforms. First, brokers will assemble and store at stock exchanges a growing proportion of certificates of listed stocks, beginning with those most actively traded, and will transfer book credits to such deposited certificates instead of the certificates themselves. They will use the same method to reduce certificate shipments which banks have used to reduce gold movements.

Second, the largest private corporations will soon begin to sell notes and shares documented by book entries on their records instead of by printed exchangeable certificates. Many mutual banks and insurance companies already use such book entries in place of certificates. But the new book entries will be salable on stock exchanges. They will be transferred from person to person by mere accounting entries, as demand deposits now are. This method of transferring corporation debts and shares will become general in all advanced capitalist countries before 2100.

The expansion of communication facilities has made obsolete once-valid justifications for local stock exchanges. Hence local exchanges will be merged into a single national stock exchange in each advanced capitalist state, before 2050. The American Stock Exchange will be merged with the New York Stock Exchange before the year 2000 in order to reduce operating costs and ensure equal protection and service to all owners of listed stocks.

Since stock exchanges render useful services to security owners, all widely owned securities, perhaps all publicly owned securities, should and therefore eventually will be listed on stock exchanges. This will vastly increase the number of transactions on stock exchanges.

In 1963 fifty-nine new corporate issues were admitted for trading on the New York Stock Exchange. This, the largest number of admissions since the exchange started keeping records, raised the total number listed to about 1,600 issues of over 1,200 companies, comprising 8 billion shares valued at some $400 billion. In spite of mergers all these totals will continue to rise steadily for 50 to 100 years. By A.D. 2000, over 10,000 issues, 100 billion shares, and $4,000 billion in value will be listed. The causes of this growth will be increasing government pressure for more complete and frequent financial reports to stockholders, the continued expansion and multiplication of American corporations, and rising public interest and investment in common stocks. Many corporations still refuse to publish the reports required of listed companies; but the SEC will compel all publicly owned corporations to publish more and more complete and frequent reports.

The volume of transactions on United States stock exchanges will continue to grow for several decades because of absolute economic growth, relative growth of corporations, and a widening public ownership of individual corporations. As government ownership expands, however, it will eventually offset these factors and initiate a long decline in the volume of stock-market transactions. By the year 2300 there will be no private securities available for private purchase, and therefore no stock exchange, anywhere in the world. Government bonds, if any, will be redeemable but not transferable.

CHAPTER VIII

Agriculture

In all advanced countries a technological revolution has long been under way in agriculture. It will certainly continue for several decades more in these countries and for a century or two in backward countries. It has already drastically reduced the proportion of the population engaged in agriculture in advanced countries, and it will do the same in all other countries. The resulting movement of people from farms and villages to towns and cities has been and will long continue to be an important cause of other social trends, such as the growth of birth control, the expansion of education, the decline of religion, the rise of social insurance, and the growth of free distribution.

As noted in the Introduction nearly all major social trends are unpopular. The more rapidly they proceed and the more serious their effects, the more unpopular they are. It is natural, therefore, that the current agricultural revolution is highly unpopular. The governments of most non-communist states have adopted many laws designed to slow it down or stop it. This has long been one of the chief purposes of American farm-relief programs. And the Department of Agriculture deliberately assembles, processes, and publishes its farm statistics in such a way as to obscure the nature, extent, and speed of the agricultural revolution in order to persuade voters that the old American way in agriculture, the family farm, is secure.

The current agricultural revolution began in the most advanced countries. It has gone further in the United States than in any other country except perhaps England. Hence a review of recent American agricultural statistics will provide the best possible basis for predicting not only the immediate future of American agriculture but the later similar development in most other non-communist countries.

Crop Farming

Like the industrial revolution, the current agricultural revolution is due primarily to the invention of new and more expensive machines which can be most efficiently used only by large multifamily enterprises. New and more expensive machines are constantly being developed, which steadily favors the large farms, and this will continue indefinitely.

In the agricultural revolution the invention of the tractor played a key role, as did the steam engine in the industrial revolution. Hence data on tractor use are significant. In 1920, American farmers owned only 246,000 tractors. By 1960 they owned 4.8 million; but one third of all farms still had no tractor. A similar expansion of tractor use is well under way in nearly all advanced countries and has begun in most other countries.

The number and efficiency of all farm machines—tractors, plows, combines, cotton-picking machines, etc.—has grown steadily during the past century and will continue to grow throughout the next 500 years. The value of farm machinery and equipment per acre will probably double every 50 years or less for the next century or two in every country. The value per farm worker will rise much faster.

Farm machines will become ever larger, more powerful, and faster. By 2200 most plowing, planting, cultivating, fertilizing, and harvesting of field crops throughout the world will be done by machines more than twice as large, powerful, and fast as the average now used in America.

Every increase in the use of labor-saving farm machinery and methods permits a single family to operate a larger farm. As a result the average size of commercial farms in America grew from about 200 acres to about 400 acres between 1930 and 1960. It will double again by A.D. 2000.

American farm population declined by 30 percent between

1930 and 1960. It will fall another 30 percent by A.D. 2000. In spite of this decrease United States farm output increased by over 60 percent from 1930 to 1960. It will long continue to grow faster than the total population. Thus, by 2000 the average commercial farm will have over twice as many acres, use about four times as much machinery, and produce three to four times as much food as in 1960.

Between 1939 and 1959 the number of commercial farms (1959 USDA definition) in the United States declined steadily from 4.1 to 2.4 million. And in 1959, 50 percent of marketed farm output was produced by 4 percent of these farms, most of which operated under crop-curtailment laws or agreements. They could easily expand their output within a decade sufficiently to replace all other farms, and in spite of numerous artificial or temporary cultural obstacles, they are certain to drive more and more small farmers out of business. The number of American commercial farms will fall below one million by A.D. 2000, below 300,000 by 2100, and below 10,000 by 2300.

In 1960 the great majority of United States commercial farms were still family farms—in other words, they used less than 1.5 man-years of hired labor—but their share of farm output had long been declining. The farms which marketed over $100,000 of farm products (at 1959 prices) increased in number from 5,000 to 20,000 between 1939 and 1959 and increased their share of farm marketings from 14 to 33 percent in this brief period. Furthermore, the number of farms with marketings over $1,000,000 per year (1959 prices) grew from 34 in 1929 to 408 in 1959.

Whether or not the current technological revolution in agriculture has already created a clear trend toward factory farming in capitalist states, it certainly will do so during the next century. By 2100 most output in North America and Western Europe will come from farms which employ over 100 workers or contain over 10,000 acres.

Such a growth of ever-larger multi-family farms is inevitable because farm machines will become steadily larger, more specialized, and more expensive; farms will require more and more specialized workers and managers as farm technology becomes more complex and more scientific; large farms can design and use more specialized buildings and fixed improvements than smaller farms; a large farm requires much less area for access roads, fences, houses, barns, etc., than small farms covering an equal area; the larger the farm, the lower the delivered cost of fertilizer, seed, pesticides, and other supplies; every increase in farm size permits a greater division of labor; and the many laws which now discriminate against large-scale farming will be gradually repealed.

Agricultural specialization has been growing for centuries in all advanced countries, and the rate of this growth has been more rapid than ever in recent years. The percentage of all farms which sell fruit, or corn, or pigs, or beans, or tomatoes, etc., has been falling steadily. Of twenty such major farm activities, the average American farm had 5.4 in 1940 and only 4.7 in 1954, a decline of 13 percent in fourteen years. This decline will continue indefinitely because all land is best suited to a single crop or crop rotation; transport costs will continue to decline; and specialization increases the scale of any farm activity and yields all the many advantages of large-scale production.

More and more working farmers will move to town. American farm land was divided into individual farms before the rise of the automobile, the tractor, and other labor-saving farm machines and practices. The general adoption of these new machines and methods has made the isolated farm home obsolete. Most American farmers could now live more comfortably in farm towns, where public utility, retail, medical, educational, and other services are cheaper and much more convenient. Moreover, moving to town will enable more farm wives and children to get off-farm jobs. As farm incomes rise and the hours of labor decline, the social, cultural, and educational advantages of town life will become ever more attractive to farm families. Finally country roads and means of transport from town to field will improve continually.

The movement of working farmers from isolated farms to town is a well-established American trend. The proportion of full-time farmers living in town rose from 5 percent in 1950 to

10 percent in 1960. It will exceed 30 percent by A.D. 2000, 60 percent by 2100, and 95 percent by 2200.

The coming radical reorganization of agriculture in non-communist states will be greatly facilitated by the growth of state ownership of farm land. It is much more difficult to persuade independent land owners to enlarge fields and farms, integrate and centralize buildings, eliminate unnecessary access roads, move from isolated homes to villages, etc., than to require tenants to do so. Moreover, nationalization of land will eliminate private unearned increment due to the rise in value of farm land ($54 billion in the United States from 1950 to 1960). For these reasons most of the world's farm land in non-communist states will be nationalized before 2100. Great Britain will be among the first, and the United States one of the last, advanced capitalist states to nationalize land.

In technology Soviet agriculture is still far behind American, but in the creation of giant farms it is far ahead. Unfortunately, giant farms are efficient only when they use very advanced methods. The Soviets organized large farms prematurely, before they had the skilled managers, workers, and machinery needed to make them a success. In the Soviet Union, therefore, the chief agricultural trends during the next generation will be the gradual adoption of more and more farm methods and machines already proven successful on large American farms. This will result in a rapid reduction of the still-large proportion (40 percent in 1960) of the Soviet labor force engaged in agriculture. By A.D. 2000 this proportion will be below 15 percent; by 2100, below 2 percent.

Soviet state farms have long been replacing collective farms. By 2050 all Soviet farms will be state farms. All farm workers will then receive regular wages instead of a share in output or profits. Wage payment is now growing steadily on collective farms and is universal on state farms.

Another well-established Soviet farm trend is a decline in the share of farm earnings paid in kind. This trend will continue, until by A.D. 2050, Soviet farm workers will receive only money income from their employer and will pay for all products not produced in their gardens.

Most Soviet farm workers, and many factory workers, now have small personal gardens and one or more farm animals. The large share of farm output produced on such holdings has been decreasing since 1945 and will continue to decrease indefinitely because large-scale production will become ever more efficient.

Chemists have already invented many synthetic fibers and foods. The production of synthetic fibers has grown rapidly and in 1960 accounted for over 12 percent of world fiber output. This proportion will continue to rise indefinitely, because the manufacture of synthetic fibers is a decreasing-cost industry and because it will benefit more from future technological progress than the production of natural fibers. By 2200 over 80 percent of world fiber output will be synthetic.

The manufacture of synthetic food has as yet made little progress, but it is certain to grow like the manufacture of synthetic fibers, and for the same reasons. Recent experiments have demonstrated that men can now subsist entirely on synthetic foods already invented; and many more will be invented. The real costs of manufactured synthetic foods will continue indefinitely to fall faster than those of agricultural products. A slow but long-continuing substitution of synthetic for natural foods is therefore inevitable. By 2100 over 5 percent and by 2500 over 50 percent of all human food will be synthetic. The chief reason for continued consumption of natural foods in the year 2500 is that many natural foods will still taste better than or different from their synthetic substitutes.

As a result of the coming improvements in farm methods and machines and the prospective growth of synthetic and sea-food production, the proportion of the world labor force employed on farms (now over 60 percent) will decline steadily. By A.D. 2100 it will be less than 30 percent, in spite of a twofold or threefold increase in world population. It will continue to fall steadily thereafter. By 2500 it will be below 2 percent. In the United States it fell from 60 percent in 1860 to 8 percent in 1960. It will fall below 3 percent by 2000 and below 0.5 percent by 2500.

Animal Husbandry

Animal husbandry is experiencing its own special revolution, which differs considerably from the revolution in crop farming. It began later and is a result of advances in technology and management rather than a result of the invention of new machines.

The chief long-run trend in the animal-husbandry revolution is specialization, which involves both separation of animal husbandry from crop farming and specialization in raising one kind of animal for one use. It is most obvious in the United States broiler industry, which has made chicken the cheapest meat in America. It has done so by concentrating broiler production on specialized factory farms, some of which house 50,000 birds per worker in broiler houses (blocks of small cages) up to 600 feet long and three stories high, and by using the most advanced feeding and care methods.

In recent decades United States egg production also has been increasingly concentrated on large specialized farms. In 1900 nearly all chickens and eggs were produced on unspecialized small farms; in 1960 most were produced on specialized farms. By 2000 nearly all will be so produced. Moreover, similar specialization has long been growing in other fields of animal husbandry.

In 1959 only 1 percent of United States hog farmers marketed over 500 animals per farm, but they produced more pork than the lowest 50 percent of all hog farmers, each of whom marketed fewer than 30 animals. Moreover, the profit per hog was much higher for the largest producers. The number of hog producers will continue to decline steadily for centuries.

The same trend is obvious in the dairy industry. In 1950 only 3,600 United States dairy farms had more than 100 cows. By 1959 this number had risen to 6,600 and there were at least 34 farms with over 1,000 cows each. The McArthur Dairy in Florida had grown to 8,000 milk cows and 150 workers by 1962. Such growth has forced thousands of small, less efficient dairies out of business.

The number of farms with milk cows decreased by half between 1950 and 1959, but the number of large dairies (sales over

$10,000) increased by 117 percent. This rapid separation of milk production from crop production has notably increased the scale of operation in both crop and milk production and has reduced costs for specialized producers in both fields. It will continue, until by 2100 over 90 percent of milk cows are owned by fewer than 1,000 dairies.

Most fattening or finishing of United States beef cattle is still done on small family farms. But big feed lots, which handle from 10,000 to 40,000 head at a time, have grown rapidly since 1940. By 1960 they had already taken over 10 percent of such finish feeding from Midwest corn-livestock farms. This ratio will continue to rise steadily, until before 2100 the big feed lots will do nearly all finish feeding.

Big feed lots do not require much space. They are not large farms, but they require a large investment. They use machinery to feed cattle and clean stalls, and they rely heavily on wage labor. They are factory farms, not family farms.

Animals are raised by man for two purposes, work and food. In advanced countries the use of work animals has been falling for over 50 years and will continue to fall indefinitely as non-animal energy sources become ever cheaper and more abundant. United States horse and mule population fell from 24 million in 1910 to 3 million in 1960. It will be below 1 million in 1980.

This trend will have significant and long-continuing effects in densely populated backward countries like India and China. In 1960, India had about 200 million cattle, which provided the chief non-human source of power in agriculture, consumed three times as many calories as the human population, and, due to religious beliefs, were little used as sources of meat. By 2200 animal power will have been almost entirely replaced by machine power in agriculture throughout the world, and cattle will be raised only as a source of beef, milk, and hides. This will free a vast amount of animal feed for human consumption.

Men have long been able to crudely control the evolution of animals and plants. Thus all the widely differing dog breeds known today are probably descended from one or two breeds first domesticated by primitive men over ten thousand years ago. In recent years men have vastly improved animal and plant-breeding methods, and this improvement will continue indefinitely.

The application of improved breeding methods during the next 500 years will produce radical changes in all domesticated animals and cultivated plants, and in some now wild. Animal-feeding costs per pound of animal product will decline steadily and indefinitely. The yields per acre of all cultivated plants will rise steadily and indefinitely.

During the next two centuries many animals and plants now wild will be domesticated and improved by breeding until they yield valuable new products at competitive costs. Expenditures on the study of wild animals (including fish and insects) and wild plants in order to discover and improve those most suitable for human use will increase tenfold by A.D. 2000 and a hundredfold by 2100. The results will be most important in Africa, where large wild animals can now produce over twice as much meat per acre as domestic animals. By 2100 several varieties of antelope, gazelle, zebra, and other herbivorous African game animals will have been domesticated.

The oceans of the world are destined to become a major source of food, raw materials, and fresh water. Shallow areas where sea mammals and food fish thrive will be vastly expanded by pushing nearby hills and mountains into the sea. These areas will then be enclosed with nets or jetties, fertilized, freed of parasites and predators, stocked with sea mammals and fish, and mechanically fished.

Long before 2500 most sea mammals—seals, walruses, porpoises, whales—will have been domesticated and improved by breeding and will be fed, herded, and slaughtered as cattle and sheep now are. They will be protected from predators and treated for diseases and parasites. Many predators and useless fish will be exterminated, or preserved only in zoos and aquariums, to increase the supplies of food fish. The proportion of world meat supplies obtained from sea mammals, now negligible, will rise steadily throughout the next 500 years and will exceed 20 percent by 2500. The growth of human population will steadily reduce the acreage of land pastures but not that of sea pastures.

Continental Landscaping

The real cost of crushing rock and moving earth has been declining for many decades and is certain to continue to decline for centuries. The use of nuclear explosives alone will sharply reduce such costs. By the year 2500 these costs (measured in hours of labor per ton-mile) will be less than 5 percent of the 1960 United States level, and world income will be one hundred times as great. Moreover, water will be cheap enough to justify irrigation of all arid or semi-arid areas.

As a result of the steady decline of earth-moving costs, governments, builders, and farmers in advanced countries have long been spending more and more money to level farm land, terrace suburban hillsides, and fill in shallow bays. Such activities will continue to expand throughout the next 500 years and will gradually achieve a radical reconstruction of the earth's surface.

Vast areas of uneven old farm land will be terraced or leveled in order to facilitate the use of wheeled farm machinery and the smooth natural flow of both rain and irrigation water. Immense tonnages of rock now lying on old or potential farm land will be crushed or removed by large new machines. By 2500 all urban and arable land will be free of stones.

Nearly all the swamps and marshes in the world will be drained, graded, and converted into farm, forest, or city land. The Pripet Marshes in Russia and the Everglades in Florida will be completely drained before 2100, except for some acreage reserved for natural-life preserves. The rivers of the Amazon drainage basin will be dammed and channeled, and the adjoining swamps drained and put to use, before 2300.

After most naturally level and rolling land has been improved and irrigated, hundreds of millions of additional arable areas will be created by partially leveling and terracing hills and mountains and by filling in shallow off-shore waters. Such projects will be started first and carried further in the best climatic regions. For instance, a large part of the Coast Ranges of California will be pushed into the nearby Pacific, and what is left will be terraced for agricultural or residential use. Most of the California shore line will be advanced five or ten miles into the Pacific by 2500. Many coastal ranges around the North Sea, the Mediterranean, the Adriatic, the Yellow Sea, and the Sea of Japan will be similarly treated before 2500. The arable land of Italy, Greece, and Japan will be increased over 50 percent by such measures. Most of the Sea of Azov, Lake Michigan, and Lake Erie will be filled in and reclaimed for agricultural and urban use. Over 20 percent of the area of the Adriatic, the Baltic, the Ionian Sea, the Black Sea, the Sea of Japan, and the Gulf of Mexico will be similarly reclaimed. The European coast line of the Mediterranean will be moved out five to ten miles on an average.

Wide land bridges will be built between Ireland and Scotland, England and France, Denmark and Sweden, Alaska and Siberia, Italy and Tunis, Spain and Morocco, Japan and Korea, Australia and New Guinea. Paved, six-lane freeways will be built across all such new land bridges, as well as throughout all continents. By 2500 it will be possible to drive over such freeways from Buenos Aires to Siberia, England, South Africa, Japan, and Australia. And long before all the land bridges required for such trips are completed, it will be possible to make them by means of car ferries across one or two still unbridged straits.

The Aral and Caspian seas will be drained of salt water by a tunnel or canal to the Black Sea and filled with fresh water from the rivers of northern Siberia. Then the Black Sea will be dammed at the Bosporus and its salt water gradually replaced by fresh. The conversion of the Baltic Sea, the Mediterranean Sea, the Red Sea, the Sea of Japan, the Gulf of California, and some other large land-enclosed seas and gulfs into fresh water lakes will be well under way, if not completed, by the year 2500.

To speed up and cheapen sea transport, many important canals will be built during the next 500 years. One or more additional canals will be constructed at sea level across the

Isthmus of Tehuantepec before 2100. The old Erie Canal across New York State will be enlarged enough to carry most ocean freighters to the Great Lakes, and an equally large canal will be dug from the Great Lakes to the Pacific (partly to transport fresh water from the Northwest to the Midwest). Before 2300, similar canals will be built from the Bay of Biscay to the Mediterranean across southern France, from the Adriatic to the Black Sea across western Russia, from the Black Sea to the Caspian and to the Persian Gulf, from the Gulf of Siam to the Indian Ocean across the Isthmus of Kra, from the Sea of Japan to the Yellow Sea across Korea.

These lists of future giant engineering projects are meant to give only a rough idea of the coming reconstruction of the earth's surface. Such projects deserve and will soon receive many monographs and books.

Fresh Water

Land, air, sunshine, and fresh water are the essential bases of all human life, and fresh water is the least abundant of these in areas most suitable for human habitation. In arid and semi-arid regions, which occupy a large share of the earth's land area, the growth of agriculture and cities has always been severely limited. And the rapid growth of population and modern industry in agricultural areas with a once-ample water supply has already produced serious shortages of unpolluted fresh water and will soon produce many more. Fortunately men have become more and more efficient in increasing supplies of cheap fresh water in all regions. Their growing efforts to increase such supplies will have major effects on the growth and location of agriculture and industry. Hence a section on fresh water is appropriate.

Annual United States water use increased 700 percent from 1900 to 1960. It will continue to increase at a rapid rate throughout the next 500 years, due to growth of population, agriculture, industry, real incomes, etc. It cannot, however, long continue to grow at the 1900–60 rate, because the marginal cost of additional water has begun to rise and will continue to rise for decades in most coastal areas and for centuries in most inland areas.

Fresh-water supplies will be vastly increased in many nations by simultaneous use of three major alternative methods: the importation by canal of fresh water from ever more distant sources; desalting sea and other salt water; and water purification and radical restriction of water pollution. Moreover, much waste of fresh water will be eliminated by ending price discrimination in water rates.

During the past century continuous technological progress has made it economic to transport fresh water by canal over ever-longer distances. In the American Southwest large amounts of water are now transported over two hundred miles, and a much longer canal is under construction. As its population continues to grow, one river after another north of San Francisco will be dammed and its water diverted to the Southwest. By 2050 water from the Columbia River will be diverted to the Colorado River. By 2100 water from the Peace and Yukon rivers in northwest Canada will be flowing to the Great Lakes, the American West, and northwest Mexico. The canal conducting water from British Columbia to the Great Lakes will be navigable, and huge blocks of hydroelectric power will be developed en route. An artificial lake over four hundred miles long in the Rocky Mountain Trench—just west of the continental divide in Montana and British Columbia—will store seasonal water surpluses until needed.

Such long-distance movement of fresh water will steadily expand in many other parts of the world. All the large Siberian rivers which flow into the Arctic Ocean will be dammed and their water diverted to arid regions in Mongolia and Turkestan before 2200. Water from the Amazon will be diverted to arid areas in Argentina, Peru, and other countries, as well as to other parts of Brazil. Water from the great rivers of central Africa will be diverted to the Sahara and Kalahari deserts. Long before 2500 all the rivers of the world will be fully used as sources of fresh water for near or distant areas.

The world supply of river water is fixed, but the supply of

sea water is unlimited, and the cost of desalting sea water is declining rapidly. In some coastal regions desalted sea water is already cheaper than transported river water, and the number and size of such regions will increase steadily throughout the next 500 years. Owing to recent and prospective breakthroughs in desalting methods, the use of desalted sea water will skyrocket during the next century; but in most inland and upland areas it will always be cheaper to use and reuse available river water than to desalt, lift, and transport sea water over long distances. The boundaries between the areas where river water and desalted sea water are used will depend upon relative costs, which will vary from region to region and decade to decade.

Desalted sea water will of course be consumed largely in lowland coastal areas, because this will minimize transport costs. As the use of desalted water in coastal areas grows, more and more river water will be reserved for inland or highland use. Later the use of desalted sea water will gradually spread inland, and river water will be increasingly reserved for ever-higher or more remote inland regions. By 2500 over half the world supply of fresh water will come from the sea.

The inland movement of desalted sea water, the repeated repurification and re-use of river water, and the improvement and spread of flood-control and irrigation dams will gradually stop or reverse the flow of more and more rivers, beginning with those in or near arid areas. By 2100 little if any water will flow into the ocean from the Nile, Niger, Indus, Columbia, Sacramento, Colorado, and similar rivers. All fresh river water will then be diverted into irrigation and urban water-supply canals in the upper reaches of such rivers.

The ever-growing use of river water for agricultural, industrial, and domestic uses in inland areas will soon begin to curtail the construction of hydroelectric power plants in advanced countries and will later cause the closing down of nearly all such plants in lowland or valley rivers. For instance, the Grand Coulee Dam power plant will cease operating before 2100, because all Columbia River water originating above that dam will then be consumed. For similar reasons the immense new Siberian hydroelectric power plants will also stop generating power, sometime during the twenty-first century. The same fate awaits the Boulder Dam power plant, on the lower Colorado River. The long canals now used to transport Colorado River water to the California seacoast will be abandoned or reconstructed to carry desalted sea water inland. All the water in the Colorado River, and a much greater quantity of imported river water, will be used in the upper parts of the Colorado River Basin.

The reversal of water flow in most large rivers will eliminate many famous waterfalls, as well as most hydroelectric power plants. Niagara Falls will stop flowing before 2200. The dams and channels built to stop and reverse the flow of water in rivers will also gradually reduce the number and severity of floods. The proportion of flood damage to national income will fall over 80 percent in advanced countries before 2200.

The farther water can be economically transported, the larger is the geographical area which should be served by a single water agency. The American Southwest has long needed such an agency. Disputes among communities in this immense region have seriously delayed and increased the costs of its major water facilities. When it becomes economical to transport water from Alaska and the Yukon to Illinois and Texas, a single continental water agency will be needed. Some cultural lag is inevitable, but by 2200 the entire North American continent will have a single water-supply agency which will plan the continent's water supply at least 100 years in advance so as to minimize the total cost of all the fresh water used. By 2300 every continent will have such a continental water agency, and all will be supervised by a single world water agency.

The growth of population and industry during the past 200 years has caused a steady increase in water pollution. Most rivers and coastal waters near urban areas are now heavily polluted with sewage and industrial wastes. Efforts to check such pollution have been growing in recent decades. They will continue to grow until they end all uneconomic dumping of sewage and industrial pollutants in river, lake, or coastal waters. By 2100 nearly all urban sewage in advanced countries will be processed near its source and converted into chemical products and purified water. Every industrial plant or area will then be required to bury, burn, or transform and utilize nearly all its waste products.

The rapidly growing costs of water purification will be increasingly allocated to the industries and people responsible for them by imposing special taxes varying with the volume of pollutants dumped. Such taxes will turn the social costs of water pollution into money costs of production. They have already proved highly effective in limiting water pollution in the crowded Ruhr River valley.

Price discrimination by water suppliers has long been customary. Prices have been based more upon estimates of ability to pay than upon costs. For instance, in 1960, Los Angeles paid $20 per acre-foot for Boulder Dam water, while nearby farmers paid only $2.25. Such discrimination is highly uneconomic. It makes money costs less accurate measures of real marginal costs and economic calculation less useful. Growing numbers of economists have condemned it. Hence the practice will be gradually eliminated. By 2100 all water in advanced countries will be priced at marginal cost (for reasons given in Chapter VI), and all users of each water supply will pay the same prices.

CHAPTER IX

INDUSTRY

IN THIS CHAPTER I shall predict technological and social trends in industry narrowly defined—manufacturing, mining, and public utilities. Only those major technological trends which affect social trends most seriously will be discussed.

Manufacturing

Modern factories in advanced countries are a product of the industrial revolution, which began about two hundred years ago in Great Britain and has since spread to one industry and one country after another. This revolution is 60 to 80 percent complete in advanced Western nations, but it has barely begun in most of Asia, Africa, and Latin America. Thus the chief trend in manufacturing in all backward countries during the next century or two will be the continuance and spread of the industrial revolution. By A.D. 2100 in Latin America and by 2200 in Asia and Africa, factory production of previously handmade items will be as customary as in Great Britain today. The coming industrial revolution in backward countries will be a major cause of many other important social trends—rise in real wages, growth of education, decline in birth rate, etc.—in all these countries.

In advanced countries the industrial revolution will continue in all as yet incompletely industrialized manufacturing industries, such as the clothing industry in Europe, but it will be far less important and prolonged than in backward countries. The major manufacturing trends in advanced countries during the next 500 years will be: a steady increase in the scale of production; concentration of production; automation; standardization of equipment and products; specialization among plants; relocation of factories nearer sources of raw materials and markets; and a decline in the share of the labor force engaged in manufacturing.

In advanced countries factories have been growing larger and larger for a century or two. The average number of employees and proprietors per United States manufacturing establishment grew from 25 in 1899 to 53 in 1958. In spite of further mechanization and automation it should exceed 80 by A.D. 2000, 1,000 by 2200, and 4,000 by 2500. By 2100 nearly all large plants will operate five or six shifts a day, seven days a week, in order to reduce capital costs per unit of output.

Average annual output per plant has of course grown far faster than the average work force. Between 1899 and 1954 value added per United States manufacturing establishment increased from \$70,000 to \$400,000 (1960 dollars). This figure will rise above \$2 million by the year 2000, above \$50 million by 2200, and well above \$1,000 million by 2500.

The real costs per ton-mile of freight transport have been declining for several hundred years and should continue to decline throughout the next 500 years. The volume of freight will grow indefinitely, and every increase in traffic over any route eventually reduces real costs. Moreover, continual technical progress in transportation is inevitable.

Each reduction in transport costs enlarges the area which can be economically served by a single factory. Hence the optimum factory size will grow steadily as transport costs fall. This is one reason why competition in manufacturing will gradually be replaced by monopoly. It also justifies the prediction that manufacturing plants will grow in size indefinitely, even after all similar plants in each region have been consolidated.

While it is easy to prove that United States manufacturing plants have been growing in size and output, it is more difficult to support another common belief, that manufacturing is being concentrated in fewer and fewer hands. The number of manufacturing firms reached a new all-time high in 1960. On the other hand, the share of assets owned by the 100 biggest firms had risen to 75 percent, and their share of all manufacturing profits to 86 percent. The remaining 419,000 firms had only 25 percent of the assets and 14 percent of the profits. Furthermore, they paid lower wages and produced inferior products. The wide gap between share of assets and share of profits suggests continued growth of concentration for an indefinite period.

Moreover, the political forces which have long opposed concentration of industry in non-communist states are steadily weakening—due to urbanization, education, propaganda, etc.—and will continue to weaken for a century or two. Hence, even if a well-established concentration trend in manufacturing in advanced countries is not now demonstrable, such a trend will soon appear and will continue indefinitely. By 2200 all manufacturing plants in each advanced country will be owned and managed by fewer than fifty national monopolies, and these in turn will be supervised by a single national agency. In several non-communist countries this prediction will be fulfilled before 2100.

Mechanization and automation of manufacturing are well-established trends in advanced countries. One evidence of this is the continual decline in the proportion of factory employees enumerated as "production workers." United States census figures reveal a decline from 92 percent in 1899 to 76 percent in 1959. Mechanization and automation of office work have slowed this decline and will continue to do so, but the decline will continue indefinitely, because it is easier to automate a factory production line than to automate clerical, professional, and managerial work. The United States figure should fall below 60 percent by 2000, below 40 percent by 2100, and below 10 percent by 2500. In a fully automated plant there are no production workers and no direct or marginal wage costs.

Competition among private manufacturing firms has resulted in an extreme over-diversification of manufactured products. Some of this is due to the isolation and independence of individual firms and much more to planned obsolescence—deliberate creation of unneeded new styles and models in order to stimulate sales. Diversification may continue to grow for a few more decades, but during the twenty-first century all advanced capitalist countries will adopt more and more measures, including the creation of monopolies, to standardize manufactured products. By 2200 the average variety of manufactured goods will have been reduced by 90 percent. This will facilitate mechanization and automation, drastically reduce inventories, lower repair costs, and help consumers to buy more wisely.

Every increase in standardization, specialization, or monopoly in manufacturing permits an increase in the scale of production, which makes mechanization and automation more feasible. And every technological advance in mechanization and automation of manufacturing increases the advantages of standardization, specialization, and monopoly. Thus these two sets of trends are interdependent and mutually reinforcing. Moreover, they will all be stimulated by long-continuing future declines in transport costs, tariff duties, language barriers, and cultural differences.

Long before 2500 the same standardized manufactured goods will be consumed in all countries. The entire world output of each kind of small valuable articles—watches, jewelry, optical goods, cameras, pocket radios, fountain pens—and of similar components of large assembled products will be produced in a single specialized automated factory. World output of a manufactured good will be divided among two or more plants only when the resulting savings in freight costs exceed the substantial savings from concentration of production in a single plant. And when two or more plants are justified, each will serve a different area. Competition between producers of the same good will end before 2200.

If concentration of all production of a good would create a plant which city planners consider too large but which is otherwise economic, the production of some parts will be sub-contracted to nearby communities. Thus my prediction of radical concentration of manufacturing does not rule out sound city planning, in particular the creation of optimum-size garden cities.

On the other hand, it does imply a continuous increase in the number of one-plant cities. By 2500 over 90 percent of all factories in the world will be located in towns or satellite cities which have no other manufacturing plant.

In advanced capitalist states freight rates are now based largely on ability to pay and are usually two to ten times as high for finished products as for raw materials. The application of marginal-cost pricing (predicted in Chapter VI) will eliminate such rate differences, and will therefore induce more and more firms to locate new factories near their sources of raw materials rather than near their markets. Nearly all remaining New England cotton and woolen textile plants will move to the South and Southwest before 2100 to be nearer the cotton fields and sheep ranches. And most clothing plants in New York City will soon follow them to be near the textile plants and nearer their customers. United States factories making products from rubber will be increasingly located near the factories producing synthetic rubber in the South and Southwest. Many other such specific predictions could be offered to illustrate the general prediction.

By the year 2500 most factories producing heavy or bulky products will be located on seacoasts or major inland waterways, because most of their raw materials and products will be transported by ship and because the majority of mankind will then prefer to live by the sea or by some great lake or river.

It is much easier to mechanize and automate manufacturing than most other economic activities. Hence the proportion of the national non-farm labor force engaged in manufacturing has already begun a long decline in some advanced countries. The proportion of United States factory employment to non-farm employment fell from 40 percent in 1920 to 30 percent in 1960. It will continue, or begin and continue, to fall in all advanced countries. The United States proportion will fall below 24 percent by 2000 and below 10 percent by 2300. In backward countries the proportion will continue to rise for many decades but should start to decline steadily in nearly all of them before 2100.

Metal Use

Rich metal-bearing ores are an irreplaceable natural resource whose limited supply has already been substantially reduced and is now diminishing at a high and rapidly increasing rate. The first nations to industrialize were able to exploit the richest ores and have already largely consumed them. They are now forced to mine poorer and poorer ores each year.

Moreover, the use of metal is still highly concentrated in a few advanced countries. Some 20 percent of the world population uses 80 percent of the world's metal output and is rapidly increasing its consumption. The coming industrialization of all undeveloped countries, whose population is soaring, will therefore produce a vast increase in the demand for all metals. By A.D. 2100 world demand at 1960 prices will be over one hundred times the 1960 supply.

World metal production probably will continue to increase for a century or two, but it cannot increase nearly as fast as potential demand at 1960 prices. The costs of production will rise steadily, and this will continuously limit the increases in output. The constant price rise will also bring about radical changes in metal use and in the mix of finished goods. Consumers will spend more and more of their rising real incomes on services and on tangible goods which will include less and less metal.

To prolong the life of domestic mineral deposits, most advanced countries will soon begin to lower their tariff duties and other limitations on mineral imports. For instance, the United States will abolish all limitations on petroleum and copper imports before 2000. Later some countries will begin to levy conservation severance taxes on all domestic mines and oil wells and will increasingly limit or prohibit non-essential uses of scarce minerals. The coming world government will make such taxes and limitations worldwide and uniform before 2300.

The manufacture of automobiles now absorbs a major share of the world output of several metals, and the coming rise in the world standard of living and population will increase the use of automobiles 1,000 percent by 2100 if no preventative measures are adopted. It is therefore certain that many measures to reduce the pounds of metal per car and to limit the growth of automobile manufacturing will be taken.

As explained in Chapter XI, all towns and cities will, before 2400, be planned and built or rebuilt so as to minimize automobile use. Private-car mileage per person within such planned cities will be reduced by 90 percent below the 1960 American level. Adults will normally walk to work and shops, and children to school. Those who do not wish to walk will use mass transport or bicycles. Private cars will be used only for pleasure trips outside residential areas and usually will be leased for short periods rather than owned.

Pleasure cars will become more compact and their engines smaller. Auto bodies and many other parts will be increasingly made of plastics. Most metal parts will eventually be designed to last for decades. More and more of the metal parts in junked cars will be renovated for re-use, and the rest will be remelted. Auto parts will be increasingly standardized and model changes drastically limited in order to facilitate re-use of old parts, as well as to reduce the costs of manufacturing and repairing automobiles. The average life of private cars will lengthen from ten years in 1960 to over twenty years in A.D. 2100 and over thirty years in 2200.

Similar design and repair principles will be applied to all machines and other goods with metal parts. More and more of their parts will be designed for repeated re-use in standardized products. And their metal surfaces will be increasingly treated so as to minimize wear and corrosion. Every machine will eventually be designed so that metal parts subjected to wear are small and can easily be replaced. Parts not subject to wear will be used in many machines before being remelted. Even scrap metal will be treated so as to minimize corrosion during storage.

The use of nickel, silver, copper, and gold in household wares will decline 90 percent before 2100. Knives and forks will be made of plastic, aluminum, or alloy steel, not silver. Copper, iron, and steel pans will be replaced by aluminum. Silver tea sets will be replaced by china. The use of lead in paint and gasoline will stop before 2100.

Tin cans will be almost entirely replaced by paper, plastic, and glass containers before 2100. Steel parts of buildings will be largely replaced by concrete and plastic. Tin and aluminum foil will give way to paper and plastic. Kitchen stoves and refrigerators will have plastic or aluminum bodies. The production of metal furniture, bed springs, lamps, etc. will stop. By 2200 metal will be used only for those few parts of essential goods which cannot be made from other materials at a reasonable cost.

Such conservation measures will prolong the life of scarce mineral deposits, but nearly all will be exhausted long before 2500. By then the greater part of the output of most metals will be obtained by processing sea water, ocean-bottom ore nodules, and ordinary rock, like granite, with nuclear power.

Mining

Competition in the drilling of wells or the digging of shafts to known mineral deposits is extraordinarily wasteful. Thousands of unneeded oil wells costing billions of dollars have already been drilled in America. Experts have protested increasingly against such waste, and more and more regulations to limit it have been adopted. These efforts will grow steadily until competitive extraction of minerals from a single oil field or ore bed has been prohibited in all non-socialist states. By A.D. 2050 almost every oil field and ore body in the world will be unitized, and new oil wells and mine shafts will be properly spaced by a single agency for each field or country.

Government regulation and supervision of private mines has been growing for over 100 years and will continue to grow for another century. In America the accident-compensation laws and safety regulations which now apply only to mines with more than so many employees will soon be extended to all mines. Social-security and minimum-wage laws will also be extended to cover all United States miners before 2050. Operators of open-cut mines will soon be required to landscape and beautify all land they have mined. All American mines will be required to reduce by 80 percent their pollution of rivers, streams, and underground water supplies before 2050. Similar trends will continue or develop in all other nations.

The proportion of the United States labor force engaged in mining rose steadily from 0.3 percent in 1840 to a peak of 3.0 percent in 1920 and then fell irregularly to 1.6 percent in 1960. The recent decline in employment in coal mining, mostly underground, has been far more rapid, from 500,000 in 1950 to about 200,000 in 1960. This decline has been caused by automation of coal mines and by growing substitution of oil and gas for coal. Similar trends have been evident in all advanced countries except the Soviet Union, where they will develop during the next few decades. They will also continue in Western Europe and America, due in part to an additional cause, the rise of nuclear power, which will become as important as coal power by 2050. On the other hand, the proportion of the labor force engaged in mining, especially coal mining, in Asia, Africa, and South America will increase steadily for a century because of their rapid industrialization.

In capitalist countries public support for nationalization of mining firms has always been relatively high, perhaps because irreplaceable mineral deposits are often regarded as national assets. As a result most mines in non-communist European states have already been nationalized, and most of the rest will be nationalized before 2000. Moreover, in all backward countries public support for nationalization of mines and oil fields, which are largely foreign-owned, is already strong and growing steadily. Hence nearly all remaining privately owned mines and oil fields in the world will soon be nationalized. The United States will be among the last to adopt such measures but will do so before 2100.

Local Public Utilities

Public utilities are industries treated by legislators and courts as invested with a public interest because they are natural monopolies which supply essential goods or services. Most local utilities—gas, water, electricity, etc.—use facilities installed in public streets. In America the majority are still privately owned, but their operations and rates are closely regulated, chiefly by state governments.

Nearly all local utilities have long been growth industries. The more advanced the country, the more of its national income is spent upon utility services. The most backward countries have barely begun to create local public utilities but are certain to expand them rapidly during the next century. And local utilities will long continue to grow faster than GNP in advanced countries, for several reasons. They are decreasing-cost industries, demand for their product is elastic, technological progress tends to increase such demand relatively fast, and urbanization will continue to raise the percentage of the population served by utilities.

The above predictions apply to established local public utilities—gas, water, light, telephone, urban transport. Several new local utilities will be created or vastly expanded in advanced countries during the next century. One of the most important will provide central heating and cooling of all buildings in an entire city or urban district. Central heating is more economical than decentralized heating in regions with cold winters and is therefore certain to become more and more common. The growing centralization of control over urban construction and property will favor its adoption. The planned cities of the future (discussed in Chapter XI) will all have central heating and/or central cooling. Hot and cold water, air, or steam will be produced in central plants and piped to all homes, as gas and water now are. Individual water heaters will be obsolete.

Another important new local utility, cable television, transmits TV programs to homes by wire, which both improves reception and makes individual TV aerials unnecessary. Cable TV has already been established in many communities, but as yet it serves less than 1 percent of the population in advanced states. By 2060 it will serve over 60 percent of this population. The cost per home will fall steadily as the percentage of homes served rises, but the gross income from such service in America will probably exceed two billion dollars by A.D. 2000. Eventually, of course, satellite rebroadcasting may obsolete cable TV.

Several industries which are now competitive will be transformed into closely regulated monopolistic utilities during the next 100 years. Among those most likely to be so treated are stock brokerage, real-estate brokerage, home delivery of milk, other local delivery services, legalized gambling, liquor stores, and used-car lots. Competition is unusually wasteful or socially harmful in these industries, and in capitalist states regulated monopoly will be a common transition stage between free competition and public monopoly.

During the past century a large number of local public utilities have been socialized, especially in Europe, and many more will be socialized, especially in the United States, during the next century. By 2100 nearly all local American public utilities will be publicly owned.

Local utilities which install pipes or wires under street paving will gradually be integrated into a single enterprise in one city after another in order to reduce excavation, maintenance, meter reading, billing, and management costs per customer. By 2100 nearly all new under-street facilities will be installed simultaneously, usually in a single ditch, and will be maintained by the same crews. All meters will be read by the same meter reader at the same time, and each customer will receive a single bill for all utility services.

In communist countries most local utility services are now free or almost free to domestic users. In capitalist countries local utility rates are nominally based on average costs or ability to pay and normally yield substantial marginal profits. These methods of price-output control will gradually be replaced by a combination of monthly service charges which cover all overhead costs and use rates which just cover marginal or direct costs. Since the latter costs vary from season to season, day to day, and even hour to hour, most utility use rates will also vary thus. A few utility services such as off-peak urban mass-passenger transport and off-peak local telephone service will be rendered without any use charge in order to save the cost of calculating and collecting charges equal to very small or negligible marginal costs. Users will pay the overhead costs of such free services in taxes or monthly service charges.

Communist states will soon restore both monthly service and use charges for domestic utility services or raise such charges high enough to cover nearly all utility costs. By 2100 public-utility rates will be similarly fixed in the United States and the Soviet Union.

Every reduction in utility use rates to or toward marginal costs will increase the use of utility services, and such rates are now far above marginal costs in America. This is another reason why public utilities will long continue to grow faster than other industries.

CHAPTER X

Commerce

In this chapter I shall predict some major trends in transportation and trade. These fields are closely related, because men transport goods from one place to another chiefly in order to sell them at a higher price. As economists have often noted, every reduction in transport costs enlarges the market for all affected producers.

Transportation

The chief social trends in transportation during the next 500 years will be: a continued decline in real transport costs per ton-mile; gradual integration of each and all means of transport into larger and more monopolistic systems; growing standardization of transport equipment; increasing containerization of freight; a further rise in the proportion of intercity freight moved by trucks; and the gradual revision of transport rates to make them measure marginal costs.

For centuries the most significant transportation trend has been a worldwide decline in real transport costs per ton-mile. For instance, between 1880 and 1960, United States railroad freight rates rose only 20 percent while wholesale prices rose some 150 percent, which means that real freight costs fell about 50 percent. This steady decline in real transport costs will continue for centuries in all countries.

Technological progress—the invention of the steamboat, the railroad, the automobile, etc.—has been a major cause of this cost trend, and such progress will continue indefinitely. Transportation is an industry in which technological advance has been and will continue to be more rapid than in most other industries, because transport is more easily mechanized than most other industries.

Furthermore, transportation is an industry in which unit (ton-mile) costs decline substantially and indefinitely as output grows. A 10 percent increase in the cost of a freight car, truck, ship, or plane can increase its capacity by much more than 10 percent. A double-track railroad costs far less per track mile to build and maintain than a single-track road and can handle far more traffic per mile of track. And nearly all other individual costs, by any means of transport, decline as the volume of freight rises. This volume will continue rising steadily because of the further growth of population and real income per person. By 2100 world freight ton-mileage will be twenty to forty times its 1960 volume. This growth would sharply reduce real transport costs, even without any technological progress in transportation.

By continuing indefinitely to broaden the market for all producers, this long future decline in transport costs will help to bring about an indefinite increase in the scale of production in nearly all other industries, an ever-growing specialization in production among plants and regions, a gradual relocation of most plants and communities, a radical enlargement of units of government, an indefinite continuation of cultural homogenization, a steady increase in the relative volume of foreign trade, and other social trends. These effects are discussed elsewhere in this book. They are noted here only to suggest the great importance of the predicted indefinite decline in real transport costs.

Perhaps the second most significant trend in transportation during the next century or two will be the continuing consolidation of independent transport firms into larger units, including the integration of different means of transport. This trend has been obvious for over a century. It has already resulted in the complete integration of all railroads in some capitalist countries and the beginning of integration of railroads with road and water lines in others, but it still has far to go, especially in America.

The number of operating railroads in the United States

reached a peak of 1,564 in 1907 and has been declining ever since, in spite of almost continuous government opposition to railroad integration. By 1960 the number had fallen to 410. This total will continue to decline steadily. It should fall below 100 by A.D. 2000 and to one by 2050.

A similar trend will prevail in all other American intercity transport industries. The number of Class I firms engaged in intercity highway freight transport reached a peak of 2,244 in 1955 but had fallen to 1,004 in 1963. By the year 2000 the total will be less than 400. Sometime late in the twenty-first century all remaining highway freight carriers will be merged into a single national highway trucking monopoly. The same thing will happen to American intercity bus companies, water transport firms, and pipelines.

The integration of all air-transport firms into national, and later international, monopolies is inevitable in the near future because air space is limited and already congested during peak hours in key areas. Monopolies will sharply reduce seat vacancy rates and will operate much larger planes, whose use will reduce congestion. The larger the plane, the lower the cost per passenger seat, and there is no known limit to plane size. By 2050 the coming United States air-transport monopoly will operate many planes seating over 1,000 passengers. By ending competitive scheduling and flying far larger planes, it will be able to carry twenty to fifty times as many passengers with little if any increase in air congestion over major cities.

After, and to some extent together with, the integration of each transport industry—rail, water, highway—these industries will gradually be integrated with each other. Railroads will initiate or expand subsidiary highway-transport operations and will purchase more and more highway-transport firms. They will also expand steadily their control over inland, coastal, and foreign water transport. By A.D. 2000 they will control 20 to 40 percent of both highway and water transport. Thereafter they will steadily expand such control, until by 2200 all American rail, highway, and water transport will be operated by a single nationalized monopoly.

Similar integration trends will prevail in all non-communist states during the next century or two. Germany, France, and Great Britain already have integrated rail systems. By 2000 they will have completely integrated their highway and rail transport systems. By 2100 all of Europe will have a completely integrated rail, highway, air, and water transport system which will be operated by a single European transport trust.

Such integration of transport firms is inevitable, because it will sharply cut transport costs, improve service, and greatly reduce the need for new investment in transport facilities. Transportation economists have become increasingly aware of such advantages for many years. Most of them now favor more integration. The chief opposition to further integration comes from transport workers and executives who fear loss of their jobs, from equipment suppliers who fear loss of sales, and from conservative ideologists who fear monopoly and big government.

The creation of a stable world government will of course greatly facilitate the integration of national transport trusts with one another. By 2200 all land transport facilities on each continent will be operated by a single continental transport agency. By 2300 all transport facilities in the entire world will be operated by a world transport trust.

The first means of transport to be organized on a world basis will be air transport, by 2100. The coming world government will demand complete integration and control of air transport in order to strengthen its military and political control.

The second form of transport to be integrated will be ocean transport. A ship can sail to any seaport, and only a single world agency can schedule all ships most efficiently.

The growing integration of transport systems will result in more and more standardization of transport equipment. By 2050 all United States railroads will use the same kinds of locomotives and freight cars for similar tasks. By 2250 all railroads in the world will do so. The same thing will happen in every other transport industry. Moreover, inter-industry standardization of jointly used equipment will increase as these industries are coordinated or merged. For instance, transferable freight containers used on two or more kinds of freight carriers will be increasingly standardized until the same sizes are used, first by all rail, water, and highway carriers in a country and eventually by all such carriers throughout the world. This will permit and be followed by standardization of all equipment used to load or unload such containers.

The shipment of freight in large re-usable package or bulk containers has been growing for decades because it sharply cuts breakage and theft losses en route and speeds up and cheapens loading, unloading, and transshipping. The coming standardization of containers and container carriers and loaders will further reduce the costs of using containers. Hence containerization will grow rapidly, especially for freight transported by ships and planes, which have the highest turn-around costs. By 2060 nearly all air freight, non-bulk ship cargo, and less-than-carload-lot rail and highway freight in the United States will move in standard containers.

The gradual integration of all transport industries into monopolies will also result in the construction of joint union terminals for all railroad, highway, and helicopter lines in each city. Most large and many small American cities still have two or more terminals for rail or highway lines, or for both. By 2100 all American cities will have union freight and/or passenger terminals used by both rail and truck lines.

Since 1900 the share of United States intercity freight carried by trucks has risen from none to 24 percent, and the gross revenue from such transport almost equaled that of all United States railroads in 1960. The freight moved by trucks is more valuable, moves shorter distances, and pays much higher rates. The chief advantages of highway transport are that it moves freight from door to door without transshipment, makes short runs much faster, and uses roads maintained largely by taxes on other users.

Highway transport will continue for some years to expand its share of United States intercity freight ton-mileage and revenues, but no long-run prediction is now feasible. Consolidation, standardization, and radical pricing reforms may enable railroads to stop or reverse this trend. In less advanced countries, however, highway transport will expand during the next few decades as it has in America during the last few decades. Thus highway transport should increase its share of world freight movement for at least 50 to 100 years.

During the past 50 years there has been a rapid shift of urban passenger transport from older mass-transport facilities to private automobiles. This shift is now 80 percent complete in large American cities, but will continue, at a much slower rate, for a few decades more. In Europe the shift is in full swing and will go on at a rapid rate for several decades. It has barely begun in Japan and Latin America but will continue to accelerate there. The Soviets now plan to minimize this shift but may change their plans later.

In any case the coming planned reconstruction of all old cities and the construction of new planned cities will eventually return nearly all urban passenger transport to public means of mass transportation. This prediction will be elaborated in Chapter XI.

The application of radical marginal-cost pricing (predicted in Chapter VI) to transport rates will drastically alter rate structures in all countries. It will sharply lower high freight rates, which apply chiefly to the more valuable goods and are usually five to ten times as high as marginal costs. It will lower railroad rates much more than highway rates because the latter are now much closer to marginal costs. It will greatly reduce empty-car mileage by sharply cutting rates for freight carried against the prevailing traffic. It will induce many more shippers to use the most economical method and route of transport when a choice is open. At present, United States freight rates for alternative means of transport or routes are often made equal in order to limit price competition.

Since transport industries are decreasing-cost industries, every increase in their scale of operations eventually reduces marginal costs. Hence the application of marginal-cost pricing to their rates will result in large and ever-rising deficits. Deficits so caused will be evidence of sound pricing, not of poor management, but they will require large, continuous, and growing government subsidies to the national transport trust. By the year 2300 such subsidies will cover 25 to 50 percent of world-freight and passenger-transport costs.

Foreign Trade and Exchange Rates

For over 400 years the great majority of businessmen and politicians in advanced states have believed that exports are more beneficial than imports. Thus a surplus of exports over imports is still called a "favorable" balance of trade.

This old mercantilistic fallacy—long rejected by orthodox economists—remains dominant in capitalist states because their businessmen find it easier to buy than to sell and because their workers know it is much harder to find a job than to give it up. As these two conditions change, businessmen and workers will increasingly realize that imports are as beneficial as exports. And I have already predicted the gradual disappearance of both conditions. The adoption of full-employment managerial, price, and wage policies will, by 2100, make it as easy to sell as to buy and as easy to get a job as to quit it, in capitalist as well as in communist countries.

The eventual establishment of a world state and the resulting disarmament will eliminate nearly all military reasons for protective tariffs. And the rapid industrialization of backward countries will eventually make the infant-industry argument for import limitation obsolete. For such reasons tariffs, quotas, and other limitations on foreign trade are certain to decline in both number and severity in non-communist states throughout most of the next 300 years. But the decline may not start for a few more decades.

Communist states have already solved the problem of expanding their internal markets and are eager to achieve "unfavorable" balances of trade by borrowing from abroad. But they still limit imports drastically and often uneconomically in order to create new industries, protect industries of military value, and simplify economic planning. These reasons will become less and less influential, and Communist imports and exports will expand greatly during the next few decades.

The many current restrictions on free trade in farm products will be relaxed more rapidly than those affecting manufactured goods because, as predicted in an earlier chapter, the proportion of the population engaged in agriculture will decline steadily for many years in all countries. Moreover, reapportionment will also reduce the political influence of rural voters in capitalist countries. And continuing difficulties in agriculture, the hardest industry to socialize, will prompt most communist states to import more and more cheap farm products for several decades.

The total value of world foreign trade has grown faster than world production of tangible goods for several hundred years. It will continue to do so throughout the next 500 years for a variety of reasons. The real costs of international freight transport will decline indefinitely, and this will broaden the market for all low-cost producers. Ever-growing specialization, integration, and automation will steadily increase the advantages of large low-cost producers. The coming gradual reduction of political barriers to foreign trade will greatly enlarge such trade. The establishment of a world government, world court, world money, world banking system, and world language will facilitate foreign trade and reduce its credit risks. The growing international standardization of education, culture, and consumption habits will raise the relative demand for imported goods. By A.D. 2500 the entire world output of each of many small manufactured goods will be produced in a single country or factory.

It may be objected that United States imports and exports rose less rapidly than national income throughout most of the nineteenth century and the first third of the twentieth. This unusual trend was due to the conquest and exploitation of the American interior by colonists who once lived on the Atlantic coast. Now that the continent is fully settled and industrialized, United States foreign trade will long increase faster than national income.

Foreign pleasure travel has also been growing faster than

world income for centuries, and it will continue to do so for another 500 years. The chief causes will be rising personal incomes, declining transport costs, and lengthening vacations. At present the richer the country, the higher the share of national income spent on travel. By 2500 the average world citizen will travel overseas for pleasure several times during his life. Currently less than one percent ever do so.

Imports, exports, and foreign travel depend upon foreign-exchange rates. During the nineteenth century nearly all economists and statesmen in advanced countries advocated fixed exchange rates, and most exchange rates were fixed for long periods. Since 1914 two world wars and the great depression have resulted in many fluctuating foreign-exchange rates. Moreover, more and more economists have come to realize that fluctuating exchange rates are less undesirable than the alternative, fluctuating domestic price levels, and/or that exchange-rate fluctuations are themselves desirable because, like fluctuations in the price of any single good, they help to balance supply and demand without government interference. I predict that expert support of flexible exchange rates will continue to grow and become more influential until all advanced countries abandon fixed exchange rates, probably before 2060. The new flexible rates will not fluctuate every hour or day but will do so often enough to prevent any balance of payments large enough to significantly affect domestic price and wage levels. Such flexible rates will greatly weaken pleas for tariffs and quotas as means of changing the balance of foreign trade or payments.

Marketing

In advanced capitalist states marketing practices have been revolutionized during the past century by the adoption of fixed prices, chain operation, new packaging methods, large-scale advertising, serve-yourself systems, supermarkets, shopping centers, etc. In less advanced states the major marketing trends during the next century will be the gradual introduction of these and other new methods already common or dominant in advanced states. In advanced states most old trends will continue for many decades, but less rapidly than in backward states because they have already gone so far. And some important predictable new trends will appear.

One of the major continuing retail trends in advanced capitalist states during the next century will be the further expansion of chain-store systems. In 1900 they handled less than 1 percent of United States retail sales, in 1930 about 24 percent, in 1960 about 34 percent. This share will continue to rise throughout the next century or two. It will reach 50 percent by 2000 and 80 percent by 2100. The trend will be similar in all advanced capitalist states.

Chain-store retailing will continue to grow because it is more efficient than one-store retailing. By integrating wholesaling with retailing, chains reduce both wholesale and retail inventories per dollar of retail sales and sharply reduce wholesale selling and delivery costs. The recent invention of computers, which can be used by central chain-store offices to control store inventories and co-ordinate retail and wholesale inventories, will make integration of retail and wholesale services even more advantageous.

Chain stores are better-managed than small independent stores because chain-store managers are trained and constantly supervised by more able superiors and are advised by experts on each phase of store operation. As a result of these and other advantages chain stores charge slightly lower prices, pay higher wages, and earn higher profits. Their growth has led to much discriminatory legislation and taxation, which will continue to slow their growth in many areas but will never stop it permanently. By the year 2050 nearly all anti-chain-store laws in advanced states will have been repealed.

In America small independent merchants have found that the best way to meet chain-store competition is to organize voluntary or co-operative chains which permit them to achieve many of the economies of chain-store operation. However, voluntary chains produce social effects—centralization of control, standardization of goods and methods, vertical integration, etc.—similar to those produced by the rise of chain stores. The rise of voluntary chains is part of the chain-store trend. But in the long run such chains will become or be replaced by integrated chain-store systems.

Another well-established marketing trend is the steady growth in the size of retail stores. Between 1930 and 1960 the number of workers (including owners) in the average American store rose from 4 to 6, and the volume of sales per store increased even more rapidly. By 2000 this number will rise above 12, by 2100 above 60, and by 2300 above 100, in spite of growing automation and city planning.

In 1960 most retail stores in every advanced capitalist state still were small family stores, most of which had no paid employees. The number of such stores has already begun to decline or will soon begin to decline in all advanced states and will decline continuously throughout the next century or two. By 2200 few if any will remain in any advanced country.

Competition between retail stores is wasteful because it results in small inefficient stores, duplication of facilities, excessive advertising, etc. The further growth of chain stores, large department stores, supermarkets, etc., will continue to reduce these wastes, but other measures will be adopted to limit and eventually end retail competition. Licensing of new private stores will be increasingly used for this purpose. And more and more large new shopping centers, housing developments, and model towns will be planned and managed so as to limit or prevent competition between nearby stores selling similar goods. By 2300 nearly all people in advanced states will live in planned model communities which have only one store in each shopping center and only one center in each neighborhood.

In the meantime wastes due to retail competition will also be gradually reduced by a continuous extension of government control over excessive advertising, false or misleading claims, fictitious sales, prices below cost, etc. Capitalist governments have made growing efforts to limit such wastes and will continue to do so as long as retail competition survives. Before the year 2000 most advanced capitalist states will begin to limit advertising to some maximum percentage of retail sales, perhaps 5 percent, and this limit will gradually be reduced to or below 1 percent by 2100. Moreover, these states will supervise advertising claims more and more carefully.

The use of brand names, which facilitates advertising and aggressive marketing, has been growing steadily in advanced capitalist states for a century or two and may continue to grow for several decades more, but this trend will be reversed during the twenty-first century, and the use of brand names will decline throughout most of the following 500 years. Brand names will become less and less useful to consumers as minimum manufacturing standards are raised and standardized. Moreover, their elimination will reduce marketing costs. Finally the rise of monopoly will make brand names less and less useful to producers.

The first industry in which the use of brand names will be radically limited or ended is that producing ethical, or prescription, drugs. Many experts have already recommended this reform, which will be adopted in some countries before the year 2000. It will greatly reduce the costs of marketing such drugs and will help doctors to select the most effective drugs.

The use of special advertised sales events to boost sales will be increasingly supervised and restricted—by curtailing the use of loss leaders, requiring more honest advertising and labeling, etc. Before 2100 most capitalist countries will prohibit sales unjustified by sound economic reason, which now make up 90 percent of all special sales.

As more and more wives work for wages, as advertising becomes more honest and informative, as consumer goods become better graded and more standardized, as retail competition diminishes, more and more consumers will order goods by mail or phone for home delivery from retail stores or warehouses. This trend will soon begin. By 2200 nearly all homes in advanced states will contain retail-order machines and catalogues which enable consumers to obtain within a few hours any standardized or graded tangible consumer good by merely punching a catalogue number on a home order-taker. And over 80 percent of all retail purchases of convenience goods—groceries, drugs, housewares—will be made at home by mail or wire. This reform will save the average housewife about an hour a day and will allow many more to work outside their homes.

In the meantime more and more cities will adopt an arithmetic or alphabetic system of street names and a uniform system of house numbers (probably 100 numbers per block in old cities) in order to reduce retail and mail delivery costs, taxi costs, and other time losses in finding individual addresses. By 2100 nearly all cities in the world will have such street name and number systems.

In order to induce more customers to shop during hours when sales are now slow (off-peak hours), retail stores will soon begin to vary their prices in regular cycles from hour to hour during the day and from day to day during the week. To avoid changing price tags, they will grant discounts on purchases during off-peak hours. Such discounts will be universally used in capitalist, socialist, and communist states by 2200. They will greatly reduce the investment in retail-store buildings and inventories required to handle any given sales volume and will therefore sharply reduce average retail markups.

Since suitable retail discounts will attract many more customers during off-peak hours, retail stores will further lengthen their hours of operation after they have begun to vary their prices from hour to hour. Other factors—more multi-shift factory operation, more women workers, etc.—will also tend to increase the average hours of store operation. By the year 2100 nearly all retail stores in advanced countries will be open over 100 hours a week, which will require at least three-shift operation.

In communist countries retail prices are often so low that demand greatly exceeds supply, and buyers must waste many hours waiting in queues to buy underpriced goods when they are available. The pseudo-Marxist dogmas responsible for such common underpricing will soon be abandoned in all communist states. The new price policy, fixing prices so as to balance supply and demand, will save shoppers hundreds of millions of hours a year, which will enable more women to take jobs outside their homes.

CHAPTER XI

Houses and Cities

The houses and cities in which men spend most of their lives will change and improve continually during the next five centuries. By 2500 almost every family in the world will have a spacious and attractive mechanized home in a beautiful garden city. The achievement of this goal will require centuries, but many specific long-run trends leading to it are already obvious.

Building

One of the major future trends in housing construction is ever-increasing prefabrication of housing. This trend has long been apparent in advanced countries, though less than 10 percent complete there, and will continue until over 90 percent of new housing is almost completely prefabricated in all countries.

Prefabrication of housing is production of housing components and houses in factories, not on the site. Of course, excavation and foundation laying must be done on the site. The prefabrication trend begins with small parts—windows, frames, cabinets, etc.—proceeds to wall and floor panels, then to complete small dwellings, such as mobile homes, and finally to large, single-family houses and units of apartment buildings.

The Soviets have already begun to assemble large apartment buildings consisting of prefabricated units. About 10 percent of all new United States homes are prefabricated mobiles. Complete prefabrication of most new housing will be achieved in advanced countries by 2100 and in other countries by 2200.

The further growth of prefabrication will help to bring about major changes in the use of building materials. In the immediate future there will be large-scale substitution of metallic walls and floors for non-metallic ones. Later the rising relative cost of metals and wood and the falling costs of plastics will result in a long-continuing gradual substitution of plastic and cement components for those made of metal or wood.

Another major future trend in housing construction is a steady increase in the average size of firms building houses. This trend has long been evident in advanced states, but it has much farther to go. It is significant because it not only reduces housing costs but permits more effective planning of entire subdivisions and communities.

Between 1950 and 1960, United States firms building 100 or more dwelling units a year raised their share of total residential construction from 32 to 74 percent. By the year 2000 over 50 percent of such units will be built by firms which build over 200 units a year. Before 2200 all new housing in each American city will be built by a single firm.

The cost of architectural plans is still a significant building cost—about 5 percent in the United States—because most plans are used only once in capitalist countries. To reduce this cost and to ensure that more buildings are well planned, both private and public agencies will steadily increase the average use of good plans. For instance, United States state and federal governments will increasingly assemble, preserve, classify, and provide copies of all architectural plans for non-prefabricated public buildings and private buildings subsidized with public funds. By 2100 the average architectural plan for a non-prefabricated structure will be used over ten times, which will reduce the cost of such plans per planned structure by over 90 percent. Of course, prefabrication itself will sharply reduce architectural costs.

In America nearly all building is subject to local codes which are supposed to assure safe construction but in fact serve chiefly to protect the vested interests of certain skilled workers, local contractors, and manufacturers of traditional building materials. Over 25,000 different local codes exist. They probably raise building costs at least 10 percent.

During the next century the number of different local building codes in the United States will decline steadily. More and more counties and states will prescribe codes uniform throughout their area. By 2100 all local and regional building codes in the United States will be replaced by a uniform national code. The preparation and revision of building codes will be increasingly entrusted to semi-independent commissions of experts relatively free from political pressure. Finally the last building code in the world will be abolished before 2300. By then all building prefabrication and assembly will be done by state trusts whose executives will need no externally formulated building rules to ensure good work.

City Planning

Nearly all cities have grown from small villages or medieval walled towns with little effective planning. The introduction of automobiles, moreover, has made even the best-planned cities designed for an earlier era entirely obsolete. Fortunately the growth of social science, the rise of large-scale construction, and the increasing centralization and professionalization of politico-economic management will result in more and more planned reconstruction of old cities and construction of new planned cities.

For over 100 years the population of old cities in advanced states has been spreading out into ever-expanding suburbs, due to growing use of railroads, buses, and private cars. This process has gone further in new American cities like Los Angeles (where 8 million people spread over 1,600 square miles) than anywhere else. These cities illustrate what will tend to happen in all advanced countries during the next 100 years.

Los Angeles now has 300 miles of freeways and will have 1,000 by 1980. Such growth of intracity freeways will be a major urban trend in all advanced countries during the next century. By A.D. 2000 London and Paris will be more completely crisscrossed by freeways than Los Angeles was in 1960. But during the twenty-first century this rapid growth of suburbs and intracity freeways will be radically slowed or reversed by more effective city planning.

In capitalist states there are three different types of city planning: municipal regulation of private construction—zoning, spacing, height control, etc.; voluntary planning by builders of ever-larger subdivisions and small towns; and construction of entire suburbs, towns, and cities planned by public agencies and built on publicly owned land. While all three types of city planning may occur in the same country at the same time, they also tend to be major stages in the evolution of city planning. The chief prediction of this section is that all capitalist states will go through all three stages and will eventually reach stage three.

Among the major new zoning, building, and subdivision rules which will be adopted during the next 100 years in most advanced capitalist states will be rules which require ever-wider setbacks from streets and other property lines, that is, more space between buildings in congested areas; aid or require consolidation of more and more small building sites into larger ones; require the provision of more and more off-street parking space; require the provision of more public-utility facilities (sewers, water mains, etc.), school sites, and park areas by large subdividers; limit increasingly the construction of apartment buildings on main through streets; and limit or prohibit the construction of additional buildings in congested districts.

While the further expansion and refinement of such government control over private builders will steadily improve city planning for another century or two, it will not produce well-planned cities. Comprehensive and sound city planning is possible only when planners fully control all urban construction in a city—the location of places of employment as well as of housing, schools, roads, parks, etc. This is one reason why capitalist governments will steadily expand their control over and ownership of business firms during the next 200 years.

The construction of planned new towns began in England around 1900, when the government built a series of garden cities around London. France, Italy, Sweden, and some other European countries have begun similar projects since 1945. But it is in the United States that the largest number of planned new cities, about fifty, are now under construction. They are being designed to accommodate more than 3.5 million people by 1980 on land now valued at over $1.5 billion. Unlike the European garden cities, they are all being built by large private corporations, including some industrial giants—Humble, Kaiser, Goodyear—who have joined with big land developers.

Such builders hope to provide better housing at lower cost by large-scale construction and to increase their profits by realizing more of the large increase in land values which always follows concentration of population. When a small builder erects a few houses or a small subdivision, nearly all of this increase in land values accrues to owners of adjacent land. When a large builder constructs an entire city, he can provide and retain all commercial and industrial sites and secure the unearned increment in their value due to population growth. He can also create local business monopolies, such as gas stations and grocery stores, and share in their profits.

In the near future the United States federal government will begin to subsidize and regulate the private construction of planned cities, and such subsidies and construction will grow steadily for 50 to 100 years. Before 2100 the United States will create a federal agency authorized to build and own such cities, and thereafter this agency will steadily increase its share of city building, until, long before 2500, it will build and own all new American cities. And the growth of government activity in this field will be much more rapid in Europe. By 2500 over 80 percent of the world's population will be housed in new planned cities or in completely rebuilt and replanned old cities.

Public enterprise will gradually replace private enterprise in building planned cities because city planning and building should be a monopoly in each area, because it will often require condemnation of private property, and because private builders cannot control the location of industrial plants. Only a collectivist state can plan and co-ordinate all economic, educational, recreational, political, and other activities in a new planned city.

Nearly all of the new state-owned and state-planned cities of A.D. 2100 to 2500 will have much fewer than 600,000 inhabitants. Most of them will be divided by wide green belts into a nucleus containing only facilities used by citizens of all satellite towns (university, central library, opera house, stadium, specialized hospitals, etc.) and the housing and service facilities needed by their staffs; and into otherwise self-sufficient satellite communities of 20,000 to 60,000 people. Each satellite will contain one or more export firms (those which export to other cities) providing jobs for nearly all local residents not employed in community stores, schools, and other local service agencies. Freeways will be confined to the green belts around communities, and the intra-community use of private cars will be almost completely prohibited.

By 2300 every new city in the world will be planned and built as a single construction project designed to house a certain population. After it has been built and occupied, no growth of population will be permitted. Rather, its population will decline slowly for several decades as the standard of living rises. During these years all residential rebuilding will be designed to house fewer people more spaciously and luxuriously. All net population growth will be housed in new cities. To enlarge a well-planned old city to house people better is as uneconomic as to enlarge an old automobile to carry more people more luxuriously.

In these planned cities of the future nearly all workers will live within two miles of their place of work, and most will live less than a mile away (a fifteen-minute walk). Since schools will be much less centralized than work places, all children will live less than a mile, and most less than half a mile, from their schools. Hence most workers and students will walk or cycle to and from work or school in good weather. Those who do not walk will ride in quiet, slow-moving buses, not in private cars. The latter will be used by able-bodied persons for intercity travel only. These transport customs will radically reduce smog and noise, cut street accidents by 50 to 90 percent, conserve scarce metals and fuels, and improve the health of nearly all citizens by requiring more physical exercise.

When entire cities are built as single projects on publicly owned farm land and all business firms are monopolies, no tenant will pay a pure land rent much higher than that obtainable from agricultural use. The average share of land rent in urban property rents will therefore be 50 to 90 percent less than it now is in capitalist cities. Each new city will be planned so as to prevent the creation of additional net land rent, for such rent would be proof of a planning error, that is, uneconomic restriction of some urban land use.

All inhabitants of planned cities will be tenants by 2200. But they will have relatively secure tenure of their dwellings as long as they can pay rent. Rents will be adjusted so as to balance the supply of and demand for each class of dwelling in each neighborhood.

In communist states—where all urban land is public property, monopoly is universal, and all construction is done by state trusts—the planned reconstruction of old cities and the construction of new planned cities is far more politically feasible than in capitalist countries. Hence comprehensive city planning will develop much faster in communist than in capitalist states during the next century. Communist countries will be building complete planned cities before 2000. They are already building many planned residential districts. They have not yet, however, adopted the policy of providing work places in each new planned district for most of its residents, and it may be several more decades before they do.

Most Soviet city dwellers now spend less than 5 percent of their wage income on rent and utilities, even when they live in new apartments. The chief reason for such uneconomically low rents is that the Soviets still interpret Marxism as implying that land rent and interest are the result of economic exploitation and should not affect house rents or plans for housing construction. This interpretation is already being questioned, and it will soon be rejected. Urban housing rents will be gradually raised, over 100 percent before A.D. 2000, until they balance the supply of and demand for each type of housing. Thereafter new housing construction will be increasingly regulated so that each new investment in housing earns rents high enough to cover both interest and land rent. As explained in Chapter V, many goods which are now sold for a price will eventually become free goods; but housing is not one of them.

The coming planned reconstruction and radical decentralization of large old cities will be much more difficult than the construction of new planned cities. The goal will be the same, but it will usually take over 50 years to achieve it after sound plans have been made. Such planning will involve many hard problems as to which old buildings, bridges, subways, etc., should be preserved and which should be wrecked.

During the next 50 to 100 years many small neighborhoods in old capitalist cities will be reconstructed so as to provide more space between buildings, but little planned city-wide reconstruction and decentralization of such cities is likely. Radical reconstruction cannot even be planned soundly until most urban real estate is publicly owned and all business firms are state monopolies.

By 2200 most plans for the reconstruction of large old cities will provide for a continuous reduction in population to a level well below one million; a division of the old city into a central nucleus surrounded by a green belt and largely self-sufficient satellite communities separated by wide green belts alongside preexisting or new freeways; the provision within every satellite of employment, schools, and shopping centers for nearly all its people; radical curtailment of the off-freeway use of private cars; and a tenfold or greater increase in the area of public parks and gardens, to be achieved largely by tearing down old buildings.

All large old capitalist cities will gradually be crisscrossed with six- and eight-lane divided garden freeways during the next 50 years. These freeways will divide giant metropolitan areas into a score or more slightly isolated communities. When planned decentralization begins, it will gradually widen the park borders of most of these freeways until they become green belts 500 to 5,000 feet wide. It will also gradually provide for sufficient schools, shops, and employment within each freeway-enclosed community to serve nearly all the inhabitants of that area. During the reconstruction period private auto traffic on off-freeway streets will be steadily restricted. And one community in each old city, or large borough of it, will be rebuilt as a nucleus to serve surrounding satellite communities.

The planned reconstruction and radical decentralization of

New York City will be especially difficult, and the resulting changes will be especially great. When this process has been completed (before 2200), almost everyone employed on the island of Manhattan will live there, within two miles of his work. Manhattan itself will be divided by wide green belts into several largely self-sufficient communities and a nucleus, each of which will provide employment and shops for nearly all its residents. The great tunnels and bridges under and over the Hudson and East rivers will then be used chiefly by tourists and trucks. If some subways are preserved, they will carry less than 10 percent of their present passenger traffic. Most of them will probably be turned into underground freeways used chiefly by trucks. Eighty percent of the land area of Manhattan will be used for parks and gardens, largely public.

By the year 2500 all buildings in advanced countries will be as attractive and well located as the most costly palaces and mansions now are. Every structure will be a work of art set apart in a beautiful garden as part of a planned ensemble. Most buildings will be painted in attractive, harmonizing colors. Many will have outside walls decorated with paintings, mosaics, and enamel panels. Smog and smoke will no longer obscure or soil them. And no noisy vehicles, planes, or other machines will be tolerated in any city.

As city planning develops, architects will increasingly beautify cities by the proper spacing and arrangement of nearby structures rather than by ornamenting individual buildings. The greatest architects of the future will be those who can plan the most beautiful urban views or perspectives for the most people, not those who can create the most beautiful buildings.

Air Purification

Urban air pollution has been increasing ever since the industrial revolution began and has become a serious menace to health and the enjoyment of city life. As real income per person continues to rise and public education expands, men are certain to attack air pollution with increasingly diverse and effective measures. Some of these measures are now predictable.

In cities like London the burning of soft coal will be increasingly restricted. Industry will be required to install more and more effective smoke-reduction devices in boilers and chimneys. The burning of coal and wood in domestic fireplaces will be gradually curtailed and eventually prohibited. Community central heating will replace more and more private furnaces in urban areas. Those industrial plants which produce the most soot and smoke will be relocated near the mines or on windy seacoasts. Oil, gas, and nuclear fuels will be substituted for coal in the power and heating plants which remain. All these methods of air purification will be generally adopted in advanced countries by A.D. 2100.

In cities more and more restrictions on the use of fume-emitting automobiles will be adopted. Since the use of such vehicles is now growing rapidly in all countries, air pollution due to the fumes will increase steadily and provoke ever more drastic control measures.

One of the first and least drastic measures will be the compulsory use of auto accessories which reduce the emission of smog-causing fumes. California has already passed such a law. The next step will be to require auto manufacturers to design cars which produce less and less fumes.

A more drastic step will be prohibition of the use of large private cars by urban residents. A Volkswagen produces far less fumes than a standard Ford or Chevrolet and is almost equally serviceable for private urban use. In a city like Los Angeles the complete substitution of small for large private cars would reduce air pollution by over 30 percent. It would also sharply reduce all other costs of private-car use. Such substitution will be enforced in most large cities in advanced countries before 2060.

Mass transportation produces far less smog than transportation of an equal number of people in private cars, even small ones. This is one reason why mass passenger transport is sure to be subsidized more and more heavily and eventually made free of charge in all cities suffering from air pollution. These policies will also greatly reduce the number of automobile accidents and the need for costly new freeways, wider city streets, and traffic-control facilities and personnel. Free mass passenger transport will be common by 2050 and almost universal in large cities by 2150.

To discourage the use of private internal-combustion cars, especially large ones, in cities with polluted air, and to cover part of the cost of free urban passenger transport, more and more cities will impose extra gasoline sales taxes. This policy will be introduced first and carried further in the United States, where gasoline is relatively cheap and air pollution relatively advanced, and eventually it will spread over the entire world. By 2060 this additional gas tax will exceed ten cents a gallon in most large American cities. It will supplement, rather than replace, other new gas taxes, such as those imposed to conserve petroleum resources and to finance auto insurance. As a result of all these new taxes, the relative cost of gasoline in United States cities will rise over 200 percent before the year 2050.

More and more buses used in urban areas will be electrified to reduce fumes. Commuter trains also will be increasingly electrified. After 2000 the use of internal-combustion motors in trucks and private cars will decline steadily. By 2100 it will be prohibited in most advanced countries.

The coming integration of all delivery services in each city (predicted in the previous chapter) will substantially diminish urban smog. It will cut the daily mileage of delivery trucks by over 50 percent. Moreover, the construction of new planned cities predicted in the previous section will eventually reduce all urban automobile use even more sharply.

As a result of such trends the air over most large cities in advanced countries should begin to improve before the year 2000 and should improve steadily for centuries thereafter. In the meantime air pollution will continue to increase in nearly all large cities in the world.

CHAPTER XII

Communication

Our primate ancestors became human only when they began to talk to one another. The mastery of spoken language was the first and greatest achievement of man. And the relatively recent invention of printing was one of his greatest achievements. Other, newer means of communication—telephone, motion picture, the radio, television—are also extraordinarily significant simply because they greatly facilitate communication.

All these means of communication will be steadily and indefinitely improved. Some of these trends, the least technical, will be discussed in this chapter; the most radical and significant will be in the use of language.

Language

During the next 100 to 200 years the share of the world population which speaks each major language—English, Spanish, Russian, Mandarin, etc.—will continue to grow steadily. In the United States, the Soviet Union, Latin America, and China the dominant language will gradually displace minority languages. In other countries the teaching and use of English, Russian, or Mandarin as a secondary language will become more and more common.

The invention and ever-growing use of printing, the telephone, the railroad, the automobile, the talking motion picture, radio, and television have exposed language minorities to more and more contacts with dominant adjacent languages. These contacts will continue to increase and to reduce the use of all minority languages. It is not economically practical to produce many good plays, movies, newspapers, books, and television programs in languages like Gaelic, Breton, and Basque. Hence such languages are certain to die. Moreover, many more widely used minority languages—such as French in Canada and Latvian in Russia—will also disappear, more slowly. North Americans who speak only French already suffer serious economic handicaps, and these will increase steadily. Furthermore, the migration of French Canadians to English-speaking areas, and Latvians to Russian-speaking areas, will continue for centuries.

The indefinite future growth of higher professional education and scientific research will favor the use of major languages. For reasons noted elsewhere, the proportion of professional men in every national labor force will continue to increase indefinitely, and such men will specialize ever more narrowly. The volume of scientific and technical information will increase steadily, and this will require professional workers to read more and more specialized and up-to-date scientific and technical books and articles. It is already uneconomic to publish many such studies in most minor languages, and it will become uneconomic to publish most of them in ever more languages as the years pass.

Every modern language includes many words of foreign origin and is constantly adding new ones. This is particularly true of small languages like Gaelic and Danish and of language minorities like French-speaking Canadians. Moreover, the rate of adoption of foreign words, especially technical terms, will increase steadily for centuries in all minority languages. And the foreign words introduced into minority languages will come largely and increasingly from major languages, especially from English, because so many more books, journals, movies, and TV films are produced in these languages. Hundreds of English words have been introduced into German, French, and Italian since 1944. This process alone would eventually create a single world language, but it will not be the sole or chief factor promoting this result.

If a world empire is established by the victor in World War III or IV, as predicted earlier, the language of the world conqueror will rapidly become the sole language of international diplomacy, commerce, science, and professional education. It will soon be taught as a primary or secondary language in all middle and higher schools in the world. By 2300 all scientific journals and books and all international messages will be written in this language, and all college graduates—over 30 percent of the world population—will read and speak it as a native or secondary language. By 2500 nearly all men will learn it as their native or secondary language, and the study of foreign languages by native users of the world language will have virtually ended.

The Romans—who had no printed books, autos, radios—were able to spread their language over some conquered provinces in two or three centuries. It will be far easier, and far more mutually beneficial, for the coming world state to spread the use of its language. Worldwide use of a single language will not only simplify the problems of world rule by reducing nationalism; it will also greatly improve international understanding, make the finest textbooks and technical journals accessible to the largest possible number of students and scientists, and end the heavy costs of the study of foreign languages, thereby freeing many school hours for other studies.

It will be much simpler to achieve worldwide use of a single basic alphabet—with supplementary letters for sounds peculiar to certain languages—than to achieve universal use of a single language. And many languages badly need a new or improved alphabet to make it easier for their users to learn to read and write. For instance, Japan and China would benefit greatly from the use of a suitable phonetic alphabet. Hence the coming world government will achieve universal use of a single basic alphabet long before it achieves universal use of a single language. All the world will use such an alphabet, probably a modified Roman alphabet, before 2200.

Language is the chief means of human thought, communication, and education. Every improvement in it improves reasoning, communication, and education, the most significant and productive of all human activities. And since modern languages are the accidental product of uncontrolled evolution among largely illiterate peoples, vast improvement is possible. The application of scientific analysis and public control to language is highly desirable and therefore inevitable.

Efforts to improve existing major languages have been increasing for 100 years. They have already achieved some minor reforms, such as the simplified spelling of a few English and Russian words and elimination of two Russian letters, and are sure to grow. They will achieve other minor reforms even before an effective world state is created, and increasingly numerous and important reforms thereafter.

It has recently been proven that children can learn to read and write English much more rapidly when they use readers which employ enough letters (about forty-four) to permit all words to be printed phonetically (one letter, one sound). Language reformers had long argued that this is true, but they lacked the funds needed to prove it. Now that this claim has been verified, British schools are planning gradual introduction of the new teaching technique. By 2050 all elementary schools in English-speaking countries will use a new standardized phonetic alphabet and a new system of phonetic spelling, both approved by agreements among English-speaking nations.

Once a new phonetic alphabet has been introduced into nearly all elementary schools, the eventual general use by adults will be inevitable. It obviously is irrational and wasteful to teach children to use an inefficient alphabet and spelling system after they have learned much better ones.

The nation which dominates the coming world government will be eager to spread the use of its language for political and economic reasons, and will be able, and increasingly willing, to use subsidies and coercion for this purpose. However, it will also continuously reform and improve its language, partly in order to enable foreigners to learn it more easily and use it more effectively.

If the coming world government is a Soviet-American condominium, the language reformers of both countries will agree upon and carry out a gradual fusion of English and Russian into a single new world language including over half the words from each of the old languages. Each language already includes many words from the other, or based on common Latin or Greek roots. Language reformers could easily achieve a common phonetic alphabet and a rapid and continuous increase in the number of such common terms by requiring teachers and publishers to adopt such an alphabet and introduce, and thereafter permanently use, a small number of Russian or English words each week. By such methods a new Russo-American common language could be created and taught to all Great Russians and Americans within a single century. This new language would not be an ideal language, however, and its creation and adoption would be followed by a long series of reforms designed to create a near ideal synthetic language.

Within 100 years after its birth the world government will establish a special public agency authorized to conduct a steadily growing program of language research and to enforce gradual but continuous reform of its major language. By 2200 this agency will be enforcing one or more minor changes in this language every month of every year. All publishers, broadcasters, and teachers will be informed of and required to adopt the language reforms.

The chief initial function of this agency will be to gradually reform the dominant natural language of the world government so that it can be spoken, written, read, learned, and understood more rapidly and can express ideas more clearly. The agency will also design and experiment on a large scale with synthetic languages. By 2300 it will have created, tested, and approved a new synthetic language which will thereafter provide a goal for subsequent language reform. The new synthetic language or goal will itself be perfected indefinitely, but it will nevertheless be a useful criterion for nearly all proposed reforms in the world language for many years. These reforms will be planned so as to bring the world language ever nearer to the ideal synthetic language. No radical sudden substitution of the latter for the former will be attempted, but the cumulative change will be so great that by 2500 no young student will be able to read any language used in 2300 without special study of it as a dead language.

I have already predicted two reforms in the world language which will gradually be adopted during the next 200 years—lengthening of the alphabet to provide a letter for each sound, and phonetic spelling. These reforms will help to shorten many words by eliminating double vowels and consonants, diphthongs, and unpronounced letters. To further reduce the time and space required to write or print any manuscript, language reformers will gradually shorten or replace one long word after another until all words containing more than four or five letters have been eliminated.

The new phonetic alphabet will contain about 30 consonants and 15 vowels, which would permit the use of 45 one-letter, 900 two-letter, and about 40,000 three-letter words. The 45 most commonly used words—like *you, me, the, is*—will all eventually become or be replaced by one-letter words. The next 40,000 most commonly used words will nearly all be replaced by two- and three-letter words. Few manuscripts contain many words not among the 40,000 most commonly used words. The works of Shakespeare contain fewer than 20,000 different words. Hence these reforms alone will reduce by over 50 percent the amount of space required to reprint any 1960 book. This will greatly reduce both the amount of library shelf space required to store any given stock of publications and the amount of office space required to file papers. Moreover, this reduction in average word length will radically increase the average reading speed.

The letters of the new printed alphabet will be designed to maximize reading speed, and those of the written alphabet to maximize a suitably weighted index of writing and reading speeds.

The formation of verb tenses will be radically simplified and standardized. Both the gender and the declension of nouns, pronouns, and adjectives will be eliminated, as has already been largely done in English. All other rules of word formation and grammar will be revised, simplified, and standardized so as to maximize an appropriate combined index of reading, writing, and verbal reasoning speeds.

To improve all reasoning, reporting, and argument, the world language-reform agency will gradually standardize the definitions of all old words, eliminate all synonyms, and regulate the coinage and introduction of all new words in the world language. All ambiguous terms will be restricted to a single meaning. The continuous progress of science will require the introduction of thousands of new standardized terms, which will make the elimination of old ambiguous or superfluous terms ever more desirable.

Of course, all language reforms which enable men to read and learn more rapidly will improve education and reasoning. By 2500 language reform alone will have reduced the time required to complete most university courses by 25 to 50 percent. Most important of all, it will have markedly increased the productivity of scientific reasoning.

Libraries

Libraries are essential means of higher education and scientific research and are rapidly becoming more and more indispensable as knowledge accumulates. For reasons given in other chapters, expenditures upon higher education and research will rise more rapidly than national income in all countries for centuries. And libraries are now grossly inadequate to service education and research. At present, marginal expenditures on research libraries benefit research far more than marginal expenditures on research. And only one third of United States elementary schools have a library. It follows that the share of GNP spent on libraries will grow very fast, even faster than that spent on education and research, especially during the next century or two. In the United States such spending (less than 0.1 percent of 1960 GNP) will increase over 100 percent before 2000 and at least another 200 percent before 2100.

The printing of books in Europe began only some 500 years ago, and the market for them was small until the nineteenth century. The vast majority of men remained illiterate and impoverished throughout these 500 years. And the volume of scientific research was negligible until a few decades ago. As a result more printed material has been published since 1900 than during the previous five centuries. And relatively even more will be published in the next 50 years. This explosive growth of printed matter and the continued rapid growth of education and research will create enormous practical problems for librarians, problems which will call for repeated radical changes in methods, as well as immense increases in expenditures.

I shall discuss here the following major trends in the functions and organization of libraries: a steady widening of the range of material preserved in libraries; growing integration of once independent libraries, first into highly co-ordinated national systems and then into a single world library system; assumption by libraries of more and more services which help readers to find needed information more quickly; the gradual concentration of all such information-organization services—cataloguing, abstracting, evaluation, indexing, information retrieval—in vastly enlarged central national libraries; agreement on an international division of labor among national libraries; the gradual substitution of microfilm for printed matter; and the continuous mechanization and automation of library operations.

As the term *library* suggests, libraries began as (and long remained) collections of books. But the range of material preserved in them has gradually broadened to include maps, prints, sheet music, phonograph records, films, etc. Large national and university libraries will continue to broaden their coverage. By 2200 the coming United States national library will preserve all written, printed, photographed or otherwise recorded matter of possible future interest to genealogists, historians, social scientists, eugenics officials, medical researchers, practicing physicians, employers, etc. Such material will include photographs, and full or summary medical, school, work, income, tax, and criminal records, for every person, living or deceased, as well as summary financial and performance records of all business firms, government units, social organizations, schools, foundations, etc., from their beginning. It will also preserve copies of a vast and growing number of news films, documentary films, feature motion pictures, and television films or tapes. In a word it will preserve all recorded material considered worthy of preservation, and more and more of such material will be so considered as scientists become ever more numerous, more inquisitive, more competent, more amply financed.

The additional costs due to this continuous widening of the range of records preserved and to the rapid increase in the output of printed matter will be partly offset by savings from a gradual reduction in the duplication of effort among libraries. By 2300 the United States will have only one great library entrusted with such comprehensive record preservation.

Nearly all American and British libraries are now locally managed, and a large city may contain ten to a hundred independent libraries. The costs of operation thus are far higher than they need be, and it is much harder than it should be for scientists and students to find the books they want. Independent local libraries duplicate one another's stocks unnecessarily and at the same time fail to stock many useful books. Sometimes they use different catalogue-number systems, which confuses readers. For these and other reasons growing integration of public and research libraries into ever-larger systems is inevitable. It will begin with integration on a city, county, or state basis. By 2100 most advanced nations will have an integrated national library system.

One of the first notable results of library integration will be the preparation of local-union card catalogues, listing all locally available library books, for each metropolitan area, and a national catalogue listing at least one copy of all books available in the nation. Many local-union catalogues will be created by voluntary local co-operation, perhaps subsidized by a state or national government, before local libraries are integrated into regional systems.

The largest United States library is the Library of Congress, one of four national libraries in Washington, D.C. It will be merged with the other three—for medicine, agriculture, and national archives—renamed the United States National Library, and vastly expanded before the year 2050. The four libraries now buy and catalogue less than half of all new publications potentially useful to American research workers and writers. They do not even buy all new British books. During the next century they will buy an ever larger proportion of all new and used publications. By 2100 the new United States National Library will have copies or microfilms of all English-language publications and manuscripts extant. By 2200 it will have copies or microfilms of all significant foreign-language publications and manuscripts extant. It will then contain over one billion different books, and over 100 billion different and separately catalogued items. In 1960 the Library of Congress had only 11 million books and 38 million items.

In 1960 the four United States national libraries spent about $40 million and employed some 4,000 people. By A.D. 2000 these figures will exceed $400 million and 20,000 people; by 2100, $8 billion and 100,000 people. Both totals will continue to grow much faster than national income and population throughout the next 500 years.

Libraries perform two quite different basic functions: they collect and preserve publications and other items and make them available to readers; and they organize the information contained in their collections in order to make it more readily available and useful to library users. I have just predicted that national libraries will vastly expand their collections; I shall now predict that they will expand their organization-of-knowledge activities even more radically. One result of this will be that the proportion of national-library personnel engaged in organization-of-knowledge activities will rise above 90 percent by 2200.

Organization of knowledge includes the preparation of library catalogue cards; the compilation of bibliographies; the making of book indexes; the preparation of book summaries and journal-article abstracts; the operation of mechanical information-retrieval systems; the standardization of terms used in all such systems; and the critical evaluation and visible grading of most books and articles. Up to 1960 most national libraries in capitalist countries had performed only the first two functions and had performed them incompletely. During the next 300 years they will perform the first two functions more and more completely and will gradually begin to perform, or co-ordinate and supervise the performance of, all the other functions.

The preparation of library cards which contain most or all of the catalogue information needed by readers is laborious, expensive, and difficult to automate. The Library of Congress now prepares and prints catalogue cards for all its books and supplies these cards to other libraries. However, local libraries still buy many books for which such cards are not available, and duplicate one another's work both in cataloguing such books and in cataloguing many books for which LC cards are available. As the Library of Congress expands its book-buying program and increases its control over local libraries this wasteful duplication of catalogue-card preparation will diminish. By 2100 all United States book publishers will be required to print LC catalogue numbers on the covers of, and include LC catalogue cards in, all books sold to libraries, and all United States libraries will use LC catalogue cards only.

National libraries will steadily increase their efforts to prepare, collect, and revise annotated bibliographies on an ever-growing number of subjects. By 2100 the United States National Library will maintain up-to-date bibliographies on all major and minor subjects. Every American writer or scientist who prepares a bibliography on any subject will send a copy to this library, and it will prepare or contract for the preparation of annotated bibliographies on every subject not yet adequately covered. It will provide free copies of all such bibliographies on request.

National libraries will assume ever-increasing control over the preparation of book indexes and summaries and journal-article abstracts in order to ensure that all books and articles are indexed or summarized in a form which allows their information to be most easily inserted in and retrieved from information-retrieval systems. By the year 2050, United States publishers of non-fiction books will be required to include an index in all their books. By 2100 they will be required to use in indexes only standardized terms approved by the National Library. By 2200 all United States book indexes and summaries and article abstracts will be prepared or edited by the staff of the United States National Library in order to ensure more consistent and informed use of the standardized terms which facilitate information retrieval.

The vast expansion of United States federal government expenditures on scientific research and development since 1930 has rapidly increased expenditures on government and private efforts to make the resulting new knowledge known and available to government contractors, government researchers, and other interested persons. Already in 1964 the United States spent $200 million on such programs—only 1.3 percent of its total R and D spending but several times as large as the combined budget of the four national libraries.

Most of these information-organization programs are now carried on by agencies outside the Library of Congress and other national libraries, but eventually they will all be assigned to the coming United States National Library.

There are several reasons why information storage and information organization will be integrated in all countries. First, the same computers can be used to store, organize and retrieve information. Second, indexers, abstracters, and bibliographers can obtain and return the publications they use or work on more easily in a library than elsewhere. Separate information organization centers require separate libraries, which increases costs. Third, all reference librarians benefit from part-time work as information organizers, and vice versa. Finally, government agencies will perform an ever-larger share of all information-organization services, because they should be free goods. By 2100 nearly all such United States services not requiring original research and publication will be performed by a single central agency, the United States National Library.

The national libraries of all English-speaking countries will agree on uniform methods of cataloguing items, indexing books, preparing bibliographies, etc., before 2100. They will also agree on a division of labor among them which will eliminate most of the unnecessary duplication of work. For instance, the British national library will thereafter prepare all library cards for British books bought by American libraries. And no two libraries will prepare abstracts of the same material or bibliographies on the same subject.

As predicted earlier, the coming world government will gradually persuade, bribe, or coerce all peoples to use a single language, first for all scientific publications and later for everything. This will eventually begin to reduce the number of translations and limit the growth in the total number of titles published in the world as a whole, both of which will slow down library expansion.

The coming world government will also create, before 2400, a single world library system which will supervise and co-ordinate the activities of all national systems. If a comprehensive, well-planned international division of labor among such systems has not been previously achieved by voluntary agreement—an unlikely achievement—such a division of labor will be planned and enforced by the new world library system. It will also plan and enforce a continuous international standardization of all scientific terms used in catalogue cards, book summaries and indexes, journal abstracts, bibliographies and information-retrieval systems.

To serve an ever-more prosperous and highly educated population while the total number of publications doubles every 50 years or oftener, libraries will revolutionize their methods of handling printed matter. Such technological advances are much more difficult to predict than social trends, but some major predictions are justifiable.

First, within a century or two all new and old publications and manuscripts will be microprinted or microfilmed on small individual plastic slides or films. This will permit great savings in library construction and operation. Hundreds of microfilmed books can be stored in the space required for one large printed book. Moreover, a book microfilmed on a single small film slide can be reproduced for less than a tenth of the average marginal cost of printing a book. Such slides can be filed as catalogue cards now are, and the book files so created can be made as accessible to readers as catalogue cards now are. Libraries consisting solely of such files will become common in advanced states before 2100.

When a reader looks up a book in a combined book-catalogue file, he will find the book he wants at the same time he finds its catalogue card. Indeed, they may be identical. He will also be able to copy the entire book on another film slide for a few cents and take the copy home with him. He will not have to fill out a request slip, take it to the circulation desk, and wait for the book to be brought from the stacks.

If he wishes to read the book at the library, he will take the microfilm slide to a nearby reading booth equipped with a projector which will display successively each page on a large screen. A research library will consist chiefly of book-catalogue files and reading booths. But since microfilm projectors will be inexpensive, by 2100 nearly all serious readers will have one or more of them in their home or office. They will usually copy the microfilm slide and take it away with them rather than read it at a library. Most specialists will have a personal library containing 10,000 to 100,000 such book slides.

This system of operation will require no mechanization or automation of library service other than copying machines and enlarging projectors, but all large libraries will be increasingly mechanized and automated even before they provide microfilms of most publications. The bulk and weight of printed books make automation of library book-delivery systems more essential than automation of microfilm libraries. The Library of Congress has already begun to mechanize and automate its book-delivery services, and many other large libraries will follow its example or pioneer in such measures during the next few decades.

While automation of large microfilm libraries will be much less essential than automation of large book libraries, it is inevitable and will yield superior results at much lower costs, especially in information retrieval. It will probably involve the use of microfilm tapes and drums, rather than slides in filing cabinets. It will permit any person at home or in his office to obtain in a few hours a microfilm copy of any book in his local library by punching its catalogue number on a retail-order device. And he will be able to obtain such copies by wire or mail from regional or national libraries within twenty-four hours. The coming United States National Library will supply such copies of any extant item ever published in any language for less than twenty cents a copy before 2200.

If a national or continental library provides such service, and if every specialist has a large personal microfilm library, no other large library will be needed in that nation or continent. Small local libraries of full-size books and magazines will continue to serve primarily recreational and elementary-school needs, but no large local or regional university or research libraries will be needed. By 2400, therefore, each continent will have only one or two complete libraries. North America will have only one, which will be located near the center of the continent for optimum mail delivery. It will then preserve and supply on request within ten hours slides of over 100 trillion different articles, books, manuscripts, typescripts, maps, architectural plans, engineering drawings, pictures, etc.

Books and Magazines

All the accumulated knowledge of man must be collected, organized, and lucidly stated in manuscripts, magazines, and books. The vast expansion of knowledge predicted in earlier chapters will therefore result in an ever-growing output of written and printed matter. In this section I shall predict the following major social trends in the production of such material: a long-continuing substitution of microfilm slides and films for paper books and magazines; gradual adoption of the practice of lithoprinting or microfilming typescripts instead of printing them; an indefinite increase in the average number of man-hours devoted to writing a non-fiction book; a long-continuing rise in the proportion of authors who live on salaries or advances largely independent of sales; the creation of national non-profit literary-agency monopolies to market all manuscripts; creation of national agencies to ensure preservation and library cataloguing of all valuable unpublished manuscripts; a rapid growth of government subsidies and activities designed to ensure the translation and non-profit publication of valuable foreign non-fiction books and articles; the inclusion in more and more new non-fiction books of various readers' aides—book reviews, biographical notes about the author, summaries, and indexes; the growth of subsidized non-profit publication; and the adoption of marginal-cost pricing, which will reduce most book prices by over 50 percent.

Since more and more new books and magazines will be published or reproduced on cheap microfilm slides in order to permit their economical storage and use in large libraries and since projectors for reading the slides will become inexpensive and ever more widely used, more and more readers will prefer to buy, read, and preserve such slides rather than books and magazines. Hence a gradual replacement of bulky paper books and magazines by cheap microfilm slides or films is highly probable. By 2100, most new book editions and magazine issues in advanced countries will be produced on slides, which will then cost less than fifteen cents apiece. By 2300 the proportion will be over 80 percent for the world as a whole.

Paper books and magazines may always be preferable to microfilm slides for certain uses—as school texts, work books, frequently used reference books, reading where no projector is available, etc. Hence the printing and sale of some paper books will continue indefinitely. But they will cost five to a hundred times as much as microfilm slides.

A typescript can be photographed on a microfilm slide or tape as easily as printed matter. It is now unprofitable to print many useful research reports and specialized books and articles because it is hard to sell enough copies to cover printing and distribution costs. Indeed, it is often uneconomical as well as unprofitable to print such typescripts. But libraries preserve and catalogue only a small proportion of useful unpublished typescripts. Therefore learned journals now print many highly specialized research reports of interest to few readers in order to get them into libraries and library catalogues. The inevitable future growth in professional specialization will rapidly increase the proportion of book and article typescripts which do not deserve printing but do deserve microfilming, preservation, and cataloguing in research and national libraries. Hence more and more typescripts will be so treated. By 2200 the great majority of new non-fiction books and articles will be so treated, and most non-fiction books and articles preserved in large libraries will be typescripts or films of them.

The average number of hours of labor devoted to researching, writing, and editing the first edition of a non-fiction book will increase steadily. Most such books are now written by individual authors in less than two full years. But collaboration between two or more authors has been growing, and will continue to grow indefinitely. By 2200 the great majority of non-fiction books will be written by teams of researchers, writers, and editors who spend together over twenty man-years on a book. By 2500 most such books will be the product of over a hundred man-years of co-operative work.

Every increase in the literature on a subject makes the preparation of a new book more laborious, and the literature on almost every subject will expand rapidly and indefinitely. Moreover, every increase in the market for a book justifies more careful preparation, and the market for books published in the coming world language will expand a hundredfold, during the next 500 years, because of the growth of population, education, real income, and cultural homogenization. Finally the vast majority of non-fiction books now being published are full of avoidable serious defects because the author has received entirely inadequate advice and assistance from his colleagues and editors and has had inadequate time and funds for research. The able reviews which authors often receive after their books have been published should have been provided the authors before publication, and they will be increasingly so provided in the future.

Most books have been written by individual authors of modest means as personal speculations. Most authors still receive no pay or profit until their books are published, and usually little if any thereafter. However, the proportion of subsidized and salaried authors has long been growing and will continue to grow indefinitely. By 2100 most non-fiction authors will be salaried experts who will be well paid whether or not any particular manuscript is accepted and published. For them writing will become a secure profession, rather than a sideline or a series of personal speculations.

At present, after an author has devoted months or years of unpaid labor to the highly speculative enterprise of writing a book or article, he must wait months or years to learn whether it has been accepted for publication. Most manuscripts are submitted to many publishers in succession, each of whom takes a month to a year to read it.

To eliminate this waste and delay, advanced countries will, before 2100, establish central national non-profit literary agencies to accept, evaluate, and forward to suitable publishers all manuscripts voluntarily submitted to them. Such agencies are most needed, and will appear first, in the largest countries. For instance, over five hundred learned journals alone are published in the United States, and the time and effort required to submit an article to one journal after another is substantial.

The first national non-profit authors' agencies will be established by learned societies, probably in the United States, before A.D. 2000. But by 2100 every advanced country will have a single national authors' agency which handles all kinds of manuscripts free of charge. This agency will continue to submit each manuscript to one publisher after another, beginning with the most suitable, until it is accepted or judged unworthy of publication. The last submission will always be to a new government agency, a manuscript-review board.

No country in the world today has an agency authorized to determine whether non-fiction manuscripts rejected by commercial and non-profit publishers should be preserved unpublished in research libraries. As a result hundreds of thousands of useful manuscripts representing many billions of hours of unpaid labor by experts have been destroyed or have remained unpublished, uncatalogued, and unread. Many famous authors—Bentham, Marx, Freud—left important rejected manuscripts. Therefore, by 2100, every advanced nation will establish a well-financed national agency authorized to preserve, print or microfilm, catalogue, and make available to library users useful contributions to knowledge rejected by all other publishers.

Until recently the function of translating, publishing, and circulating valuable new foreign-language books and articles was performed entirely by profit-seeking publishers and scholar-scientists with little spare time and funds. In recent years several departments of the United States federal government have spent increasing amounts to translate, publish, and circulate foreign-language publications of special interest to them. Their chief concern has been to determine social conditions in communist countries and to aid, and reduce unnecessary duplication of, scientific research. The latter function will become ever more important. Most books and articles useful to scientists cannot be profitably translated and published by private publishers. But a book which would sell only a few copies may easily save a million dollars in research costs. Hence all national governments will continue for centuries to increase their expenditures on the translation, publication, and circulation of foreign-language books and articles.

As the amount of human knowledge, the number of non-fiction books, and the multitude of potential readers grows it will become more and more desirable to help readers choose books more intelligently. Therefore publishers will be increasingly induced or required to publish as a part of each new non-fiction book a brief review, or résumé of reviews, by one or more competent and impartial authorities. By 2200 all new non-fiction books will include such authoritative evaluations. And in publishers' announcements, library catalogues, and bibliographies, all listed books and articles will be marked with symbols indicating their evaluation by competent critics.

In recent decades more and more new books or book jackets have included a brief biographical note on the author. This practice will spread until it becomes universal (before 2100 in advanced states), and the notes will become ever longer and more informative. The more original and controversial the book, the longer such notes will be. By 2500 they will include, in addition to a summary of the author's education and experience, such revealing details as his I.Q., his university grades, his religious and political affiliations, and professional evaluations of his other major publications. Such information will help readers to allow for the author's biases and evaluate his conclusions.

Finally more and more authors of condensable non-fiction books and articles will be required to summarize them, usually in fewer than 10 percent of the words in the full text. This practice, already common in some kinds of learned journals, will spread to all other non-fiction journals and books before 2100. Such summaries will be increasingly required because they will help readers to find and review the literature on any subject far more rapidly, and this saving of time will become more and more essential as the volume of literature on every subject grows. As noted earlier, those who prepare such summaries will soon be required to use agreed standardized terms in order to facilitate economical organization and retrieval of information.

The proportion of non-fiction books and magazines published by non-profit agencies—government departments, university presses, learned societies—has long been rising in all advanced capitalist states. It will continue to rise for centuries. By 2100 most publishing in all countries will be done by non-profit agencies; by 2200, over 80 percent.

The average size of book and magazine printing plants and firms has been growing for over 100 years and will continue to grow indefinitely. By 2200 all such printing in the United States will be done by a single firm, which will locate its regional plants so as to minimize the sum of printing and delivery costs.

The number of independent book and magazine publishers will, however, remain large in all advanced capitalist states and will again become and will remain large in all communist states. By 2100 advanced countries will heavily subsidize most independent publishers in order to preserve and expand the publication of free, varied, and controversial opinion. And the coming world government will continue the policy or at least resume it after it has become politically secure.

As predicted in Chapter V, average-cost pricing will be largely replaced by marginal-cost pricing during the next 200 years. This trend will reduce book prices relative to other prices because the marginal costs of publishing a book are unusually low. They do not include any research, writing, typing, typesetting, advertising, and other such non-direct costs. Moreover, authors' royalties measure no real marginal cost and will therefore eventually be excluded from marginal money costs. And the coming growth in authors' salaries and in the number of hours of labor devoted to researching and writing non-fiction books will steadily increase the deficits due to marginal-cost pricing of books and magazines. Finally the introduction of microfilming as a means of original publication will radically reduce the marginal costs of publication and greatly increase these deficits. By 2200 income from the sale of books and magazines will cover less than 10 percent of the costs of writing and publishing those sold. Obviously the effective demand for and use of books and magazines will rise steadily as prices fall toward marginal costs and as the resulting deficits grow. These deficits will be treated as costs of education and research and will be covered by revenue taxes.

Magazines financed partly by advertising now sell at prices much closer to their marginal costs than books do. Therefore the application of marginal-cost pricing to such magazines will reduce their prices much less than the prices of other publications.

Newspapers

The merger trend long obvious in most industries has been especially rapid in the newspaper field, because the wastes of competition are here unusually large. In spite of a 120 percent increase in United States newspaper circulation between 1910 and 1960 the number of daily papers declined some 30 percent, chiefly because of mergers. In 1910 most American cities of over 10,000 population had two or more independent local papers; in 1964, only 68. By A.D. 2000 this number will fall below 20; by 2100, to zero.

This trend exists in nearly all advanced capitalist states. The number of daily papers in France fell from 230 in 1938 to 82 in 1965, and eight Parisian dailies folded between 1948 and 1965. By 2100 competition among local newspapers will have almost ended in all countries.

A continued decline in competition among local papers is inevitable, because such competition is highly uneconomic. It at least doubles the total costs of news collection and editing, advertising solicitation, and typesetting, the chief costs of publication. A monopoly can produce a much better paper at a much lower cost. And variety of editorial opinion can be preserved or increased by methods other than competition.

The rise of national newspapers, predicted later, will restore some competition in many one-paper cities by giving readers a choice between the local paper and one or more national papers, but this revival of competition will be temporary.

During the last 100 years more and more of the news and editorial items printed in local newspapers has been provided by syndicates. This trend will continue indefinitely because syndicated material is usually both better-written and cheaper. The trend has been, and will continue to be, favored by the growth of newspaper chains and by a steady reduction in the cost and time required to transmit syndicated material. By 2100 nearly all outside news and feature stories published in local papers will come from syndicates. Such material will be typeset by remote control from regional or national offices.

Newspaper chains have been expanding in nearly all advanced countries for almost a century. In 1964, 560 American dailies, with 40 percent of United States circulation, were owned by chains. This share will rise above 60 percent by A.D. 2000 and above 90 percent by 2100.

The further expansion of newspaper chains and the growing use of syndicated material typeset by remote control will lead eventually to the creation of more and more national newspapers —papers which serve the entire nation. In small advanced countries, like England, metropolitan newspapers have long been becoming more and more national, merely by expanding their out-of-town circulation. But in large countries, like the United States, national newspapers will have to be printed in local or regional printing plants, as the *Wall Street Journal*, America's first national daily newspaper, now is.

All non-local news and feature items in each regionally printed national newspaper will be written elsewhere and will be typeset by remote Linotype operators or typists. Only supplements containing local news and announcements will be written and typeset locally.

Few local newspapers will survive to become national newspapers, so the rise of the latter will rapidly reduce the total number of newspapers. Moreover, competition among national newspapers will end before 2200 in most countries for the same reasons that competition among independent papers in cities has long been declining. By 2200 only one daily English-language paper containing general non-local news will be published in North America, and only one such Russian-language paper in the Soviet Union.

Centralization of newspaper ownership will not result in centralization of control over newspaper editorials and syndicated commentators. As explained in Chapter III, all advanced countries will soon begin an ever-intensifying effort to require all newspapers to give appropriate or equal space to competent advocates of all sides of every controversial social issue, especially during electoral campaigns. As a result all newspapers will become less and less biased or partisan throughout the next 500 years.

The continued growth of newspaper monopoly and of public demand for well-rounded discussion of controversial issues will result in ever-increasing government control over private newspapers in advanced non-communist countries. Capitalist governments will increasingly require equal or fair treatment of competing political parties and candidates, more free space for campaign speeches and advertisements, limitation of monopoly profits, refusal of dishonest or misleading advertisements, etc. In other words, daily newspapers will soon be recognized and regulated as public utilities.

In backward countries many newspapers will be taken over by the government before they are treated as regulated utilities. In most advanced capitalist states the press will not be socialized until after it has become a closely regulated public utility. Socialization will initially take various forms—municipal, provincial, and national ownership, consumer co-operatives, producer co-operatives—but by A.D. 2200 nearly all daily papers in the world will be owned by national governments and edited by professionally chosen journalists.

Even under private ownership and competition the staffs of

daily newspapers have been increasingly professionalized. The proportion of American journalists who have university degrees has long been rising and will continue to rise until all reporters and editors have degrees in journalism or in the subject they most often write about.

As social ownership of the press develops, more and more newspapers will be entirely managed by professional journalists. In the beginning such managers will be appointed by higher co-operative or government officials, but eventually all will be chosen by regional or national professional associations of journalists, in order to minimize political control over the press.

The rise of socialism has already eliminated most advertising in newspapers and magazines published behind the iron curtain. It will produce similar results in all other countries before 2200. Since most advertising is socially wasteful, special taxes or quotas on advertising will soon be enacted in some capitalist states and will multiply and grow thereafter. The gradual elimination of most advertising from newspapers will equally reduce the space given to publicity stories tied to advertising.

Radical changes in newspaper news and feature content are inevitable. Capitalist newspapers now play up crimes, divorces scandals, accidents. Such stories grossly impair the administration of justice and cause an enormous amount of personal embarrassment and unhappiness. Many witnesses lie or withhold evidence in order to avoid harmful publicity. As men become more intelligent and better educated, they are sure to limit and eventually prohibit more and more stories liable to have such effects. All criminal and divorce proceedings will become secret before 2100. Even the court decisions will then be transmitted only to officials and private persons who need such information.

It is customary for readers to preserve newspapers for a few days only. Hence editors will eventually eliminate all printed matter which should be preserved more than a few days—fiction humor, popular science, how-to-do-it stories, memoirs, etc. Such matter will be printed in books, which can be more easily preserved, passed on to others, and made available in libraries. When advertising has been curtailed by 90 percent, and all newspapers have become monopolies, their editors will have little reason to try to build circulation by including non-news items in papers. And it is wasteful to print items which ought to be preserved, in daily papers which are not preserved. Separate publication of feature material will permit readers to buy only the printed matter they want.

The gradual elimination of advertising, crime and scandal stories, comics, fiction, and other non-news items will make United States newspapers thinner and thinner. In 1960 big-city papers averaged over 50 pages an issue; by 2200 this figure will fall below 12.

The marginal cost of printing and delivering such newspapers will be small. Moreover, it will be socially desirable to encourage universal reading of them. Hence they will become free goods, financed entirely by taxation, before A.D. 2200.

Radio and Television

Radio and television broadcasting are recent and extremely significant inventions. In the long run they will together have almost as much influence on social trends as the invention of printing. They will become major instruments of education and the most popular of all means of entertainment everywhere. They can provide nearly all forms of aural and visual entertainment—sports, concerts, ballets, plays, variety shows—at a far lower cost per spectator-hour and in a far more convenient place—the listener's home—than any other means. Moreover, their cost advantage will increase steadily and indefinitely as their audiences grow, as their library of expensive-old-program tapes expands, and as the wage costs of competing live entertainment continue to rise.

The extraordinarily rapid and general purchase of radio and TV sets in advanced countries is clear evidence of the already great advantages of broadcast entertainment. Most Americans now spend over two hours a day listening to radio or TV programs. By A.D. 2100, 80 percent of all the world's population will devote even more of their time to such entertainment and education. As real wages rise in backward countries and as the real costs of producing radio and TV sets continue to decline, more and more of the world's population will buy receivers, and more and more broadcasting stations or channels will be used. By the year 2000 most European and American families will have three or more radio sets and two or more TV sets. By 2200 most Asiatic families will have this many.

Today the average TV set receives well only two to six broadcasting stations, and the average radio, only ten to twenty. By 2100 the TV figure will be over fifty in advanced countries and the radio figure over one hundred. No two alternative channels will then broadcast the same program at the same time. All radio and TV programs in each metropolitan or regional area will be co-ordinated by a single office in such a way as to provide optimum variety and listener benefit during every hour of the day and night. All major new live theatrical performances—plays, musicals, concerts, ballets—will be recorded, broadcast, and periodically rebroadcast without cuts, delays, or advertising breaks. The TV audience for nearly all such productions will be over a thousand times as large as the live theater audience. And radio stations will broadcast a wide variety of university courses, poetry and fiction readings, symphonic music, etc., as well as popular music, throughout the day and most of the night.

In America community TV antennas have already begun to replace individual antennas, especially in fringe areas, and this trend will continue. In 1960 fewer than 3 percent of United States television sets were connected to a community TV antenna. By 2060 over 80 percent of sets will be so connected, and community antenna service will be a major public utility. Such service will eventually eliminate the dangerous and ugly forest of antennas now so conspicuous in urban areas. It will also increase the number of programs which the average TV set receives, and improve most reception.

Radio and TV advertising may continue to grow for a few decades more, but it almost certainly will be reduced by 90 percent before 2100. The costs of broadcasts will be increasingly paid by governments. Pay-TV may grow for a few decades, as a temporary means of eliminating commercials and financing superior programs, but it will not long endure because charging a price for listening to a broadcast greatly reduces the total benefits to consumers without reducing the cost of broadcasting. All prices will eventually equal marginal costs, for reasons given earlier, and the marginal cost of allowing one more person to listen to a TV broadcast is always zero.

The marginal costs of programs most suitable for radio broadcasting—victrola records, lecture tapes, news programs, etc.—are already low, but a good new TV program may cost several hundred thousand dollars. As audiences continue to grow and average real wages continue to rise, it will become economic to spend ever-larger sums on individual new programs. But the more expensive the programs, the more frequently they will be rebroadcast. By 2100 most TV broadcasts in English-speaking countries will be reruns of old programs, which may have cost over a million dollars to produce and some of which may be over a hundred years old. TV connoisseurs will by then appreciate the finest old programs as much as musical connoisseurs now appreciate Beethoven and Bach.

Creative Artists

The number of professional authors, artists, and composers has increased much faster than population in all advanced countries for centuries. According to the United States census the number of American authors rose from some three thousand in 1900 to seventeen thousand in 1950.

This trend will continue indefinitely, probably throughout the next 500 years, for several reasons. The steady reduction in the hours of labor will give all men more time to read, listen to music, and enjoy works of art. The steady rise in real personal incomes will enable men to pay for more and more of such recreation. The growth of education and the progress of eugenics will make men more able and eager to enjoy ever-finer works of art. Automation may reduce the number of performers, but it will increase the demand for creative artists.

A second major trend in artistic creation will be steadily growing government support of creative artists—novelists, poets, dramatists, composers, painters, sculptors. For a few decades more this trend will be largely due to international and cold-war competition for cultural prestige. But other motives will become increasingly important, and eventually dominant.

Charging a price for the right to reproduce or perform a work of art reduces such reproduction or performance, and therefore the pleasure derived from the work, without reducing its cost. Rights to reproduce or perform works of art will therefore eventually become free goods. Copyrights and copyright royalties will be abolished in most countries before 2100. But when creative artists cannot sell rights, they must be liberally supported by the taxpayer. This will soon become a major reason for state support of creative artists.

By 2200 the great majority of full-time creative artists in all advanced countries will be entirely supported by their government. Their ample salaries will be based in part on the volume of sale of reproductions, or the number of performances, of their works, but such payments will not be treated as costs of reproduction or performance and will not be large enough to enrich any artist or his heirs. The artists supported by governments will be increasingly chosen by their own professional associations and schools, rather than by bureaucrats and politicians.

To increase the numbers of highly creative artists in some fields, the Soviet government has already established specialized boarding schools which accept only the most gifted and promising students and then give them a thorough professional artistic education free of charge. All other advanced countries will follow this example in more and more fields of art. By the year 2200 most highly gifted artistic children will be recognized before age twelve and offered a free professional education. At present less than one gifted artistic child in a hundred in any non-communist country receives such recognition and education.

A new work of art resembles a durable machine because it yields a flow of benefits over a long period of time. Indeed, fine works of art are far more durable than any machine. They can yield ever-growing real income (pleasure) for centuries. Hence governments will eventually treat the salaries of creative artists as investments yielding permanent incomes. In other words, they will increase such spending until the resulting annual real income yields only the market rate of interest on the investment. They will therefore spend many times as much on artistic creation as would private persons or firms, who later must recoup their entire costs in a short time. Moreover, most of the real income produced by new works of art takes the form of consumer surplus and cannot be recouped by private persons.

CHAPTER XIII

Education

In Chapter I, I argued that when well-established trends in social reform or expert opinion are lacking, one can safely predict the future by assuming that needed social reforms advocated by able reformers will eventually be adopted. The development of education since the French Revolution supports this argument.

In 1792, Condorcet submitted a radical and farsighted report on education to the new French Legislative Assembly. He recommended that education should become a function of government; state education should be universal and free; both sexes should be educated; coeducation should be practiced; scholarships should be established to aid all poor students; extension classes for adults should be created; classical subjects should be largely replaced by scientific and vocational courses in secondary schools and universities; the teaching of religious dogma in state schools should cease; teachers should be given tenure; and all schools should be supported by local governments, aided by central governments. In 170 years Condorcet's proposed reforms have all been largely adopted in the most advanced countries, and there is ample evidence that they will be increasingly adopted in more and more countries during the next century. This should increase the confidence of the reader in long-run predictions based partly or wholly on the proposals of able contemporary reformers, especially educational reforms.

Elementary Education and Child Care

As Condorcet predicted, the growth of public education has been one of the most significant social trends during the past 170 years. Public education was negligible in 1800. Today nearly all children aged seven to thirteen in advanced countries attend school, usually a public school. And in America most children aged fourteen to seventeen are in public secondary schools.

During the next century public education will grow and improve rapidly in all backward countries. In 1960 less than 40 percent of children aged seven to thirteen in backward non-communist countries were in school. By A.D. 2000 this proportion will rise above 60 percent and by 2100, above 90 percent. Educational expenditures per elementary school pupil will rise even faster.

In 1800 less than 15 percent of the world's adults were literate. By 1960 this share had risen to about 55 percent. It will exceed 70 percent by 2000, and 90 percent by 2100. Furthermore, the average reading speed and vocabulary of literate persons in countries now literate will increase steadily and substantially.

Between 1870 and 1960 the proportion of United States children aged six to thirteen enrolled in school rose only 40 percent (from 70 to 99 percent), but the average number of days attended per year rose 100 percent, from about 80 to 160, thanks to more regular attendance and to prolongation of the average school year from 130 to 180 days. The enrollment rate cannot rise much further, but the average number of days attended can and will continue to rise for many decades, due chiefly to a further lengthening of the school year. Long summer vacations were perhaps justifiable when children disliked school and most teachers and pupils lived on or near farms which needed their help to plant and harvest crops. Such vacations represent a serious cultural lag in urbanized countries where children enjoy school and need far more vocational education. By 2100, United States schools will be in session 260 to 300 days a year.

While nearly all children aged seven to fourteen in advanced countries now attend school, the proportion of those aged two to five who attend pre-school institutions is still small. Although attendance had been growing for over 100 years, in 1965 only 66 percent of United States five-year-olds attended kindergarten, and only 15 percent of four-year-olds were in nursery schools. In May, 1966, the influential Educational Policies Commission recommended that the school-entry age should be reduced to four, so that all four- and five-year-olds could attend public nursery schools and kindergartens. This recommendation will gradually be adopted by more and more local school districts. By 2000 nearly all five-year-olds will be in kindergarten, and by 2060 nearly all four-year-olds will be in nursery school. Moreover, public and professional support for pre-school education for two- and three-year-olds will continue to grow. By 2200 nearly all such children will attend school. Similar trends will occur contemporaneously in all advanced countries, and 50 to 100 years later in all other countries.

The hours of operation of pre-school child-care institutions—now commonly three hours a day in the United States—will gradually lengthen, until by 2100 they will exceed the working hours of working mothers.

As the term *pre-school* implies, kindergartens are not now considered schools, and they give little formal education. This condition will change greatly. Superior children can learn to read and write or typewrite well before age six, which would permit a badly needed acceleration of their education. Hence instruction in reading, writing, and arithmetic will soon be introduced into kindergarten classes for superior children in advanced countries. Further progress in the science of education and continual eugenic reform should make it possible and customary for an ever-growing proportion of children to start such education at three or four and achieve current American third-grade standards by age six.

It has long been customary for many wealthy families in advanced countries to start their children in boarding school at ages eight to twelve. As noted earlier, it is usually safe to predict that what the rich do today the poor will do eventually, when their incomes have risen sufficiently. And the Soviet Union is planning a vast long-run expansion of its small boarding-school system.

Of course, wealthy families now choose boarding schools for social as well as educational reasons, and public day schools can and will be greatly improved. But boarding schools will always be able to choose their students much more selectively— according to interests, needs, and ability—because they draw students from much larger areas. And, as predicted later, much more specialization and channeling in education is inevitable. Moreover, boarding schools can improve education for nearly all classes of students by supervising after-school play and study more effectively.

The chief disadvantage of boarding-school education has been an undue separation of children from their families. This will gradually be reduced by sending children to boarding schools nearer their homes and allowing them to spend several hours at home every day or week if the parents desire it.

The sciences of education and child care are still new and undeveloped. Professional care of children throughout the day and night will become more and more advantageous, especially for underprivileged, mistreated, handicapped, and gifted children. Sending children to boarding school will simplify housekeeping and permit more mothers to work outside the home. For these reasons the proportion of children aged ten to eighteen in boarding school will continue to rise throughout the next 500 years in all countries. By 2500 most such children in all countries will attend boarding school.

For much the same reasons nurseries, nursery schools, and kindergartens will steadily increase their daily hours of operation and the number of operating days per year throughout the next 500 years. By the year 2300 most pre-school children in advanced countries will spend over eight hours a day, over 300 days a year, in such institutions. By 2500 nearly all pre-school children in the world will do so. And by then such institutions will offer, and many parents will accept, sixteen- to twenty-hour-a-day care for such children.

Religious control and influence over education has been declining for over 200 years and will long continue to decline. The percentage of children enrolled in church schools and the time given to religious indoctrination in public schools will both continue to fall steadily throughout the next 500 years.

Owing to peculiar conditions—Catholic immigration and a large Negro population—enrollment in church schools in the United States has grown faster than enrollment in public schools for several decades. This distinctive trend may continue for some time, but like all reactionary trends, it is bound to reverse.

When large-scale Catholic immigration into Protestant America began over a century ago, the Catholic-Protestant conflict was much sharper and the Catholics were far weaker politically than in 1960. The creation of a separate school system to preserve their faith was more defensible then than now. It will become less and less defensible, and more and more expensive, in the future. Moreover, Catholics will become less and less devout. Hence the gradual decline of their school system, serving 5 million pupils in 1960, is inevitable, though it may not begin for a decade or two. The first obvious major trend will be the gradual closing down of elementary schools, beginning with the first grade. A growing number of liberal Catholics have advocated this curtailment. By 2100 nearly all Catholic elementary and secondary schools in the United States will have been closed or merged into the public-school system.

Secondary and Higher Education

During the past century the growth of secondary and higher education in advanced states has been far more rapid than the growth of elementary education. This will continue until nine out of ten children in the world receive a complete secondary education and some higher education.

The chief factors responsible for this trend have been and will long continue to be: the steady rise in real incomes per family; the spread of birth control; the previous expansion of elementary education; the ever-increasing need for technical and professional training; and growing realization of the full economic and political benefits of secondary and higher education. Furthermore, eugenic advance will become a major factor promoting higher education after 2100.

The United States has long led the world in the development of secondary and higher education. In 1900 only 13 percent of American children aged fourteen through seventeen were full-time students. By 1940 the rate had risen to 73 percent and by 1960 to 90 percent. Similar but less rapid trends have prevailed in other advanced countries. By 2100 over 90 percent of all adults in advanced and semi-advanced countries will have completed twelve years of education; by 2200, over 90 percent of all adults in the world.

In 1870 less than 2 percent of American young people aged eighteen to twenty-one attended higher schools. This rate rose steadily and rapidly to 12 percent in 1930 and 25 percent in 1964. It will exceed 40 percent by A.D. 2000, when most American youth will remain in school to age twenty.

Similar growth trends have prevailed in all advanced countries during the last 100 years and will continue indefinitely. Japan and the Soviet Union have come closest to achieving United States levels of higher education. In non-communist Europe only 10 percent of young people aged eighteen to twenty-one were full-time students in 1960, but student achievement levels were higher than in America. These levels will fall as the proportion of youth in school rises. By 2100 over half of all European youth will stay in school to age twenty, and over 20 percent will earn university degrees.

In Great Britain the percentage of young people (eighteen to twenty-three) enrolled full-time in higher schools rose from about 1 percent in 1900 to about 8 percent in 1960. The government now plans to increase this rate to 20 percent in 1978. By the year 2000, Britain will exceed the 1960 American rate.

Future increases in higher education outside Europe and North America will be much more rapid, because they will start from much lower bases. Thousands of new higher schools will be established in Latin America, Asia, and Africa during the next 100 years.

By 2200 over 20 percent of all adults in the world will have a university degree, and this proportion will thereafter rise steadily to at least 60 percent by 2500, when the average I.Q. will be over 120. Moreover, the proportion with graduate degrees will rise much faster. By 2500 over 10 percent of all adults, and over 20 percent of United States adults, will have an M.A., a Ph.D., or their equivalent.

Formal adult education, both cultural and vocational, has been expanding relatively in all advanced countries for 50 to 100 years. It will continue to expand relatively for centuries.

As the hours of labor are reduced, adults will have more time for formal cultural education, and as real personal incomes rise, they will be able to afford more such education. The steady lengthening and improvement of pre-adult education and the adoption of ever more effective eugenic measures will produce more and more adults interested in further cultural education.

Technological progress is now so rapid that skilled and professional workers must be periodically or continuously retrained to enable them to compete with more recently trained men. Such further training is often profitable to both employers and workers. In recent decades many large United States corporations have rapidly increased their expenditures on vocational training for their employees. In 1964, General Electric spent $45 million on such education, even though most of the benefits accrue to its workers, who may leave at any time. The United States federal government sends most of its military officers back to school for postgraduate professional study. Soon it will require or pay for such adult education for all its civilian professional employees and executives. Nearly all teachers, physicians, surgeons, dentists, and psychiatrists now need much more continuing professional education than they get, because of the rapid progress of their sciences. They will be given more and more such education in the future. By 2400 over one third of the world labor force will consist of professional workers (including executives), and on the average each will spend 10 to 20 percent of his working life taking additional professional courses. Similar but less extended adult vocational study will be increasingly required of skilled and semi-skilled workers. In sum, throughout the next 500 years all workers will spend more and more of their adult life in vocational education classes.

Since the year 1800 higher education for women has grown much faster than higher education for men. As late as 1830 higher education for women was still negligible, even in the most advanced countries. By 1870 women were receiving 15 percent of first university degrees in the United States, a pioneer in this field, and by 1960 about 35 percent. A similar but less rapid development took place in other advanced capitalist states and, more recently and rapidly, in communist states. All countries will experience such a trend, either new or continued, during the next century or two. By 2200 the world will provide a higher education to almost as many women as men, and all higher schools will be coeducational.

In non-communist countries secondary and higher schools still discriminate against children from lower-income families by charging fees, by enforcing entrance requirements more difficult for them to meet, by failing to provide adequate scholarships, or by other means. As a result over 80 percent of all university graduates in non-communist countries come from families with above-median incomes and probably less than 4 percent from families with incomes in the lowest 25 percent. Such discrimination has long been declining and will continue to decline for centuries. By 2100 less than 65 percent of university graduates will come from families with above-median incomes. And the proportion of graduates from families with incomes in the lowest 25 percent will more than treble, to above 12 percent.

Government financial support of American higher education has been rising for over 100 years. It rose from 8 percent of the educational and general income of higher schools in 1880 to about 45 percent in 1960. It will continue to rise for another century or two, reaching 70 percent by 2000 and 90 percent by 2100.

The share of the federal government in such support has risen much faster, from 6 percent in 1920 to 18 percent in 1960. It should reach 40 percent by 2000 and 80 percent by 2100.

The above figures apply to the support of higher schools. The living costs of the students make up another almost equally large cost of higher education. In communist countries most such living costs are now covered by government scholarships. All advanced capitalist countries have long been moving slowly toward this goal and will continue to do so. By 2200 nearly all secondary and higher education in the world will not only be tuitionless but will require no payment of living costs by parents. All university students will receive liberal stipends or loans.

The gradual elimination of class discrimination in higher education and the future expansion of such education will create a new kind of ruling class, or power elite, in every country, one based upon personal ability and graduate university education, not upon inherited feudal titles or family wealth. Membership in it will be earned, not inherited, and will increasingly demonstrate superior ability and education.

The continued rapid expansion of public support of higher education will induce non-Catholic private colleges and universities, which are especially numerous and important in the United States, to specialize more and more in kinds of education not provided by large public institutions. Many private universities—Harvard, Yale, Princeton, Stanford, etc.—will soon eliminate the first two, later all four, years of undergraduate education and will specialize in graduate education and research. Those which continue to offer undergraduate education will specialize increasingly in superior education for gifted undergraduates. The proportion of undergraduate students in private higher schools will fall from 40 percent in 1960 to less than 10 percent in 2100.

Curriculum

The continuous substitution of useful or vocational courses for largely cultural courses—dead languages, foreign languages, literature, etc.—is an old and well-established educational trend in all advanced countries. It will continue for another century or two in these countries and much longer in less advanced countries.

America has long led the way. Between 1910 and 1960 the proportion of secondary-school students enrolled in Latin classes fell from 50 to 8 percent. It will fall below 2 percent by 2000. The proportion studying modern foreign languages fell from 33 to 20 percent; it will fall below 10 percent by 2000 and below 1 percent by 2500.

The time saved by reducing cultural education and by increasing both the hours per year and the years of education will be largely devoted to directly useful education—vocational and professional subjects, hygiene, child care, etc.—and to indirectly or socially useful subjects, such as history and the social sciences. By 2050 all European countries will stress vocational education more than the United States does now. For instance, European secondary schools will then devote many more class hours to driver education than to Latin. By 2100 over 90 percent of all school leavers in advanced countries will have learned a trade or a profession.

In 1962, 10 percent of new women college graduates in the United States had earned degrees in English and only 0.1 percent in engineering. By 2100 the English rate will fall below 2 percent, and the engineering rate will rise above 4 percent.

This shift from cultural to vocational education has been and will long continue to be largely a result of the growth of applied science and of the rise in the proportion of middle- and lower-class children in secondary and higher schools. Upper-class adults find the display of cultural knowledge a satisfying means of conspicuous consumption, and a century ago most students in good secondary and higher schools came from the upper classes. Moreover, what is cultural to a lower-class child may be useful to upper-class adults. Finally some subjects which were once primarily vocational, like Latin, are now primarily cultural, and their undue retention is a pure cultural lag.

Few secondary and higher students now take courses in logic or scientific reasoning, and most logic courses feature deductive rather than scientific thinking and neglect the causes of illogical reasoning. In the future such courses will increasingly concentrate on inductive reasoning, semantics, personal and social prejudices, and other causes of illogical reasoning in politics, business, and personal affairs. The study of logic, renamed the study of scientific reasoning, will eventually cover the causes of all illogical reasoning, as well as the theory of sound reasoning. This transformation of logic and the growth of science will make the subject ever more useful and popular for centuries. By 2200 nearly all secondary and higher students will be required to take separate courses in scientific reasoning each year they remain in school. Moreover, teachers of all other secondary and higher subjects will devote more and more of their time to teaching students *how* to think instead of *what* to think.

Educational Methods

The foregoing predictions on education deal almost entirely with the range and length of education. I shall now offer some predictions concerning methods of education. Such predictions are more difficult to make, especially for the latter part of the period covered, because great advances in the science of education are inevitable. Contemporary educational theory is naive and controversial because little scientific research on education has been done.

One of the major educational trends during the next 500 years will be a rapid increase in expenditures on educational research and development. In spite of recent rapid growth such expenditures in the United States in 1965 amounted to only $72 million, about 0.1 percent of total educational costs. This share will exceed 1 percent before 2050 and 3 percent before 2200. By 2500 over 6 percent of world educational spending will be on applied educational R and D. Such spending will of course lead to many new methods of education which are now unpredictable.

However, some major reforms in these methods are predictable. The most important broad general trend in methods of education during the next 500 years will be ever-growing individualization of education, fitting education to the need, interest, and ability of the child. At present nearly all children in a school district go through the same educational process in public elementary and secondary schools. In each school system different schools teach the same subjects in the same way, and the pupils in each classroom take the same tests, carry out the same assignments, and listen to the same teacher. All this will change gradually, but in sum radically. Education will be individualized by classifying and channeling pupils, by using different teachers, texts, and methods for each class of students, by developing and using teaching machines and other methods which allow students to study alone and advance at their own speed, and by giving each pupil more and more private tutoring and personal counseling. The continual improvement of psychological and educational testing will make such methods of individualizing education more and more feasible and effective.

One of the chief specific individualization trends in advanced states during the next century will be the growth of educational channeling: classification of pupils according to learning ability and their assignment to one of three or more differently taught classes, or educational channels. Superior students will be grouped together and taught by superior teachers using appropriate texts and methods scientifically designed. They will start their formal education earlier, go through it more rapidly, and cover more material while doing so. By 2100 they will enter secondary schools and universities at least one year earlier than average students. Specialized teachers, texts, and teaching methods will also be used in classes and channels restricted to average or inferior pupils.

Such specialization will speed up the learning of all students, because it will permit teachers to use more suitable and effective methods and texts in all classes. At present most teachers bore the superior students and talk over the heads of many inferior students. The few teachers who interest the bright students usually talk over the heads of many average, as well as of most inferior, students.

The first major step in the introduction of educational channeling will probably be classification into three large classes—

a superior third, a middle third, and an inferior third. By 2500 five or more channels will be used for normal children.

Advanced countries now have a few special schools for severely handicapped children—feeble-minded, deaf, blind, etc. Such schools will be established in all countries and will be expanded to care for nearly all children needing such education, before 2300.

Geniuses and near geniuses (I.Q. over 140—1.3 percent), hereafter called gifted children, need special education as much as severely handicapped children. Moreover, special attention to them would be far more socially productive. Most progress is due to the contributions of gifted people, and such people would be far more productive if specially educated and aided throughout their lives. Hence special schools for gifted children are certain to multiply indefinitely. By 2400 nearly all gifted children in the world will attend highly specialized classes or schools from age two to age twenty-four.

The number of students trying to enter the best American and European universities is already so large that some now admit only the top 10 percent of all applicants. And several states of the Union have deliberately established two or more channels of public higher education. For instance, California has state universities for the gifted and near gifted (upper 12 percent of high-school graduates), state colleges for the superior (the next 30 percent), and junior colleges for all lower-ranking high-school graduates. Such classification and channeling of higher-school students will continue to grow and spread in all countries during the next century or two.

The most significant recent development in educational methods has been the development and pioneer use of self-teaching or programmed teaching materials, including those used in teaching machines, which permit each student to study alone at his own pace and receive constant confirmation of his progress and correction of his mistakes. The use of such materials and machines will increase for centuries, until it is worldwide and almost universal in all suitable subjects and classes. This will do more than any other trend to individualize education. Different series of programmed material will be developed for each of five or more different educational channels in each subject, and within every channel each student will be free to proceed at his own pace. The use of programmed material will enable nearly all students to progress more rapidly, because it will provide constant approval or correction of each student's work.

While the individualization of education within each school and school district will continue indefinitely, the standardization of methods used in different schools, school districts, and nations will continue throughout the next 500 years. Since this standardization will result in large part from gradual integration of school administration, it is discussed more fully in the following section. But it is worth noting here that such standardization is a form of cultural homogenization and a product of all the factors responsible for cultural homogenization. For instance, the great increase in educational research will result in the discovery of many unquestionably superior methods of instruction and therefore in ever wider use of such methods.

The use of educational films will increase steadily for centuries. The proportion of schools and classrooms equipped with film projectors and screens, the number of educational films produced each year, and average expenditures per film will rise in all countries until every pupil in the world spends several hours a week looking at expensively produced educational films, each planned for use in a specific educational channel. By 2100 most United States science teachers will use films of demonstration laboratory experiments instead of performing such experiments themselves, and most history teachers will use films as supplements or aids to all study of the daily life, economic activities, military campaigns, architecture, etc., of past ages. All university lectures will be delivered on film, radio, or TV rather than in person. This growing use of film will be furthered by a continuous increase in the size and wealth of school districts, by further centralization of control over national school systems, by growing standardization of curricula and teaching methods, and by scientific research in teaching methods. Furthermore, the gradual elimination of unemployment will steadily weaken teachers' opposition to all labor-saving methods of education.

Lectures by professors, now the chief means of higher education, will be increasingly replaced by reading, individual study of programmed material, tutoring, and writing. Any lecture can be printed or filmed and then read or heard by students. Moreover, in those few cases where lectures are needed, printed or filmed lectures permit students in all universities to read or hear the best lectures by the ablest teachers. The survival of personal lecturing by professors is a perfect example of the featherbedding practices they often note and deplore in other occupations. University lecturing began before the invention of printing and was useful only as long as suitable books were unavailable.

Such reforms will greatly reduce the amount of live class instruction. Teachers will devote more and more time to personal tutoring and to reading student reports, and less and less to classroom instruction. By 2100, pupils and students in advanced countries will spend over 60 percent of each class day in independent use of programmed material or watching films and TV broadcasts. Much of the remaining time will be spent in writing reports and compositions. Little time will be spent in class recitation or in listening to live class instruction.

The use of true-false examination questions has grown steadily for over 50 years in the United States, the country where they have become most popular. Their use will continue to grow for centuries in all countries because they permit more objective grading, enable supervisors to evaluate instructors and educational methods more accurately, make the personal grading of examinations much easier and faster, and facilitate mechanization of such grading. Support for the use of true-false questions is higher among experts than among teachers. Many teachers fear being displaced by machines, but this fear will decline steadily. By 2100 most secondary-school and higher-school examinations in nearly all countries will consist largely or entirely of true-false and other questions which can be graded by machine.

The growth of real income per person, the reduction in the

number of children per family, and the gradual mechanization of routine teaching duties will permit all schools in advanced countries to devote more and more teacher hours to personal tutoring of students. In 1960 the average American pupil received much less than thirty minutes a month of private personal tutoring and counseling. By 2100 he will receive over two hundred minutes a month of such personal attention; by 2500, over four hundred.

This will require a steady increase in the proportion of the labor force devoted to teaching, for teachers, like other workers, will work fewer and fewer hours per month, while school hours and years will be prolonged and school vacations radically curtailed. In 1960, teachers and professors made up 2 percent of the United States labor force. By 2100 this ratio will rise above 4 percent and by 2500 above 8 percent, of a relatively larger labor force. For the world as a whole the trend will be much faster, but the ratios achieved will be lower.

The number of pupils per teacher in United States elementary and secondary schools fell slowly from 35 in 1870 to 27 in 1960. This decline will continue for centuries, in spite of great technological progress in teaching aids. By 2000 the figure will fall to 24, and by 2100, to 18 or less, due chiefly to birth control, rising personal incomes, growing parental demand for more personal attention to their children, and growing teacher demand for an easier work load. By 2500 the average pupil-teacher ratio for the world as a whole will be less than 6 to 1, for the school day will be more than twice as long as the work day for teachers.

School Administration

The major trends in school administration during the next 500 years will include gradual equalization of average expenditures per pupil in different areas of each country; continued centralization of control over local schools; standardization of texts, equipment, buildings, and teacher training; professionalization of educational administration; and increasingly scientific evaluation and incentive payment of teachers.

American public schools are financed by local school districts, which vary greatly in wealth and in the desire to support education. As a result expenditures per pupil vary enormously both within states and among states. The ten most backward states spent less than $200 per pupil in 1956, while the ten most advanced spent more than $350. The bad results of such differences are being increasingly recognized, and more and more efforts to reduce them are being made. Such efforts are certain to continue until by 2100, spending per pupil will be almost equal in all school districts. This result will be gradually achieved by consolidation of school districts and by a steady increase in state and federal aid to local school districts. A similar equalization trend will arise or continue in all other countries where spending per pupil now varies substantially among school districts.

During the past century or longer the administration of public education has been increasingly centralized in all advanced states by the consolidation of independent school districts and by the steady expansion of regional or national control over such districts. These trends will continue indefinitely. During the next century they will be especially marked in the United States and in other countries with a highly decentralized school system.

In 1930 the United States still had 130,000 independent local school districts. By 1960 this total had declined to some 32,000. It will decline well below 10,000 by A.D. 2000 and below 100 by 2100.

As late as 1918, 70 percent of United States public elementary schools were one-room schools. As a result of school consolidations made possible by the use of buses this figure had fallen to 18 percent by 1960. It will continue to decline indefinitely, falling below 2 percent in 2000 and 0.1 percent in 2100.

The number of United States elementary schools declined from about 247,000 in 1930 to 111,000 in 1960, and the average number of pupils per school rose from 93 to 336. The first of these trends will continue for several decades. The second will go on indefinitely, except when special elementary schools for special classes of pupils—gifted, handicapped, etc.—are being rapidly established.

Eventually, probably during the twenty-second century, all

United States public elementary, secondary, and higher schools will be integrated into a single national educational system financed and managed by a national department of education.

During this long process of integration, textbooks, school buildings, teaching methods, and curriculums will become more and more standardized. By 2200 nearly all American teachers will be trained in the same way and will use the same texts, teaching methods, examinations, and grading methods in similar classrooms and school buildings. Of course, educational experimentation will be far more extensive than now, but it will affect less than 1 percent of students each year.

One of the early results of this integration and standardization of American education will be the adoption, probably before 2000, of state laws or rules which permit all professionally trained teachers to teach in all states. At present most teachers are allowed to teach in only one state. The requirement that teachers obtain a state teaching certificate, in addition to a university degree in education, will soon be abolished.

The creation of a stable world government, the growing use of a dominant world language, the economic development of backward countries, and many other trends will gradually make educational texts, buildings, equipment, methods, and curriculums more and more similar throughout the world. By 2500 the world will have a single educational system financed and supervised by an educational agency of the world government. Most texts will be similar throughout the world. This will justify and result in a hundredfold greater investment in the preparation of the average new text, film, or teaching procedure.

Another major trend in school administration during the next two centuries will be the gradual substitution of expert for lay control of education. In the United States in recent decades this trend has taken the form of increasing consultation with and employment of professional educators by the politicians and laymen charged with school administration. This trend will continue for many decades, owing to increasing lay respect for expert opinion, the growing complexity of educational problems and theory, and continuing consolidation of school districts. Well before 2200 school administration in most countries will be completely entrusted to professional educators chosen by their colleagues or their professional associations. Governments will retain control over total expenditures on education but will relinquish all control over the spending of educational appropriations. The reasons why such professionalization of administration is inevitable were given in Chapter III.

The use of salary differentials based largely on demonstrable differences in teaching efficiency will grow steadily during the next two or three centuries. Teachers' salaries are now based largely on education and seniority, because until recently it has been impossible to evaluate teaching ability objectively. But the recent development of standardized true-false and other examinations which can be impartially graded enables administrators to evaluate teaching ability far more scientifically than before. And such standardized examinations will be steadily improved. Hence administrators will rely more and more upon comparison of such examination results, with suitable allowances for variations in student ability, to determine teachers' salaries. By 2200 nearly all teachers' salary differences will be based largely on such examination results.

CHAPTER XIV

HEALTH CARE

HEALTH CARE comprises the services rendered by doctors, dentists, psychiatrists, nurses, hospitals, nursing homes, and related personnel. In the world as a whole the value of such services has long grown much faster than income. The more advanced the country, the more income it devotes to health care.

It is much easier to mechanize and automate the production and distribution of tangible goods than the provision of personal services. Moreover, the demand for health-care services is more elastic than the demand for most tangible goods, and it will therefore continue to rise faster than personal incomes. Furthermore, scientific research will improve health-care services faster than it improves food, clothing, and shelter. Finally, birth control and medical progress will increase the relative number of aged persons who require much more health care than others.

For such reasons the proportion of the world's labor force employed in the provision of health services will continue to rise for centuries. This proportion is now below 1 percent. It will rise above 3 percent by A.D. 2100 and above 10 percent by 2500, when it will be larger than that employed in manufacturing, agriculture, or retailing.

Medical Care

The major social trends in medical care during the next 500 years will be: a continual rise in the share of world income and labor force devoted to medical care; a long expansion of compulsory medical care; the provision of more and more free medical care; ever-increasing government regulation of private medical care; growing specialization in medical care; the gradual replacement of individual by group medical practice; socialization and co-ordination of private hospitals and clinics; growing preservation, centralization, and organization of medical records; more and more spending on medical research; and the integration of all medical services and facilities into ever larger systems.

Between 1900 and 1960, Americans increased their spending on medical care from 3 to 5 percent of national income. It is therefore remarkable that the ratio of physicians to population fell 25 percent from 1900 to 1930 and remained constant from 1930 to 1960, while it rose steadily in other advanced countries and the world. The United States decline and stabilization was due to various peculiar or temporary factors—the rapid establishment of higher educational requirements for doctors and rapid increases in the use of telephones, autos, nurses, new drugs, and hospitals. For reasons given in the previous section, however, the relative employment in health services will increase steadily for centuries. Hence the ratio of physicians to population will soon begin to rise and will continue to rise indefinitely.

In 1962 the average American M.D. served some 760 persons, a figure typical of advanced capitalist countries. The Soviet Union had achieved a lower figure, about 620 (using the narrower United States definition of M.D.). The number of Russian M.D.'s (Soviet definition) rose from 23,000 in 1913 to 480,000 in 1962. Most advanced capitalist nations will achieve the 1962 Russian ratio before the year 2000. By 2500 the ratio for the world as a whole will be less than 200 persons per M.D.

In 2500 the average American will visit a medical clinic at least once a month. Doctors will work only twenty hours a week, will spend much of this time reading medical literature and attending classes, and will give patients more personal attention than they now do. Thus the average M.D. will serve less than 200 persons.

In advanced countries the amount of compulsory medical care has long been growing. It will continue to grow indefinitely, and the growth will be especially notable during the next two centuries. By 2100 all American children and adults will be required to undergo semi-annual medical examinations, several kinds of inoculation, and treatment for any infectious or serious non-infectious disease. All pregnant women will be required to accept prenatal medical care. All newborn infants will be submitted to compulsory medical tests and treatments. The rapid future growth of medical knowledge will develop more and more tests and treatments which will be made compulsory. Freedom to become and remain sick and a burden upon one's family and community will be increasingly restricted in all countries throughout the next 500 years.

During the past century medical researchers have discovered more and more ways in which polluted drinking water spreads disease, and advanced countries have adopted more and more measures to purify and medicate water. Both discoveries and control measures will continue to multiply. Long before 2500 nearly all drinking water in the world will be elaborately filtered to kill all disease germs and viruses and will have a variety of chemicals and drugs added to it. Such medication of drinking water will reduce heart trouble, tooth decay, and other diseases. It will be one kind of compulsory medical care.

The proportion of world medical care paid for out of public funds has risen continuously since 1860. Great Britain, the Soviet Union, and several other countries already provide over 70 percent of such care free of charge, and this share is substantial in all advanced countries. It will continue to rise. By 2100 over 80 percent of medical and dental care will be free in nearly all countries, including the United States.

In the United States the next major step toward free medical care will be adoption of compulsory medical and hospital insurance for most workers under sixty-five, probably before 1980. Later, health insurance will be extended to all citizens, and benefits will steadily be raised until they cover over 80 percent of all medical expenses. In the meantime labor unions will continue to demand and obtain more private health insurance partly or wholly financed by employers. But as public health insurance expands, these private insurance systems will gradually be ended.

Later, free provision of most medical care will become universal, because many, perhaps most, people do not voluntarily buy enough such care. A less intelligent minority fails to understand the value of such care, and a fearful minority needs to be induced or forced to accept such care. Moreover, medical care, like education, yields large benefits to society—such external economies as protection from contact with disease germs, lower taxes for relief, less crime and delinquency—which society ought to pay for.

Free provision of medical service is merely universal compulsory medical insurance, with taxes replacing individual premiums. It will replace health insurance because taxes to finance free health care need not be related to individual risk or credited to individual insurance accounts.

Government regulation of private medical care has been growing for many years in all advanced countries and will continue to grow as long as private medical care survives. Every expansion of public health insurance results in new government regulations concerning fees and medical services. And every increase in the efficiency of government justifies additional government control over the manufacture and sale of drugs and over private medical services. The more numerous and complex the drugs and medical services offered, the greater is the need for competent public supervision. It is therefore inevitable that all countries will continue to increase and intensify government regulation of patent medicines, ethical drugs, drug advertising, and medical practices.

Growing specialization in medical training and practice is an old and worldwide trend. In 1930 only one United States doctor in six was a specialist. By 1950 the proportion had grown to 36 percent. In 1964, 61 percent called themselves specialists, and 70 percent of new M.D.'s began specialized training. Both the number of specialties and the proportion of doctors who are narrow specialists will continue to grow in all countries throughout the next 500 years. Every increase in medical knowledge and in the volume of medical service makes specialization more beneficial. Practice makes perfect, and only specialists get enough practice. Surgical death rates for non-specialists are much higher than those for specialists, and among specialists the death rates are lowest for those who specialize most narrowly.

General practitioners will restrict themselves increasingly to preliminary diagnosis, referring more and more of their patients to specialists for final diagnosis and treatment. Before 2100 they will be denied the right to perform operations and to treat patients for any serious disease, except when specialists are unavailable, in all advanced countries. Preliminary medical diagnosis will become a new specialty, and later, like all 1960 specialties, will be divided into narrower specialties—preliminary diagnosis of eye complaints, etc. By 2500 all doctors in the world will be in new specialties much narrower than most 1960 specialties.

The growth of specialization in medical practice will increase specialization in medical education, eventually throughout the entire course of each student's training. Specialized medical education in America now begins only after the student has obtained his M.D. degree. But there is no good reason why an eye doctor should learn to name and designate all the muscles, bones, and veins of the entire body, or to treat diseases which do not affect the eyes. Over half the medical training now given the average specialist is relatively useless to him—much less useful than more specialized training would be. Moreover, medical knowledge will continue to grow rapidly and indefinitely; hence medical schools will soon begin to eliminate more and more general training from the education of specialists. This reform will radically shorten the basic medical education of most specialists.

The sixth major social trend in medical care will be the replacement of individual medical practice by group medical practice in ever larger clinics. This trend will promote and be promoted by increasing medical specialization. It will enable more and more patients to visit their family doctor and specialists at the same office, will facilitate face-to-face consultation among doctors, and will reduce rent, equipment, and secretarial costs per doctor. In 1960 less than 20 percent of United States doctors and dentists were salaried employees of or partners in medical clinics. By 2100 over 80 percent will work full-time in clinics or hospitals as salaried employees. Such institutions will grow in size and become local monopolies, as public schools now are. By 2500 most local clinics will employ over 50 doctors and over 150 other persons.

The proportion of clinics located in or next to hospitals will rise for many years. By 2100 most practicing doctors in advanced countries will work in hospitals or in clinics attached to hospitals. This will permit them to visit their hospital patients much more easily and frequently, will reduce clinic and hospital operating and construction costs, and will give doctors easier and quicker access to hospital laboratory, X-ray, and other facilities.

The governments of capitalist countries will increase the output of free hospital care by subsidizing private hospitals ever more liberally, by building new public hospitals, by providing more compulsory hospital insurance, and by nationalizing private hospitals. The use of these methods has been growing for many years. Up to 1960 the United States had relied chiefly on the first two methods, but Great Britain had nationalized most private hospitals. By 2100 nearly all remaining private hospitals in non-communist countries will have been nationalized.

Most American general hospitals are small, local, and independent. They will steadily become larger, less local, less competitive, more specialized. They grew in average size from 80 beds in 1920 to 135 in 1960. They will reach 200 by A.D. 2000 and 400 by 2100, when no city will have competing hospitals, that is, hospitals offering the same service to the same people.

Specialization among hospitals will increase indefinitely. The most serious, difficult, novel, or unusual operations and medical treatments will gradually be concentrated in specialized hospitals which serve entire regions or nations. Eventually all new operations and treatments will be pioneered in such institutions, which will often continue to be the sole places where they are available. Existing national clinics, like the famous Mayo Clinic, will specialize more and more in new or difficult medical care not available anywhere else in the country.

The progress of medical science has already greatly increased the number of medical examinations and laboratory tests per patient in advanced countries, and this trend will continue indefinitely. Since most private medical care in non-communist countries is competitive and uncoordinated, the results of the examinations and tests are rarely preserved, collected, and made available to all doctors who treat the same patients later or to medical researchers. The coming socialization and centralization of medical care and the growing interest in medical research and eugenic reform will result in the systematic assembly and preservation of more and more medical reports on every citizen. By 2100 all such United States records will be kept in a central national research library long after the patients concerned have died. When a person moves from one area to another, his complete medical file will automatically follow him. And medical administrators will increasingly use such files to evaluate individual doctors.

Until recently the governments of advanced states spent little to support health-related research, but such spending has grown rapidly since 1940. In that year the United States Congress voted only \$3 million for such research, but the figure reached \$186 million by 1957 and almost \$1 billion by 1963, when it was twice as large as similar private investment. This remarkable growth rate cannot long continue, but the figure should exceed \$4 billion by 2000. Public investment in such research will grow faster than GNP in all countries for centuries. By 2200 the world will invest over 1 percent of world GNP in health research, a rate at least ten times as high as the 1960 rate, and 90 percent of such investment will then be publicly financed.

As predicted earlier, more and more medical care will become a function of government, like education. In the United States and most other advanced capitalist states, public health care is largely provided by local units of governments. During the next two centuries this function will gradually be shifted from local government to regional and national government. By 2200 nearly all health services in advanced countries will be provided by national agencies. One minor but typical result of such integration will be that American doctors will be allowed to practice in every state in the Union. And American patients will get similar and equally good medical care wherever they live.

The establishment of a strong world government will result in gradually increasing efforts to integrate and standardize health services throughout the world. By 2500 the world government will have a world health agency which will supervise medical education and care throughout the world. It will concentrate many difficult operations and treatments in highly specialized hospitals too large and specialized for small nations to support. It will control the entire world output of drugs, vaccines, and other medical supplies, many of which will be produced in only one plant. But it will not provide equal medical care throughout the world. Such care will still vary widely with average real income.

Psychiatric Care

All the ten general medical predictions offered in the previous section are valid for psychiatric care also. But some additional predictions concerning psychiatric care are worthwhile.

Psychiatry is a relatively new science. It has barely reached the stage of development achieved by medicine a century ago. The recent discovery of tranquilizers and energizers corresponds to the discovery of anesthetics and narcotics from 1840 to 1860. During the next century (1960–2060) the progress of psychiatry probably will be as rapid as the progress of medicine since 1860.

Moreover, personal expenditures for psychiatric care vary with family income and education far more than do those for medical care. Working-class families in advanced countries appreciate and obtain much good medical care but little if any psychiatric care. Therefore, as real wages rise and public education expands and improves, public demand for psychiatric care will continue to rise more rapidly than the demand for medical care, whether or not psychiatric progress is faster than medical progress. For these and other reasons the number of psychiatrists and expenditures on psychiatric care will increase much faster than their medical counterparts in advanced countries during the next century or two, and later in all other countries.

During the twenty-first century periodic psychiatric examinations will be made compulsory in advanced countries, first for failing or disturbed schoolchildren and adults, later for all persons. By 2200, psychiatric examinations will be required of all persons in the world at least once a year, and treatment for many curable nervous disorders will be free and compulsory.

Psychiatry began as the study of serious mental illness, then called insanity. Later, psychiatrists expanded their field to include mild mental illness, or neurosis. A major trend in psychiatry will be increasing study and care of ever milder neuroses, those common among so-called normal people. By 2300, psychiatric examinations and care will be as acceptable and conventional among normal persons as other medical examinations and treatments now are. Almost everyone suffers from minor mental ills, and these should receive treatment as soon as it is possible and available.

The widespread use of drugs to treat neurotic and psychotic persons, though new, has already produced notable results. Many more new and improved drugs will be developed. By 2500, drugs for treating effectively nearly all types of neuroses and psychoses will be available, and many neuroses too mild to be noticed or treated today will be treated. Drugs will be used to change moods, to improve mental functioning, to reduce nervous tension, and to make people more energetic, as well as to treat neuroses and psychoses. The average normal adult will then consult his psychiatrist more often than his dentist.

In advanced countries, where suffering due to hunger, cold, and disease has largely been eliminated, most pain and unhappiness is due to neurosis, psychosis, mental depression, and other mental illness. During the next 500 years progress and growth in psychiatric care will do much more to increase well-being in such countries than will progress and growth in medical care.

Most mental illness is due to heredity or to undue and alterable social pressures, such as harsh or unwise treatment by parents, mates, employers, peers, police. In the future psychiatrists will devote more and more of their time to suggesting and promoting eugenic and social reforms designed to diminish the causes of mental illness and unhappiness. Moreover, treatment of individuals will rely less and less on psychoanalysis, and increasingly on drugs and control of alterable conditions at home and at work. The predicted indefinite further increases in social control over home life, education, and business will enable psychiatrists to advise ever more effective measures to reduce or eliminate the environmental causes of mental illness.

Much juvenile delinquency and adult crime are due to bad care of very young children by defective or emotionally disturbed parents. In the long run, such parents will be eliminated by eugenic measures, but during the next 300 years compulsory psychiatric examination and treatment will be increasingly used to detect and treat such parents and to dissuade or prevent disturbed persons from becoming parents. By 2300 most young people who fail to pass appropriate psychiatric and medical tests will be sterilized.

Alcoholism and narcotic addiction are still treated primarily as criminal rather than psychiatric problems. Known alcoholics and drug addicts now spend far more time in jail than in hospitals. Indeed, most of them never receive any psychiatric care. This situation will change greatly during the next century. More and more alcoholics and drug addicts will receive psychiatric rather than police care. By 2100 over 90 percent of all alcoholics and addicts in advanced countries will receive effective psychiatric care or be permanently segregated in psychiatric institutions, rather than sent to jail or prison or allowed to become derelicts.

To facilitate early detection and treatment of alcoholics and drug addicts, tests for these conditions will eventually be included in the compulsory periodic examinations predicted earlier. All paroled alcoholics and addicts will be required to take such tests weekly or monthly for a long period after their parole. Such measures will be adopted in most advanced countries before 2100.

Psychiatrists who treat drug addicts will increasingly be allowed to prescribe maintenance doses for their patients, primarily in order to reduce crime.

Since most alcoholics and addicts cannot afford to pay for the psychiatric treatment and institutional care they need, advanced countries will provide more and more such care free of charge, until by 2100 it will nearly all be free.

Cigarette smoking is almost as harmful as the use of narcotics, and is a hundred times as common. Hence psychiatrists will soon spend far more time curing cigarette addicts than curing narcotic addicts.

The growing demand for psychiatric care predicted above will help to bring about radical reforms in the education of psychiatrists. American psychiatrists are now required to have both an M.D. and a Ph.D. degree, which usually demands over six years of graduate work. And psychiatric knowledge will expand tenfold during the next century. Therefore the training of psychiatrists will become more and more specialized. The scientific and medical courses of little use to psychiatrists will gradually be dropped and replaced by more useful and more specialized courses. Psychiatry itself will break up into many specialties, and students in each specialty will concentrate increasingly on courses useful only or chiefly to them.

Suicide and Euthanasia

Suicide is a major cause of non-natural death in advanced countries. Because of Christian condemnation of suicide, many, perhaps most, suicides in Christian countries are called accidents; but in the United States, 20,000 suicides were reported in 1960, more than twice the reported murders. And attempted suicides, which are not tabulated, greatly outnumber successful suicides.

Among the young and middle-aged, suicide is largely due to preventable, often temporary, causes. Thus suicide rates rose sharply during the great depression, and in Germany and Japan in 1945. Recent advances in medical care, real wages, social insurance, etc., in the United States have reduced the urban suicide rate by over one third since 1912. Future social and medical progress will continue to reduce suicide rates among persons under sixty for centuries.

Suicides by persons temporarily depressed or in great pain will be discouraged and prevented more and more effectively. Doctors will be given increased power to commit such persons to institutions where they will be closely watched and carefully treated until the danger of suicide has passed. Anti-depression drugs will be steadily improved and more widely and promptly used.

While suicide rates among the young and middle-aged are likely to decline indefinitely, suicide among the aged will almost certainly increase for centuries. Religious prejudice against suicide will continue to decline, and the proportion of the very aged in the population will grow for centuries. The older one is, the more rational suicide becomes if one is chronically sick or unhappy. By 2200, aged persons who commit suicide to reduce the burden they impose upon relatives and society will be praised rather than condemned by public opinion in all countries.

Euthanasia—painless killing of defective infants and painfully dying adults—has long been illegal in all advanced states, but public support for it has been steadily growing, especially among the best-educated. The major arguments against euthanasia are theological and will therefore count less and less as the years pass. I predict, therefore, that euthanasia will become legal in most advanced states before 2100 and common long before 2500.

Mercy killings of seriously deformed or defective children and of dying persons in great pain will be among the first classes of euthanasia to be approved. Of course, approval by a committee of experts will be required. Once mercy killing in the most extreme circumstances has been approved, the limitations on such killing will be repeatedly relaxed, so that it can be applied to an ever larger number of defective infants and painfully dying persons. It is most unlikely, however, that euthanasia of adults against their wishes will ever be approved, for the mere possibility of such mercy killings would make serious illness more fearsome and therefore more harmful.

CHAPTER XV

Family Life

PREDICTIONS which affect family life most directly and which have not already been made in earlier chapters will be dealt with here. Some overlapping with preceding chapters—especially those on work and wages, housing, and education—is unavoidable, but it has been minimized.

Feminism

The terms *feminism* and *feminist movement* denote an important group of social trends illustrating the decline in female subordination to males. This subordination is economic, political, and educational, as well as sexual and marital, but it is convenient to discuss feminism in this chapter.

Throughout nearly all of recorded history wives have been subordinate to their husbands. Words like *obey* are still included in most marriage vows, even in the most advanced countries, where wives have become less and less obedient for centuries. This long-run trend will continue in all countries until women have equal legal rights and exercise them. The word *obey* and its synonyms will be omitted from more and more marriage vows. By 2100 it will be used in less than 10 percent of all wedding ceremonies in advanced states, and most major family decisions will be made by mutual discussion and agreement between husbands and wives, not by male edict.

In most if not all advanced countries, wives are still required by legal or canon law to submit themselves sexually to their husband, often even if he has a venereal disease, and to use no birth-control means disapproved by their husbands. All such civil and canon laws will be repealed by 2200.

In most countries it is still legal for husbands to punish their wives physically when they are disobedient. This ancient privilege, embedded in Anglo-Saxon common law, will be legally withdrawn in all advanced states by 2100 and in other states by 2200.

In democratic states voting was long restricted to males. British and American women were not granted equal voting rights until 1920, but the advance of female suffrage has since been rapid. It will continue until women have equal voting rights in all nominally democratic states.

The number of elected female legislators and public officials, which has risen steadily since 1920, will continue to grow indefinitely. By A.D. 2100, 30 to 40 percent of legislators in advanced democratic states will be women. Great Britain, the Soviet Union, and the United States will all have one or more female chief executives before 2200.

In 1860 the United States had no female lawyers. In 1960 about 3 percent of all lawyers were women. By the year 2000 the rate will be above 6 percent; by 2100, above 30 percent. In 1960 only 3 percent of judges and less than 1 percent of federal judges were women. Both rates will rise above 30 percent by 2100.

Medical care, like education, is one of the professions for which women are better qualified than men. The fact that only 10 percent of American doctors are women is therefore prima-facie proof of continued gross discrimination against women. In Russia three out of four medical students are female, and in Great Britain, one in four. Such ratios will continue to rise, until before 2200 most doctors in the world will be women.

It has long been believed that women are more religious than men. Recent public opinion surveys have justified this popular belief. But the number of female priests and ministers is still small. During the past century, however, their influence and number rose steadily in advanced states. Christian Science and several other new sects were founded by women. By 1960 there were over 6,000 ordained or licensed female ministers (2 percent of the total) in America. This percentage will rise steadily in more and more countries. By 2200 over one third of all Protestant ministers will be women. By 2500 most priests, ministers, and theologians in the world will be women. Already over two thirds of active United States church members are women.

Until recently all educational systems discriminated markedly against females. Higher education for women is little more than a century old in the most progressive countries. There has been a rapid and continuous decline in such discrimination since 1830, and this decline will continue indefinitely. More specific predictions were given in an earlier chapter on education.

The customs of giving children their father's family name and of requiring a woman to take her husband's family name are both results of male domination of women. Hence they will weaken gradually as such domination declines. Long before the year 2500 most married women will continue to use their maiden name after marriage, and most daughters will take their mother's maiden name.

A century ago the property rights of women were much inferior to those of men in all advanced states. Thus the Napoleonic Code gave husbands full control over the property of their wives. Indeed, French wives were not even allowed to sign checks until after World War II. While there has been a continued increase in female property rights in all advanced states during the past century or two, women have not yet achieved equal property rights in any non-communist state. But such achievement is inevitable, and it should come during the twenty-first century in nearly all advanced states. It will include community property laws which entitle wives to claim or bequeath half the increase in family wealth during their marriage.

Sex

In an earlier section on birth control I predicted that contraception, abortion, and voluntary sterilization would soon be legalized, steadily improved, and ever more widely used. These advances will make sexual intercourse more frequent and pleasant. Many other previously predicted social trends—better health care, education, etc.—will have similar results.

The Christian belief that normal sexual gratification is sinful outside marriage and low or degrading within marriage has been declining for centuries and will continue to weaken indefinitely. It will gradually be replaced by a pagan, humanistic belief that sexual satisfaction is as wholesome and desirable as the pleasures of eating, drinking, and sport. Long before 2500, efforts to increase sexual satisfactions will be as numerous and as respectable as efforts to improve the flavor of food and the aroma of wine. Most such efforts are now generally considered obscene, perverted, degrading, or sinful.

It follows that all laws against obscenity, unnatural but harmless sexual acts, homosexual behavior between consenting adults, pornographic books and performances, adultery, premarital sexual intercourse, voluntary prostitution, etc., will gradually be weakened and in time repealed. In many urban areas of advanced countries juries already are often reluctant to convict for some of these offenses, and they will become more and more reluctant. Many sex laws will become unenforceable before they are repealed. And courts will interpret laws against obscenity, perversion, and pornography ever more liberally. More and more books and pictures now legally condemned as obscene or pornographic in Christian states will be declared legal without any relevant change in the law. Later, of course, the laws will be repeatedly liberalized, and eventually repealed.

These changes in attitudes and laws will result in a long-run increase in the production of sexually stimulating books, pictures, movies, and television shows, and in the creation of books, pictures, etc., which are far more stimulating sexually than any now produced.

The risk of contracting a venereal disease has long been a major factor restricting extra-marital sexual intercourse. Although VD rates in advanced countries have fallen fairly steadily since 1900, some 650,000 Americans under twenty contracted a venereal disease in 1960. The advance of medical knowledge and the adoption of more and more compulsory physical examinations and medical care will steadily reduce VD rates during the next century. By 2100 they will be negligible in nearly all countries.

The Kinsey studies revealed that the United States ratio of premarital sexual intercourse had been growing slowly for 50 years. The further reduction of VD and the spread of birth-control knowledge will cause this trend to continue slowly in all Christian countries for another century or two, though it will be temporarily reduced by the spread of childless trial marriage.

Commercial prostitution is an ancient evil which is extremely difficult to suppress in free-enterprise societies. By assuring full employment of women, by making personal incomes far less unequal, by drastically limiting the use of money, and by further regulating or replacing private enterprise, advanced non-communist countries will be more and more successful in restricting commercial prostitution and will greatly reduce economic incentives to voluntary individual prostitution. The coming decline in VD rates and the continuing revolution in sexual attitudes, however, will continuously reduce social disapproval of voluntary prostitution. Hence such prostitution will remain or become legal and will long survive, even in nations with full employment and high real wages.

Illegitimate birth rates and trends in them vary widely from country to country. The continued spread of birth control and the further liberalization of divorce laws should soon start or should continue a long decline in these rates in all countries. The United States rate rose from 3.8 percent of all births in 1940 to 5.2 percent in 1960. It may rise a little more, but will fall below 1.0 percent by 2100.

For thousands of years moralists have taught that society should discriminate against unwed mothers and their children in order to discourage illicit sexual relations, but such discrimination has declined steadily for centuries in advanced countries. The further changes in sex attitudes and laws predicted above will bring about a continued improvement in the treatment of unwed mothers and their children. By 2100 nearly all laws which discriminate against them will have been abolished. In the meantime legal procedures, records, and documents which now describe or publicize illegitimate births will be revised so as to minimize public knowledge of individual cases and thus reduce embarrassment to the persons involved.

Child Care

As predicted in an earlier chapter on education more and more public child-care services for pre-school children will be provided outside the home. The hours of operation of all child-care agencies and schools will steadily be lengthened until they care for children throughout the time most working mothers are away from home. And the proportion of children in boarding child-care institutions and schools will increase slowly, until by 2500 most children over ten, and many younger, will sleep and eat as well as study outside the home. Long before this expansion of boarding agencies is so complete, children will wear pre-school or school uniforms supplied, mended, and laundered free of charge by the state, will eat one or two free meals at school, and will receive free medical care at school. Such measures will greatly reduce the homemaking work of wives.

Expert opinion that much adult misbehavior, failure, and illness can be traced back to the mistreatment of very young children by their parents has been growing for 50 years and will continue to grow for many more. The growth and spread of this view and the increase of knowledge concerning child care will result in steadily increasing state supervision of parental child care. Schools will offer more and more courses in this subject until all students or parents are required to study child care. Government agencies to supervise parental child care will be created or enlarged, and their authority will be repeatedly increased, until by 2200 all advanced states will supervise the home care of all children.

For most homes this supervision will be slight. It will merely confirm periodically that children are being properly cared for. But for the minority of homes which now produce the great majority of juvenile delinquents, problem children, criminals, alcoholics, and drug addicts, such supervision will eventually become very close. Supervisors will first try to improve child care in such homes; if this fails, they will have the parents sterilized and remove the children to foster homes or boarding schools. Of course, the provision of more and more free or subsidized birth-control aid and advice will gradually reduce the number of children in such homes. Together with other reforms, public child-care supervision will reduce the proportion of United States juvenile and adult delinquents by 80 percent before 2200.

Due chiefly to the progress of medical care, the percentage of children who are part or full orphans has been declining steadily in peacetime in advanced states for a century or more. In the United States the percentage of full orphans declined by 90 percent between 1920 and 1960, and that of partial orphans by 70 percent. These trends will continue indefinitely but at decreasing rates in advanced states and will arise or continue for decades at increasing rates in the most backward states.

The proportion of American orphans cared for in institutions has also been declining for over 50 years, largely because of the growth of adoption and of financial grants to widows and foster parents. In 1960 about 100,000 children were adopted, and over 2.3 million children benefited from aid to dependent children. Fewer than 150,000 remain in orphanages. By 2100 the last United States orphanage will have been closed.

On the farm nearly all aged parents used to live with one of their children. This custom was carried to the city by rural migrants but has long been declining among urban families in advanced states. It will continue to decline indefinitely.

Every rise in average real wages and pensions permits more aged urban parents to maintain their own homes. And every advance in medical care for adults enables more parents to live and work to a ripe old age in good health and unwidowed. Hence the proportion of aged parents able and eager to maintain a separate home is much higher in advanced states than in backward states. It will continue to rise slowly until the great majority of aged parents in all countries live apart from their children. They will therefore become less and less available as housekeepers and baby sitters.

Housekeeping

Industrialization, urbanization, and technological progress in housekeeping have already revolutionized home life in advanced states, but most of the changes are still incomplete and will continue for decades or centuries in these states. In backward states they have barely begun and will therefore speed up and continue much longer.

In farm families most husbands, wives, and older children work at home. In the city nearly all husbands, many older children, and many wives work outside the home for wages. The percentage of American wives (husbands present) who work outside the home rose from 5 percent in 1890 to 30 percent in 1960. It will rise above 40 percent by 2000 and above 80 percent by 2200.

Since 1917 the Soviet Union has pioneered in increasing the proportion of women who work outside the home. In 1960, women made up 48 percent of the Soviet labor force. Heavy military losses in World Wars I and II were partly responsible for this high ratio, which may decline slightly when the male-female ratio becomes normal. By 2300, however, over 45 percent of the labor force in all countries will be female.

The chore of personal shopping for groceries and other convenience goods will gradually be lightened by the growth of mail-order and telephone-order buying and home delivery. In America the rapid growth of automobile use has caused a temporary trend away from telephone ordering and home delivery, but this trend will reverse itself, probably before 2000, and thereafter such purchase of convenience goods will expand steadily.

By 2200 most retail buying of convenience goods will be done by means of communication devices which connect each home with the nearest retail store or wholesale warehouse. These devices will permit any person to order from his home by punching or dialing catalogue numbers, and most orders will be delivered within a few hours. Standing orders will be delivered regularly without repeated ordering. A single delivery service will handle all home deliveries—mail, milk, groceries, clothing. Within apartment buildings nearly all retail deliveries will be completed by mechanical means, without disturbing the tenants. The shift from personal shopping to home ordering of retail goods will save the average family several hours a week and greatly diminish street traffic and store parking lots.

America has long led the world in the invention and use of labor-saving cooking and housekeeping aids—electric refrigerators and freezers, vacuum cleaners, washing machines and dryers, contour sheets, drip-dry clothing. The number and efficiency of such aids will continue to grow throughout the next 500 years, and their use will rise steadily in all countries. By 2060, Europe will have as many electric refrigerators, washing machines, hot-water heaters, garbage disposals, etc., per thousand persons as the United States had in 1960; by 2200 all Asiatic and African countries will be as well or better equipped. And increasing co-operative use of the most expensive items—washing machines, ironers, dryers, floor polishing machines, etc.—will make such equipment more and more productive, especially during the next century or two, before they are universally available.

Another long-obvious trend which will continue indefinitely to reduce the burden of housekeeping is the development and use of more and more prepared foods—canned, frozen, powdered, baked, etc. The sale of prepared and semi-prepared food will continue to increase faster than total retail food sales for centuries. By 2100 most home-prepared meals in advanced countries will consist largely of fully prepared food which is merely opened, seasoned, and warmed at home. And most dishes will either be discarded or washed, dried, and stored in automatic dishwashers.

In homes where husbands and wives both work, the more arduous or time-consuming chores—window washing, floor scrubbing, laundry, rug cleaning, etc.—will be increasingly turned over to outside professionals, who will use more expensive, more specialized, and more wisely chosen equipment and materials and will be much better trained in such work than housewives. By

2100 over half these housecleaning chores in Western countries will be performed by such specialists; by 2300, over 90 percent.

In advanced societies the share of the labor force employed as domestic servants has been falling for 50 to 100 years, and it will continue to decline indefinitely. In the United States it fell from 7.5 percent in 1870 to 2.6 percent in 1960, and it will fall well below 1.0 percent by 2100.

The less advanced the country, the larger the share of the labor force employed as domestic servants. Economic progress raises the real wages of servants faster than the real incomes of the average upper-class family, and the growing use of labor-saving housekeeping utensils and machines reduces the need for domestic help. Both these trends will continue for centuries in all countries. By 2500 less than one family in a thousand, in any country, will have a full-time domestic servant.

The previously predicted growth in world population and in concentration of population in areas with superb climates and pleasing views will make the land most suitable for residential use ever more valuable. Furthermore, families will continue to become smaller, and children will be at home less and less of the time. Also, housing is cheaper per square foot in apartment buildings, and the cost of heating and air conditioning is less. Finally, by housing more people in apartment buildings, city planners can enable many more people to walk to work, schools, and shops and can solve smog and traffic problems more easily. Hence more and more people will live in apartment buildings, which will become ever larger and taller.

From 1900 to 1930 some 20 percent of new United States urban dwelling units were in multi-family (three or more) buildings. Due to the great depression and to the growing use of automobiles, this ratio fell sharply after 1930, and averaged about 13 percent over the next 25 years. After a low of 8 percent in 1955 it rose to a new all-time high of 34 percent in 1963. It should reach 40 percent by the year 2000 and 70 percent by 2100.

In more crowded advanced countries the proportion of apartment-house dwellers is much higher than in America, and the automobile has not yet had its full decentralizing effect; but in the long run, apartments will replace more and more single-family dwellings in their cities for the same reasons as in the United States. This trend will simplify housekeeping and make it easier for wives to work outside the home.

Marriage and Divorce

Since men and women are usually almost equal in number, most marriages have always been monogamous. But polygamy has been common among the upper classes of many societies. It still is practiced legally in some backward countries and illegally in all advanced capitalist countries. As incomes become less unequal, between men and women and between rich and poor, both legal and illegal polygamy will decline steadily. The number of countries which legally permit polygamy will fall to zero by 2100, and the proportion of men who can afford to support a mistress as well as a wife will decrease for centuries throughout the world.

The vital problem of how to increase the number of happy marriages has received little attention from scientists, primarily because the funds available for such research have been insignificant. One of the most important future social trends affecting marriage will be a rapid and continuous increase in spending on such research. By 2100 such spending will exceed $2 billion a year in the United States.

The limited research already done shows that marriages between persons with similar education and/or interests are much more apt to be happy than other marriages. Fortunately, educational trends will increase greatly the number of such marriages. As explained earlier, coeducation in secondary and higher schools will continue to grow, and secondary and higher education will continue to expand, until most young people are attending coeducational schools when they decide to marry. Moreover, students will be increasingly segregated according to ability and interests in ever more specialized secondary and higher schools.

As a result more and more young people will marry current or recent fellow students with similar ability, education, and interests.

In capitalist Europe and Latin America marriages between fellow students or graduates at the same university are now probably less than 0.2 percent of all marriages. This rate will rise above 2 percent by 2000, above 6 percent by 2100, and above 20 percent by 2500. Moreover, rates for marriages between university graduates with degrees in the same subjects will rise much faster. By 2200 over 20 percent of all male doctors in the world will be married to female doctors—as compared with less than 1 percent in 1960—and many more will be married to nurses and scientists.

Such marriages will greatly increase the proportion of gifted children, as well as of happy husbands and wives. Hence governments will take more and more effective measures to promote these marriages.

Ability, education, and interests are not the only factors which markedly affect marital happiness. Sexual, emotional, and other factors are significant. As scientific research reveals more about such factors, parents, young people, educators, and government officials will give them more and more attention. By 2200 all secondary and higher schools in the world will teach their students how to select a mate wisely. All students will be carefully tested to discover and measure traits which should be considered in marital decisions. The information obtained will be used more and more by social directors and parents to throw similar marriageable young people together, and it will be increasingly revealed to the dating partners considering marriage.

During the past century the annual number of American divorces has gradually risen from about 3 percent to over 25 percent of the annual number of marriages. Similar trends prevail in all advanced states which have liberal divorce laws. And the more advanced the country, the more liberal are its divorce laws. Furthermore, the great majority of experts on family life advocate more liberalization of divorce laws. Therefore divorce laws will be further liberalized and divorce rates will continue to rise in all countries. Most European rates should reach the 1960 American level by 2060.

The United States divorce rate is much more difficult to predict, because it is already so high. It will not rise nearly as fast as European rates, but it should rise another 50 percent by 2060. In those American states with the most liberal divorce laws, such as California, it is already 50 percent above the national average. Furthermore, religious objections to divorce are certain to weaken indefinitely. On the other hand, progress in education, birth control, marriage counseling, and eugenics should soon check and eventually reverse the rising trend in the United States divorce rate among families with children. This trend probably will turn down permanently before 2100.

Although they have changed greatly during the past century, legal divorce procedures are still costly and irrational, even in the most advanced nations. They are usually handled by lawyers and judges untrained in psychology, psychiatry, and marital problems. They often require or induce bitter public trials which are widely reported in the press. Fortunately a growing number of experts on marriage and divorce have urged that divorce cases be handled by professionally trained experts working in complete privacy and free to use their best professional judgment, and such proposals are certain to be adopted more and more widely. By 2100 all divorces in advanced countries will be handled privately by professional non-legal experts employed by administrative agencies. Parents with minor children will be increasingly required to accept reconciliation aid and advice over a period of months before being granted a divorce, but no person who persists in demanding a divorce will be denied one for more than a year.

Granting freedom of divorce to childless couples—inevitable before 2100 in most countries—amounts to sanctioning trial marriage. Eventually this will be recognized, and trial marriages will be legally distinguished from semi-permanent (child-producing) marriages and separately regulated. By 2200 most young couples in advanced countries will be encouraged by their parents and their marriage counselors to practice childless trial marriage for one or two years before formally entering a semi-permanent marriage. Long before 2500 such trial marriages will be compulsory in all countries, but divorce after a trial marriage will always be voluntary.

Legal and social acceptance of birth control and trial marriage, full employment for young men and women, and state-subsidized higher education will remove many barriers to early marriage. It seems likely, therefore, that, by 2200 most people in advanced countries will enter their first or only trial marriage before age eighteen and will try two or more trial marriages before entering a semi-permanent marriage. On the other hand, the growing practice of childless trial marriage will help greatly to reduce the divorce rate among married couples with children.

The Western custom of requiring men to pay alimony to their divorced wives arose in the Middle Ages when wives owned little property and could rarely earn a living. Yet nearly all divorced husbands are still required to pay alimony in advanced countries where women own much property, can usually earn a living, normally remarry after divorce, and often have no minor children by the husband. This is a perfect example of a cultural lag. Sweden has already virtually abolished alimony. More and more experts are recommending a radical reduction in the number, amount, and duration of alimony awards. Such recommendations will gradually be adopted in all countries. By 2100 few divorced wives in advanced countries will receive alimony for more than one year.

Imprisonment for non-payment of alimony is now fairly common in America. Condemned by a growing majority of experts, it will be ended in nearly all states of the Union before 2000.

Alimony payments are distinct from child-support payments. The latter will continue to rise in advanced states for 50 to 100 years as real wages and the number of divorces rise. However, the growth of childless trial marriages, government child-support subsidies, and free services for children—educational, medical, etc.—will reverse this trend in such states during the twenty-first century.

Friendship

Nearly all people want more friends or more congenial friends than they now have. The recent migration of a large part of the population of advanced states from farms and villages to towns and cities has disrupted traditional ways of making friends, and many city dwellers have failed to find sufficient new ways. Loneliness is common and depressing among them.

For these reasons social scientists will become increasingly interested in the problem of promoting congenial friendships and social activities and will spend ever larger sums on relevant research. Such expenditures, negligible now, will exceed one billion dollars a year in the United States by 2200. They will result in better and better methods of making and keeping suitable friends.

To promote wise friendship and marriage, all governments will eventually establish special agencies. These agencies will design suitable cultural, medical, psychiatric, and other tests and require all children and adults to take them. The results of these tests will be used to bring together congenial people in each school, plant, and neighborhood. Full-time professional social directors will be employed in each large school, plant, or neighborhood to promote suitable friendships and marriages by making needed introductions and by arranging social gatherings for congenial prospective friends and mates. These directors will introduce all new students, workers, and residents to those old ones with whom they are most likely to be congenial. And they will continue thereafter to facilitate and promote friendship between such persons.

It is noteworthy that the growing segregation of school and college students by ability, predicted earlier, will greatly increase the number of satisfying long-term friendships formed in childhood. Moreover, extensive research on friendship formation will suggest many new methods of making and keeping friends, some of which will be suitable for repeated use by individuals. Such methods will eventually be taught to all students in school.

By 2200, when most housing will be state-owned and state-managed, many neighborhoods and apartment houses will be restricted to residents whom social directors have determined to be most likely to form congenial friendships or who have already formed such friendships. Equalization of personal incomes will gradually lower many traditional bars to congenial social life.

Finally the continuous future growth of scientific vocational guidance and of vocational segregation due to the growing concentration of like activities in ever larger plants and offices will promote social relationships among like-minded and congenial workers. Men with common vocational interests and experience have much more to talk about than other men.

CHAPTER XVI

Crime

Many changes and trends predicted in previous chapters will affect future developments in crime prevention and detection, criminal trials, and the treatment of criminals. Progress in child care, education, health services, the provision of full and suitable employment, and social insurance will be especially effective in reducing crime. In this chapter trends in other and more direct methods of reducing crime and detecting and treating criminals will be predicted.

Crime Prevention and Detection

The functions of directly preventing and detecting crime and catching and treating criminals are now performed badly, even in the most advanced countries. Great changes are inevitable.

Scientific research on these functions has barely begun. It will expand a hundredfold during the next century or two. By 2200 the world will spend more on such research than it now spends on weapons research. This research will develop many entirely new methods of preventing crime and catching and treating criminals.

It is already possible to predict some major changes in these methods. First, all police and penal functions will gradually be transferred from local to regional to national to world government and integrated into a single world system. In the United States most metropolitan areas now have several, and some have twenty to fifty, independent police forces, each with its own crime records, jail, radio communication system, purchasing office, etc.

These will be increasingly merged into larger units, until by 2100 no county or metropolitan area will have more than one police force. Then these regional police forces will be merged into state police forces or into a single national police system. In the meantime the functions and staff of American state police forces and the FBI will grow much faster than those of local police. By 2200 all nations will have merged their local and regional police and penal systems into national systems. By 2500 all such national systems will have been merged into a single world police system.

This gradual integration of police systems will permit and result in an ever-growing specialization of function among policemen and among prisons. Detectives will specialize more and more in certain classes of crime. Parole officers will specialize increasingly in handling one class of parolees. Prisons will be designed and run to handle ever narrower classes of prisoners.

Third, the training and education of all police, parole, and prison officials will gradually be improved, prolonged, and specialized. By 2100 nearly all police chiefs and prison wardens in advanced countries will have Ph.D. degrees in police or prison work, and most police and parole officers will have university degrees in their fields.

Fourth, regional and national police systems will gradually assemble more and more complete files containing the names, addresses, photographs, descriptions, signatures, fingerprints, voice prints, occupational records, car types and license numbers, police records, etc., first for every known delinquent or criminal and later for every citizen. New methods of identifying any person from his signature, photograph, vocal record, hair, blood, etc., will be developed. By 2100, national police offices will have machines which can almost instantly identify and pull or copy the file card of any person when presented with a uniquely identifying fact or combination of facts. Local police will be able to present such data by wire or wireless and secure an almost immediate reply.

The accumulation of the data needed for such files will be speeded up by requiring ever larger groups of citizens to provide such data. By 2200 all people in the world will be required to provide their government with all data useful for police work, social research, eugenic reform, and other social purposes. Moreover, every person will then have an identification number indelibly inscribed on his body, and all police data will be filed according to these numbers.

Fifth, lie detectors will continually be improved and used more and more often in criminal investigations. By 2060 nearly all criminal suspects will be required to take improved lie-detector tests, and all parolees will be required to take them weekly or monthly for several years. By 2200 all persons over some minimum age, perhaps twelve, will be required to take lie-detector tests annually. The first question will be, "Have you committed any crimes the past year?" Only if the answer to this question arouses suspicion will further questions be asked, each designed to narrow the area of suspicion as rapidly as possible.

Sixth, wire tapping and electronic eavesdropping by police will remain or become legal in all countries, and equipment used for these purposes will steadily be improved. Police will soon be able to identify voice prints almost as accurately as they can now identify fingerprints. It usually is more desirable to reduce crime than to preserve personal privacy. Moreover, as police and courts become more honest and competent, the danger of blackmail or unpleasant publicity due to such invasions of privacy will steadily diminish. Policemen will eventually learn to keep personal secrets even better than physicians now do.

Seventh, the use of cash to buy any good worth more than a small sum (five dollars?), the possession of cash in excess of a certain amount (one hundred dollars?), and the use of more than one checking or savings account for paying living expenses will be increasingly restricted and eventually prohibited. These restrictions will be applied first to parolees in advanced countries, and before 2200 to all persons in the world. Police will be increasingly authorized to examine the resulting, ever more informative, personal bank statements without any court order. Eventually bank bookkeeping machines will automatically pick out for police inspection suspicious personal bank statements, such as those containing unusual deposit entries.

Eighth, the ownership of firearms by private persons will be gradually restricted and eventually prohibited. This prohibition will be effectively enforced throughout the world by 2100. More and more police will stop carrying firearms. They will in time be armed with new weapons which temporarily blind, paralyze, or tranquilize their human targets and do not seriously wound or kill them. Target and hunting rifles will be available for temporary use in suitable surroundings but will be locked up in clubhouses otherwise. All new guns will soon be test-fired, and the resulting bullet markings noted and recorded, so that police will be able to identify the source of bullets found at the scene of a crime. In the meantime, while criminals are still able to obtain firearms easily, police will increasingly be equipped with bulletproof vests and helmets, when dealing with armed criminals.

Ninth, more and more countries will allow doctors to prescribe free or cheap habit-forming drugs for poor addicts under their care and to do so indefinitely on a sustaining basis for addicts who cannot be induced to voluntarily stop using drugs. Much crime is due to the efforts of addicts to obtain drugs or the money to buy them at high prices from illegal vendors. If addicts could obtain sustaining doses from doctors, most of this crime would stop. Only thrill seekers would then buy from illegal vendors, and they would never be in fear of withdrawal pains. This reform, already partly adopted in Great Britain, will be adopted in the United States before 2060. Support for it among experts has grown steadily in recent decades.

Tenth, many forms of gambling will be legalized in most American states before 2060 in order to reduce drastically the large revenues criminals now secure from illegal gambling and to divert more gambling profits to public treasuries. Laws against gambling are now difficult to enforce. Public and expert support for the creation of state lotteries and carefully regulated and stiffly taxed legal private gambling has been growing. Hence many American states will create profitable state lotteries before 2100 and/or will license private gambling houses.

But gambling will not remain legal indefinitely. As governments and police agencies become more efficient, as men become better-educated concerning the harmful effects of gambling, public opinion will again turn against legal gambling. By 2300 both commercial and high-stake private gambling will be universally illegal. And these future anti-gambling laws will be effectively enforced with ease, because all substantial cash payments will then be made by bank check or credit.

To eliminate temporarily another major source of criminal revenue and power, most countries which have made commercial or individual prostitution illegal will repeal the relevant laws before 2060. Later, when police forces have become much more honest and efficient and criminals have become far less numerous, commercial (but not individual) prostitution will again, or for the first time, become illegal in all countries.

Finally more and more cities, states, and countries will begin to reward private citizens who aid the police in detecting crimes and catching criminals. At present nearly all persons who aid the police are penalized. They lose time in informing the police, are not adequately paid for time spent as witnesses, often are insulted or humiliated in court, and occasionally are threatened or punished by criminals. By 2100 most countries will have adopted a system of liberal pecuniary and honorary rewards which will make it normally profitable, as well as honorable, for nearly all citizens to aid the police.

Criminal Trials

Radical changes in criminal-court procedure are inevitable during the next 500 years, and the most significant will come during the next century or two.

First, the wide differences in such procedure among different countries, even among the most advanced countries, will be gradually reduced, until by 2500 all nations will have almost the same criminal-court procedures. This adoption of more and more uniform procedures will be largely due to the growth of scientific criminology, to the general factors making for cultural homogenization (discussed earlier), and to the rise of an increasingly centralized world government. Since European court procedures have long been, and will long continue to be, more advanced than African and Asiatic procedures, the result will be continued Europeanization of African and Asiatic procedures.

Mankind has as yet spent only negligible amounts on the scientific study of criminal-court procedures. During the next century or two it will spend an ever larger share of its GNP on such research. Experimental courts will be established in most advanced countries before 2100, and these courts will scientifically test all old and new hypotheses concerning the efficient operation of criminal courts. The pursuit of absolute moral justice will gradually be replaced by efforts to achieve socially expedient verdicts more economically. By 2200 investment in such scientific research will exceed 10 percent of the world's annual expenditures on criminal court trials. It now amounts to much less than 0.1 percent of such expenditures.

Third, criminal trials will become increasingly private. The Canons of Professional Ethics of the American Bar Association will be amended before 2000 to prohibit the release by lawyers of any material relating to a trial, either before or during the trial. And American judges will soon begin to use their rule-making and contempt powers to prevent police and other law-enforcement officers from releasing any information about persons charged with crimes until the trial is over. Newspaper comment on criminal trials will be more and more restricted, until by 2100 nearly all trials will be completely private. Even the verdicts will eventually become confidential, except perhaps in trials of wide and justifiable public interest. By 2200, United States criminal investigations and trials will be as confidential as medical examinations and diagnoses now are.

Fourth, the Anglo-Saxon rule that persons accused of crime cannot be required to take the witness stand or testify against themselves will be gradually relaxed, and completely abandoned before 2100. This rule was adopted in an age when torture was widely used to force confessions, as a means of making such coercion less useful to undemocratic governments. Of course, police still commonly resort to undue physical or psychological pressure to obtain confessions, but such practices have long been declining and will continue to do so. Hence the only justification for the rule against self-incrimination will gradually weaken.

Fifth, more and more testimony and evidence obtained by means of lie detectors will be admitted and used in criminal trials. Such evidence is now inadmissible in United States courts on the ground that it results in self-incrimination or that it is unreliable. Self-incrimination will be allowed before 2100, for reasons noted above. Lie detectors will become more reliable. And the argument that evidence should be rejected unless it is completely reliable will become less and less influential. Scientists welcome evidence which suggests that any significant claim is *probably* true, even when the probability is low, and judges and criminologists are certain to become more and more scientific.

Sixth, evidence concerning previous proven or charged offenses will be collected and considered in all criminal trials before 2100. There never has been a good reason for excluding such evidence. Unqualified juries may of course give such evidence undue weight, but this argument may be used against the submission of any relevant evidence. Information concerning previous crimes is as relevant in a criminal hearing as information concerning previous illness in a medical or psychiatric examination.

Seventh, defendants in criminal trials will be increasingly defended by public defenders—criminal lawyers paid by the state—who will be given more and more adequate funds and staff to gather evidence and hire experts. The first public-defender office in America began its work in Los Angeles County in 1941. By 1964 the number of such offices had risen to 186, but 3,000 counties still lacked such an office. By 2100 all advanced governments will provide free and adequate tax-supported legal aid to all indigent persons accused of crime. By 2200 all criminal lawyers will be civil servants assigned to cases by their superiors. The best criminal lawyers will then be as available to the poor as to the rich.

Eighth, the proportion of accused persons held in jail until their trial will decline steadily, for several reasons. The average amount of bail required from most classes of accused persons will decline, costs per dollar of bail will fall, and the accused will become more affluent. Police will become more and more efficient in finding accused persons who flee to avoid trial, which will make high bail requirements less and less necessary. And holding innocent men in jail is costly and harmful to the innocent.

Ninth, the proportion of accused persons who are required to post bail to obtain their freedom pending criminal trial will decline rapidly in advanced countries. As police become more efficient, the need for bail to ensure appearance in court will decline. Moreover, requiring bail discriminates unreasonably against men unable to secure bail or pay its costs. A growing number of lawyers and experts have protested against such discrimination, and a few American courts have recently begun to reduce it. By 2060 nearly all Americans accused of crime for the first time will be released without bail pending their trial. Only felony parole violaters accused of new felonies will then be held in jail until their trial, and rich and poor will be treated alike.

Tenth, corruption, discrimination, and wasteful competition among bail bondsmen will steadily be reduced, both by increasing government regulation and by creating private or public bail-bond monopolies. Most states of the Union will establish bail-bond monopolies before 2060.

Eleventh, the use of juries in criminal cases will decline steadily until it finally is abolished, probably before 2100 in the United States. Juries were originally introduced to protect the accused against biased or subservient judges chosen by undemocratic rulers. As governments become more democratic and judges become more impartial, the justification for juries in criminal cases steadily weakens. Moreover, impartial judges are much superior to jurors as judges of the facts, as well as of the law, because they are better-educated and far more experienced in the evaluation of evidence. Finally, the use of jurors is much more costly than the use of judges alone. Indeed, it is so costly that United States police and prosecuting attorneys have had to induce 80 percent of all indicted persons to plead guilty and give up their right to a jury trial. Censurable methods are used to obtain guilty pleas and confessions—holding prisoners in jail until trial, denial of competent legal advice, the third degree, reduction of charges—but are excused by the need to reduce the number of long, costly jury trials.

Twelfth, the rule that persons accused of crime must be proven guilty beyond a reasonable doubt will be abandoned and replaced by a rule based upon statistical probability theory—perhaps that when the odds supporting guilt are 7 to 3 or better, conviction is justified. The present rule was developed during an age when most felons were executed. It has allowed many dangerous criminals to escape conviction and commit new crimes. It is often said that it is better to acquit the guilty than to convict the innocent. This once plausible maxim is dubious now and will certainly become false when convicts are properly treated by trained scientific penologists. Nearly all first offenders will then be paroled, and few if any innocent persons are likely to be convicted twice. Finally verdicts of guilt will eventually state the probability of guilt, just as some medical diagnoses now do, and scientific treatment of convicts will be affected by this probability finding.

Thirteenth, the practice of compensating persons acquitted of criminal charges, now rare, will spread until it becomes universal. Millions of innocent persons have been arrested and tried at great inconvenience and cost to them. Such errors are inevitable in any court system, but the costs should be borne by society, not by a few innocent members. Public and expert acceptance of this principle is growing and will result in more and more laws to compensate acquitted persons for legal costs, lost wages, and personal worry or humiliation. Full compensation should be universal by 2200.

Fourteenth, the rule that a man cannot be tried twice for the same offense will be repealed. It is as unsound scientifically as the rule that a sick man may not be examined twice for the same illness. It may once have been politically justified by governmental persecution of persons by means of repeated trials, but the obvious long-run solution of this problem is to improve governments, not to prohibit retrials of acquitted persons when important new evidence has been uncovered. Requiring governments to pay the full costs of all trials of acquitted persons will also greatly reduce the danger of persecution. By 2100 retrial of acquitted persons on the same charge will be legal in most advanced countries; by 2200, in all countries.

The use of torture and harsh, prolonged pre-trial confinement to secure confessions or guilty pleas from criminal suspects will decline steadily and indefinitely. This trend has long been obvious to historians, but many give the false impression that it has neared its limit, especially in advanced democratic countries. In fact, many, perhaps most, American police forces still use mild torture, called the third degree, or the threat of such torture to secure confessions. And district attorneys often allow suspects to remain in a cold, overcrowded, or dirty jail for weeks or months in order to secure a guilty plea. The growing use of lie detectors, wire tapping, fingerprints, and other scientific methods of crime detection will continue indefinitely to make mistreatment of suspects less defensible. Increased central supervision of local police forces and jails will also reduce use of the third degree. For instance, the United States government will soon begin to interview released jail and prison inmates to determine whether they were mistreated. By 2060 physical mistreatment of criminal suspects will have declined at least another 50 percent, and statistics to demonstrate this trend will be available.

Sixteenth, the adversary system of conducting criminal trials will be abandoned by 2100. Prosecutors and defense lawyers will gradually be replaced by impartial investigators and experts paid by public agencies. This reform will end efforts by hired and biased lawyers to hide or distort the facts, intimidate witnesses, and use purely emotional arguments. It will speed up trials, reduce court costs, and give poor men more equal chances for a fair trial.

Seventeenth, legal training of criminal lawyers and judges will be increasingly replaced by training in criminology, penology, and psychiatry. The criminal-court judges of the year 2200 will be psychiatrists who have specialized in the study of criminal behavior, not lawyers who have specialized in criminal law. And they will conduct all criminal trials more like 1960 insanity hearings and medical examinations than like 1960 criminal trials.

Finally, the common modern rule that criminal trials should consider only the specific charges in a formal criminal indictment will gradually be abandoned. When a doctor examines a patient, he does not look for evidence of certain diseases only. He looks for evidence of any disease, and his diagnosis reports all diseases or defects found. Court trials will become more and more like medical examinations in this respect as well as in others. At present judges carefully exclude evidence of crimes not specifically charged in the indictment. By 2200 all judges in advanced countries will allow and consider evidence of any crime when considering serious charges. Every felony verdict will then be a judgment on the entire past life and current character of the accused, not merely a judgment concerning a single criminal charge.

The Treatment of Criminals

During the past 200 years the most important social trend in the treatment of criminals has been a humanitarian one, the continuous replacement of punishments by less severe ones. This trend will continue for many years, especially in backward countries, but the most significant general trend throughout the next 500 years will be the further replacement of punishment or protective detention of criminals by ever more effective corrective treatment. This latter trend is not new, but it will grow faster and continue much longer than the humanitarian trend.

The precise forms these general trends take will be increasingly determined by scientific research, expenditures on which will rise relatively for centuries. Nevertheless, many specific changes and trends are predictable. The annual number of executions will continue to fall steadily, fines will increasingly replace prison sentences, the proportion of convicts who perform suitable labor will rise, more and more convicts sentenced to prison will serve indeterminate terms, a growing proportion of convicts will be paroled, and work paroles will be increasingly used.

In 1800, England still had over one hundred capital crimes. Petty thieves and children were often hanged publicly. In 1960 the United States had only seven capital crimes. By 2000 neither the United States nor Great Britain will have any capital crimes.

The annual number of criminals executed has been declining for over 200 years in nearly all countries and will continue to decline, until by 2100 no prisoners will be executed anywhere in the world. In this trend the United States has lagged behind other advanced countries. Several European countries abolished capital punishment in the nineteenth century, and others in the twentieth. But United States executions still averaged 167 (82 Negro) a year in the 1930's. This annual average fell to 72 (38 Negro) in the 1950's, and to 21 (8 Negro) in 1963. It should reach zero before the year 2000.

The proportion of criminals who are fined rather than imprisoned will increase steadily for centuries. As real wages rise, as unemployment is reduced, as personal incomes become less unequal, as the police and courts become more efficient and punishment therefore more certain, monetary fines will serve ever more effectively as deterrents to crime. Moreover, imprisonment will become more and more costly as real wages rise. And most criminals can be treated by psychiatrists and otherwise re-educated or reformed as easily outside as inside prison. Finally, fines collected from criminals can and will increasingly be used to compensate the victims of crime, which itself will prove a useful part of the re-education of criminals. By 2200 over 90 percent of all sane felons will be fined rather than imprisoned. It will be easy to collect large fines on the installment plan when all personal income passes through a single state bank, as predicted in Chapter VII.

A growing majority of criminologists have advised that all prisoners should be steadily employed at suitable work while in prison. Breaking rocks or other such hard labor is rarely suitable. Nearly all prisoners with work skills should perform work which uses or increases such skills, and untrained workers should be trained and employed at work which they can, and probably will, continue after leaving prison. This expert advice has been and will long continue to be increasingly followed by prison officials. The gradual elimination of unemployment, predicted earlier, will help to reduce public opposition to useful employment of convicts in non-communist countries. By 2100 all convicts in advanced capitalist countries will be steadily engaged in suitable work or vocational training. This goal has already been largely achieved in communist countries.

In recent decades more and more convicted criminals have been given partially indeterminate prison sentences instead of fixed terms or have been given substantial time off for good behavior. This trend is both humanitarian (because it reduces most prison terms) and corrective (because it induces better behavior). It will continue, until by 2100 all criminals sentenced to confinement will be given completely indeterminate terms and will be released from confinement whenever their psychiatrists consider this desirable.

The use of parole or conditional release has grown greatly during the past century, and it will continue to grow until it becomes universal. More and more convicted first offenders will be fined and immediately released on parole. And a steadily growing proportion of released prisoners will be on parole. Moreover, as prison sentences become fewer and shorter, parole periods will become longer and parole supervision more intensive and efficient. By 2200 most first-time felons will be heavily fined and released on parole, but the parole period will last for years and will include periodic lie-detector tests and compulsory psychiatric treatment.

In America paroles are now commonly granted by state parole boards consisting of well-meaning but untrained men unacquainted with the prisoners who come before them. This method will gradually be replaced by a system which permits professional prison wardens and psychiatrists to grant parole at their discretion to men under their care. This reform will be completed in all American states before 2100.

Many prisoners who are not good risks for immediate full parole are good risks for work parole, that is, for release from prison each working day during working hours and the time required to go and come from work. And work parole makes it much easier to provide suitable work for prisoners. Hence the practice of work parole will grow steadily. By 2100 work parole will become a customary transitional stage between full imprisonment and full parole.

It is difficult for convicted criminals to secure employment, and many former convicts return to a life of crime because they cannot find work. Hence all advanced countries will gradually adopt increasingly effective measures to provide jobs for all released criminals. However, it would obviously be unreasonable to provide work for criminals but not for unemployed non-criminals. And there are many other reasons why all governments will assure jobs to all who want to work. As predicted in Chapter V, such reasons will soon induce all advanced countries to ensure suitable jobs for all who want to work, including former convicts.

The Volume of Crime

We know little about the amount of crime and the number of criminals in advanced countries, because scientific research on these questions has been grossly inadequate. Available statistics on reported crimes have usually been prepared by policemen untrained in criminology and statistics. Moreover, America has fifty states with different criminal definitions and laws and thousands of independent police forces, each free to interpret and prepare statistics in its own way. And many crimes are unreported. As predicted earlier, all these conditions will change gradually but radically during the next few centuries, and these changes will make criminal statistics more and more accurate. By 2100 most advanced countries will have reasonably complete and accurate statistical data on all aspects of crime.

The best crude estimates suggest that the United States had about two million hardened criminals in 1950, of whom only 170,000 were in prison. Thus such criminals made up about 3 percent of the male population over seventeen years of age. Whether this proportion had risen or fallen significantly during the previous century is unknown. But future trends in crime prevention, criminal-court procedure, and treatment of criminals (predicted earlier in this chapter), and in wages and employment (predicted in earlier chapters) will begin to reduce the relative volume of crime and the proportion of criminals in the United States before 2050, and this decline will continue throughout the next 500 years. By 2500 the proportion of hardened male criminals in the United States, and in all other countries, will be less than 0.1 percent.

On the other hand, reliable future studies of crime may well reveal that the volume of crime increased in the United States and other advanced countries during most or all of the twentieth century, due to such temporary factors as rapid urbanization and the introduction of the automobile, both of which facilitate crime and the escape of criminals. These and other temporary crime-promoting factors will cease to operate in the long run, while most long-run crime-reducing factors will continue to operate indefinitely.

CHAPTER XVII

Religion and Philosophy

In each field of thought, human reasoning passes through three major stages of development: the religious or theological stage, in which conclusions are based ultimately on revelation; the rational or philosophical stage, in which conclusions are ultimately based on the light of reason or rational intuition; and the scientific stage, in which conclusions are based on systematic observation of phenomena. Since most thinkers in some fields of thought and many thinkers in every field of thought are still in the first or second stage of intellectual development, even in advanced countries, this famous Comtean theory of inevitable intellectual evolution suggests many valid predictions concerning future intellectual and social changes.

Nearly all of the social trends and changes predicted in earlier chapters of this book will be partly, often largely, due to the spread and improvement of scientific thinking. However, men usually adopt more scientific ways of thinking without realizing that they are abandoning pre-scientific ways of thinking and acting. Indeed, they often go to great lengths to persuade themselves or the public that they are not abandoning such older ways of thinking. Hence, few of the trends in opinion or social behavior predicted in previous chapters are commonly thought of as changes in religion or philosophy, or as the result of such changes. In this chapter, I shall predict social changes which are most likely to be widely recognized as such changes, or the result of such changes, and which have not been discussed in earlier chapters.

Religion

Although churchmen consider religious faith and practices to be supremely significant, they have made little effort to prepare reliable statistics on major trends in religious opinion and behavior. During the next few centuries, they will steadily expand scientific research in these fields, and this will enable them to improve their methods of operation and propaganda. At present, however, the lack of reliable data on past religious trends makes scientific prediction of specific future trends relatively difficult. Nevertheless, a number of important religious trends can be scientifically predicted.

The principal world-wide religious trends during the next 500 years will be a continuation of seven trends long obvious in the West: a steady decline in the proportion of people who are religious—i.e., believe in a personal god or gods who answer prayer and reward men on earth and/or in a future life; a continuous decline in the proportion of religious persons who are fundamentalists by 1960 standards; a weakening of sectarianism in old sects; a continual world-wide growth of religious dissent; an ever-increasing separation between church and state; a long decline in church control over education, charity, and other non-religious activities; and a continuous decline in superstition. Furthermore, all Asiatic and African religions will be steadily Westernized throughout the next 500 years.

In the absence of relevant data on public-opinion polls, the most significant evidence of the long decline of religious faith in Europe and America is the steady rise of science. Most significant new scientific theories were condemned as heretical or atheistic by religious leaders. Copernicus, Bruno, Descartes, Galileo, Priestley, Erasmus Darwin, Charles Darwin, and Freud all feared and suffered from religious persecution. The rapid rise of science since 1500 is therefore proof of a steady decline in religious faith, at least among educated men.

Additional evidence of this decline is to be found in the continuous curtailment of government support of religion in advanced countries. During the sixteenth century European governments executed or severely punished hundreds of thousands of persons for witchcraft, heresy, dissent, or other purely religious crimes. Since then persecution of religious dissenters has continuously and obviously declined in Europe and America. Taxation to support religious organizations has been steadily reduced. Innumerable blue laws have been repealed. Many other illustrations of the curtailment of government support of religion could be cited. Since all governments are responsive to public opinion, this long and continuous trend suggests an equally long and steady decline in religious faith in advanced countries. And what has happened in such countries since 1600 will happen in less advanced countries during the next 300 years, insofar as it has not already occurred there.

American churches have published crude data which suggest a 300 percent increase in church membership (as a proportion of population) between 1850 and 1960. However, when adjusted by competent statisticians, these data actually reveal a decline from 1906 to 1940, and a rise from 1940 to 1960. This reversal of a previous longer trend was due to war and to cold war. United States church membership will resume its long-run decline as soon as the cold war, and the resulting increased economic and political pressures against non-religious persons, have eased sufficiently. Improved religious statistics will soon verify this prediction.

The scant available data on Sunday-school membership, church attendance, and, especially, donations to churches in Great Britain and the United States all suggest declining long-run trends. For instance, donations to eighteen representative American Protestant churches declined from 1.3 percent to 1.05 percent of personal income between 1930 and 1952, while average real personal income rose about 50 percent. If religious faith had not diminished, religious giving (a luxury expenditure) would have risen, and much faster than average real income.

Scientific opinion surveys of English and American university students have repeatedly revealed that they consider themselves less religious than their parents and that they are less religious than the general population. Other opinion surveys have shown that university professors are less religious than their students, and that the most eminent professors, scientists, and authors are less religious than their colleagues.

The long decline in religious faith and practice is due to the invention of printing, the growth of education and science, the movement of peasants to the city, the rise in real wages and in leisure to think and read, etc. All these factors will continue to operate throughout the next 500 years. Moreover, eugenic reforms will raise average human intelligence steadily after 2100. Hence religious faith and practice will continue to decline for centuries.

In recent decades normal long-run religious trends have been seriously distorted in certain countries by political and police measures. For instance, church attendance in the Soviet Union has been artificially and temporarily reduced below normal by Communist-party pressure. On the other hand, church attendance in several non-communist lands has been artificially and temporarily stimulated by political propaganda which identifies atheism with communism. A similar temporary religious revival occurred in England for similar reasons after the French Revolution. To determine normal long-run religious trends, one must look at countries less involved in the cold war and at pre-1940 or pre-1914 trends in the United States and the Soviet Union.

During the next century or two the most important general trends in religious opinion among believers will be from conservative to liberal religious views, not from theism to atheism. Religious people will continue to abandon the less plausible and satisfying dogmas of religion, such as those concerning hell, the devil, angels, the virgin birth, divorce, birth control, miracles, etc. They will pray and attend church less and less often. Atheism and agnosticism will continue to grow, especially among university graduates, but will not soon become dominant in countries where religion is free. In general the average Protestant will be as liberal theologically in 2300 as Unitarians are today.

Catholic dogmas and opinion will also move steadily to the left. The proportion of Catholics who use birth-control methods condemned by their church has risen steadily for over a century.

Liberal Catholic clergymen have increasingly called for a change in their church's official stand on birth control. It is almost certain, therefore, that the pope will approve one or more additional and more effective methods of birth control in the near future. Before 2100 he will approve all birth-control methods endorsed by the medical profession. He will also approve artificial insemination, euthanasia, marriage of priests (already approved by most United States priests), more liberal divorce laws and other such reforms. In the year 2200 the great majority of the Catholic clergy will be married men and women with small families limited by birth-control methods now condemned by their church. And priests, bishops, and all higher clergy will be chosen or elected by their subordinates, as in Protestant churches today.

Cremation of the dead was illegal or unpracticed in all Christian states in 1860. Most Christians still object to it for fear that it will prevent resurrection of the body after death or for other reasons. Nevertheless, the number of cremations in the most advanced countries has risen steadily and rapidly for over 60 years—to 3 percent of American, 20 percent of British, and 25 percent of Australian deaths. In such countries cremation is much more popular among the upper classes than among the lower. Moreover, religious objections to cremation will certainly decline, and the costs of burials, already high, will rise indefinitely. Hence cremation will continue to spread. By 2100 most corpses in all advanced states will be cremated. By 2500 nearly all corpses in the world will be cremated.

Belief in sectarian dogmas peculiar to any religious sect or group of sects—such as the belief that the Koran or the Bible is divinely inspired—will of course decline everywhere much more rapidly than belief in basic, universal religious dogmas, such as belief in gods, prayer, or a future life. The fact that sectarian beliefs are far less widespread than basic religious dogmas proves that they are less plausible or less satisfying or appealing than the dogmas. Growing inter-sectarian communication and contact and growing education will make most men ever more skeptical of distinctive or peculiar religious views. Opinions on religion, like those on every other subject, will become more and more uniform throughout the world for much longer than 500 years.

The practice of circumcising male infants soon after birth is now almost universal in some Christian lands—notably, the United States—and is rare in others, like Finland, which provide excellent medical care. It is a purely traditional sectarian religious practice and will therefore tend to decline faster than belief in basic religious dogmas. In 1960, 95 percent of all United States infants were circumcised, at a minor but significant cost in money, pain, and death. By 2100 this proportion will fall below 60 percent; by 2200 below 30 percent; and by 2500, below 5 percent.

The Christian practice of infant baptism is another sectarian religious custom which will decline throughout most of the next 500 years. It is essentially magical rather than religious, since infants do not understand it. All such purely magical or ceremonial practices will decline faster than beliefs in basic, more universal religious dogmas.

In all countries polytheism will continue to give way to monotheism, which is a more plausible and advanced religious dogma. Among Christians this trend will end in near universal acceptance of unitarianism as a dogma, not as a sect. Among Catholics it will result in a long decline in the proportion of prayers to saints and the Virgin Mary. Among Hindus and Buddhists it will result in the degradation of all minor gods and goddesses. By 2500 all great religions will be as insistent on monotheism as Moslems are now.

The decline of sectarianism among Protestants has recently brought about several mergers of similar Protestant sects. It will produce additional mergers throughout the next 500 years. But the effects of such mergers will be partly, perhaps largely, offset by the continuing creation and growth of new sects and religions. Christians will not unite in a single church or in a few large churches during the next 500 years.

The fourth major worldwide religious trend will be the continuous growth of religious dissent among religious people. This general trend is several hundred years old in the West and will continue for many more centuries. It includes two distinct component trends: the creation and above-average growth of new sects within old religions—like Mormonism, Christian Science, and Soka Gakkai; and the above-average growth of old minority sects and religions in areas previously relatively homogeneous in religious belief.

While belief in old sectarian dogmas will continue to decline among members of old (pre-1960) sects and religions, many new sects and religions will arise and flourish. This trend has long been obvious. New sects and religions have appeared continually and have often grown faster than old sects. It seems likely, therefore, that by the year 2500 most religious people will belong to sects or religions founded after 1960.

In the future, as in the past, almost every successful new sect will experience an initial period of missionary evangelism and fundamentalism. But thereafter the opinions of its members will steadily become more conventional and universal until most members have abandoned nearly all sectarian beliefs. Thus the continual creation and growth of new sects will not prevent a decline in sectarian differences among religious people as a whole.

In all countries where one sect or religion is now dominant, minority sects and religions will grow faster than it for centuries. In Catholic countries Protestantism will gain steadily in relative numbers and power, and vice versa. Moreover, non-Christian religions will do the same in all Christian countries, and vice versa. These trends will be continuously promoted by missionary activity and by international travel, study, and migration.

This relative gain of minority religions and sects will usually be slow. It will not materially change present religious ratios in many countries during the next century. But differences in population growth will seriously alter such ratios in the world as a whole in the near future. Since Asiatic peoples are growing much faster than Western peoples, the proportion of Christians in the world population declined from 35 percent in 1900 to 28 percent in 1960. It will decline below 20 percent by the year 2000 and below 15 percent by 2100.

The growth of new sects, the general decline in religion, and the liberalization of theology will inevitably bring about the disestablishment of those few sects which are still established. In 1750 almost every country had an established church. Since then the proportion has steadily fallen. This well-established trend is certain to continue. The number of experts who endorse it increases yearly. Disestablishment will be complete in all countries before 2100.

The use of public taxation or compulsory tithes to support religious worship is also certain to decline. It has long been opposed by non-religious people and by those sects which have been discriminated against. And today a growing number of religious liberals are criticizing the policy of taxing non-believers for the benefit of believers. All religious taxes and subsidies, including tax exemption, will end before 2200.

The use of government powers to support religion in other ways will steadily decline. The phrase "In God We Trust" will be removed from American coins, stamps, postmarks, and public buildings. Government support of military chaplains will end. The practice of opening legislative sessions with prayer will end. The use of religious oaths in court proceedings and in swearing in public officials will end. All these changes will be completed in the United States before 2200.

In the world as a whole the proportion of pupils taught in church schools has been declining for 200 years, and it will continue to decline for centuries. Peculiar local conditions may, however, increase the proportion of pupils in church schools in America for a few more decades. Thereafter the United States will follow the world trend.

Persecution of religious minorities is as old as religion and still persists in many countries. For instance, some Catholic countries still oppress Jews and Protestants, especially Protestant missionaries. And most communist states harass all religious groups. Such persecution, however, has been declining for centuries. It will continue to decline slowly for centuries more as men become better-educated, more intelligent, more prosperous, and less religious. By 2300, Jews and Protestants will be treated almost as well as Catholics in Spain, Jews will be treated as well as

Moslems in Egypt, and Moslems will be treated as well as Hindus in India.

Most religious organizations perform important non-religious functions—social, artistic, ceremonial, philanthropic, medical, psychiatric. Churches will continue to perform some of these functions for centuries, and these activities will continue to help keep many non-religious persons in religious organizations, but as these functions are taken over more and more fully by the state and by secular private organizations, non-religious church activities will steadily decline. One obvious evidence of this will be a gradual decline in the share of GNP spent by religious groups on charity and hospitals. By 2200 over 90 percent of all charity and 99 percent of hospital services will be provided by secular agencies in all countries.

The border line between religion and superstition is difficult to determine. One man's religion may be another man's superstition. But there are also many superstitions which are not commonly recognized as a part of any major contemporary religion—astrology, phrenology, belief in fortunetelling, fear of the evil eye, belief in witches and sorcerers, etc. Even in advanced countries most people still believe in one or more superstitions. But such faith will decline slowly and inevitably, for the same reasons that faith in more honored and respectable religious dogmas will decline. This trend will continue throughout the next 500 years, and will often be demonstrated by public-opinion polls.

It is far more difficult for an occidental to predict specific minor or regional religious trends in the Orient than to predict similar trends in the Occident. As noted earlier, my seven general religious predictions apply to the entire world. The most significant additional prediction about the Orient is that all oriental religions will gradually be westernized. For instance, Hindu and Buddhist polytheism will give way to monotheism. And their emphasis upon devils and unethical acts of their gods will steadily decline. All Moslem sects will abandon their endorsement of polygamy and the segregation and subordination of women before the year 2200. Most Hindus will become beef eaters by then. Such illustrations could be multiplied indefinitely, for nearly all the peculiar dogmas and practices of Oriental religions will be abandoned before 2500. Religion is largely the product of social conditions, and Oriental social conditions will continuously be westernized.

Ethics

For over two thousand years both priests and philosophers have taught that personal conduct should be governed by fundamental, universal ethical or moral principles. All major religions contain such principles. The Greek philosophers made ethics a major branch of philosophy, and most modern philosophers still believe that ethics is a distinct and important branch of knowledge. This belief is pre-scientific and unscientific. It will gradually die out.

The continued decline of religious thinking will of course include the decline of religious ethics. But most educated non-religious persons in advanced states still accept some other pre-scientific ethical theory, one based on reason rather than on revelation. All such beliefs are certain to weaken and decline.

Many famous ethical problems are pseudo problems, that is, are senseless. The common question "What is the meaning of life?" is nonsensical. Words and signs have meanings; objects and processes do not. It is possible to discuss and investigate the purposes of men, as social scientists do, but it is futile to try to answer any question concerning the meaning or purpose of life.

Sensible ethical questions deal with meaningful problems of social and personal conduct, problems which scientists can, and will, eventually attack and solve. Since many men demand solutions to unsolved problems of conduct, they are willing to accept unscientific ethical rules until scientific rules are available. But the rapid advance of applied science constantly reduces the demand for such ethical rules.

The rise of science has produced an ever-growing number of pure and applied sciences which deal with personal conduct or social behavior—medical sciences, psychiatry, criminology, sexology, social sciences. As a result more and more men seek advice on personal conduct from doctors and other applied scientists, not from priests or philosophic moralists. This trend will continue for centuries. Scientists will learn how to treat many more personal ills, how to solve many more personal problems; and men will become ever more confident of obtaining successful treatment or advice from applied scientists, and ever more skeptical of that given by moralists.

One obvious and measurable result of this trend has been and will long continue to be a decline in formal instruction in ethics. By 2500 few if any schools or universities will give courses in ethics, and the number of students in such courses will be negligible. In the near future, however, the study of philosophic ethics may rise temporarily as more men abandon religious ethics and seek an unscientific alternative.

Another measurable result will be the change in public opinion toward ethics. A public-opinion survey today would probably show that more than 90 percent of university graduates believe that ethics is and should remain a distinct field of knowledge. By 2200 this percentage will fall below 50 percent; and by 2500, below 10 percent.

One of the most popular moral dogmas in advanced countries is the doctrine that men have certain inalienable natural rights. American laws and court decisions contain many references to and applications of this doctrine. The gradual abandonment of ethics and the rise of applied science—in this case, applied social science—will cause a long decline in the efforts of legislators and judges to interpret and apply doctrines concerning natural rights. Such efforts may increase for a few decades more, but they certainly will decline during the twenty-first century and will almost end before 2500.

Many writers have predicted that ethics will become scientific. They usually advocate some form of utilitarianism. But men do not need to be urged to do what is expedient. They only need to be convinced that one course of conduct is more expedient than another; and this is the function of applied scientists. Unless moralists urge men to do what is inexpedient, they have no separate function.

Conduct that is expedient for the individual is often inexpedient for the community. Many moralists have tried to reconcile this conflict by teaching that men have a moral duty to do what benefits the community. Unfortunately it is impossible to conceive of any method of verifying this doctrine. One can test the hypothesis that certain conduct benefits the community, if *benefit* is suitably defined, but one cannot conceive of a method of testing the claim that such conduct is moral. In other words, the claim is senseless.

When a philosopher asserts that certain conduct is ethical, he may prove that he, or society, approves of or desires such conduct, but he does not make a sensible and therefore verifiable statement about the conduct itself. Increasing awareness of this is inevitable and will increasingly discredit all ethical doctrines.

The problem of inducing individuals to refrain from conduct which harms society and engage in conduct which benefits society is of course eternal and immensely significant. Practical men have always tried to solve this problem by persuading society to reward men for socially beneficial conduct and penalize them for anti-social conduct. Social scientists have increasingly accepted the principle that the chief function of government is to create rewards and penalties which make private interest more identical with public interest. During future centuries all laws governing personal conduct will be revised repeatedly in order to approach this goal more closely. Many such specific changes have been predicted in this book. All of them will result from and promote the decline of morality, which is never needed to urge or justify expedient conduct.

Ideology

As used here the term *ideology* denotes a social philosophy, a body of social theory largely based upon "reason" rather than on revelation or scientific observation. Some or all of the practical conclusions of an ideology may be true. The distinctive feature of an ideology is not false conclusions but conclusions (true or false) supported chiefly by pre-scientific arguments.

The major ideologies of our time are those which support Marxist communism and competitive capitalism, and the following discussion is largely restricted to them. Every major ideology, like every major religion, includes many sects, but a discussion of individual sects would require more space and more expert knowledge than I have.

The cold and hot wars between communists and capitalists, which began in 1917 and are likely to continue until a strong world government is established, resemble in many ways the religious conflicts which divided and devastated most of Europe in the sixteenth and seventeenth centuries. The communist-socialists of the twentieth century are playing a role similar to that of the Protestants in the Reformation. Marx, like Luther, led a dogmatic, puritanical, radical revolt against the abuses of an established order. Even in personal character there are many marked similarities—intolerance, opportunism, belief that the end justifies the means, etc. Many other significant resemblances between the current ideological cold war and the old religious wars might be mentioned. But the above should suffice to suggest that the future course of the modern conflict can be illuminated by reviewing the course of the older one.

The major conclusion which this analogy suggests is that the conflict between capitalism and communism will not be quickly or peacefully won by either party but will continue indefinitely and become less and less bitter. However, the invention of nuclear weapons has at last made world conquest and world rule by a single great power possible. Moreover, as explained earlier, a world state is the only means of freeing mankind from the danger of nuclear war and is therefore likely to be created before 2100. If it is established by a victorious United States or Soviet Union, it may temporarily impose the ideology and economic system of the victor on all countries. Fear of such a result has intensified the cold war, which itself makes World War III and a world government imposed by conquest more probable.

If communism and capitalism both survive indefinitely, however, the conflict between them will become less and less bitter. Each system is certain to adopt more and more theories and practices of the other. Communists will reintroduce rent, interest, and profits; and capitalist states will steadily expand public ownership, free distribution, and social security. Such compromise trends are suggested by the policies of the Counter Reformation and the major Protestant sects from 1700 to 1960.

Furthermore, if either Russian communism or American capitalism is imposed on most or all countries by the victors in World War III or IV, this dominant system will gradually be revised to incorporate more and more features of the other system, and more and more of the many other economic reforms predicted in this book. The economic system of 2500 will be more scientific than communist or capitalist, regardless of the outcome of the contemporary struggle. In the long run, social science will replace social ideologies.

Comte's theory of intellectual evolution suggests the most significant prediction about ideologies, namely, that their influence will gradually and indefinitely weaken as men advance from philosophic to scientific reasoning. It also partly explains the long relaxation in the Catholic-Protestant conflict, which occurred during the rise of modern philosophy and science. Religious wars have diminished in number and force because men have become less religious. During coming centuries men will become less and less ideological.

As philosophic thinking gives way to scientific thinking, more and more men will reject the dogmas of ideologists and accept the conclusions of social scientists. Statesmen will gradually learn to experiment with proposed social reforms on a small local scale rather than apply them immediately to the nation or world as a whole. Social thinkers will increasingly present their new ideas as hypotheses deserving experimental testing, not as rational certitudes. Instead of opposing most or all social reforms for ideological reasons, conservatives will merely insist on thorough testing of plausible reform proposals. Communist states will experiment with more and more capitalist practices, and capitalist states with more and more communist, socialist, and anarchist practices, or proposals. Thus, whether the coming world government is initially capitalist or communist or both, it will evolve in the same direction as a result of scientific testing of new and old reform proposals. And until such a world state is created, both capitalist and communist states will become more and more similar as a result of the increasing use of scientific social observation and experimentation. Ideologies will, however, remain influential for another century or two.

CHAPTER XVIII

Science

As explained in the previous chapter, all human reasoning evolves through three major evolutionary stages—the religious, the philosophic, and the scientific. It is proper, therefore, to discuss science immediately after religion and philosophy. In this chapter I shall predict the major social trends in scientific work (not in scientific thought) during the next 500 years.

Scientific Research

Men do not undertake scientific analysis or research to discover the causes of events which they believe are directly determined by supernatural persons or causes—witches, spirits, angels, devils, gods. Some pioneer scientists were agnostics or atheists, but they carefully avoided expressing opinions which might provoke severe punishment. Many more were deists, who believed that a divine first cause set the universe in motion but thereafter failed to alter the course of events. But whatever their professed faith, all scientists have always acted as if the events they investigate are determined by observable and predictable causes. And actions speak louder than words! Thus the rise of science and scientific research is a result, as well as a cause, of the decline of religion and philosophy.

Since religious belief was strong and almost universal among educated and influential men until recently, and since it takes many years to create a theory and methodology of scientific analysis, the most useful scientific theories and methods of research are very new. The rapid rise of modern science began only 400 years ago, and 95 percent of all scientific research has been conducted since 1900.

Heavy public spending on scientific research and development is recent and is confined to a few fields in a few advanced countries, chiefly the United States and the Soviet Union. In 1920 new United States investment in R and D was only $140 million (1960 dollars), or 0.1 percent of gross national product. This investment rose to $0.8 billion in 1940 (0.4 percent of GNP) and to $22 billion in 1965 (3.3 percent of GNP). Thus the share of GNP devoted to R and D rose over 3,000 percent in 45 years. Obviously it cannot do this again in any succeeding 45 years. The United States will, however, invest 5 to 6 percent of its GNP in R and D in the year 2000 and over 10 percent in 2100. This rate should continue to rise slowly throughout the remainder of the next 500 years, but it is unlikely to exceed 20 percent in A.D. 2500.

In 1930 the world spent some $1 billion (less than 0.1 percent of world GNP) on R and D. By 1965 the annual total had risen to perhaps $50 billion (2 percent of GNP). In A.D. 2000 it should exceed $250 billion (4 percent of GNP). By the year 2500, R and D will absorb between 10 and 20 percent of world GNP, which itself will be at least a hundred times the 1960 GNP. In other words, world spending on R and D will increase five hundred to a thousand times by A.D. 2500. Furthermore, unpaid voluntary R and D will become a popular hobby of workers, who will then be far better educated and will work for wages less than twenty hours a week.

As a result of the rapid growth of scientific education and research, 90 percent of all scientists who have ever lived are now alive. Moreover, this condition probably has existed for over 200 years. Obviously it cannot continue for many years more. By 2200 less than 50 percent and by 2500 less than 20 percent of all scientists will still be alive.

Scientific research will continue to grow relatively throughout the next 500 years, because educational and eugenic progress will make men ever more aware of the vast potential gains from R and D, because a steady rise in real income per person will permit ever higher expenditures on R and D, because research work is unusually interesting and satisfying, and because it often yields data which make further research even more promising. Every major breakthrough suggests additional research projects. In all other fields successive increments of investment usually yield diminishing returns, but in R and D they have long yielded equal or greater returns. The latest major inventions—penicillin, television, atomic-power plants, computers—are those which can most benefit mankind per dollar of cost. One reason for this is that every increase in world population increases the benefit from any new invention.

Furthermore, the average marginal social return from investment in non-military research has long been and will long continue to be far above the marginal returns from investment in most other fields. This is true in all capitalist countries, because capitalists consider only the private gains from research, and these are less than half of the social gains, most of which go to consumers as consumer surpluses and external economies, and because a firm usually captures only a minor part of total private gain. The governments of all advanced countries have therefore heavily supplemented private spending on research, though they have not yet come close to the optimum level in any field except perhaps military research.

In Chapter VI, I predicted that all cost prices will eventually be fixed so that they measure the marginal real costs of production. The marginal real cost of using any technological process or invention is nil. But capitalist producers are now required to pay patent royalties for the use of most new processes and inventions. This uneconomic policy will gradually be abandoned in all capitalist states. By 2100 the use of new processes and the manufacture of new inventions will be free of royalty costs in nearly all countries. This reform will greatly increase the social gain from the use of new processes and inventions, which will induce all countries to invest still more in research and development.

Over half the world's 1960 investment in R and D was devoted to military (including space) research. This extreme concentration on military R and D will continue until a stable world government has arisen and has disarmed most of the world. Thereafter military R and D spending will fall rapidly to less than 1 percent of total research spending.

For military reasons research in the natural sciences, notably physics and chemistry, has grown much faster since 1940 than research in other fields. The achievement of a secure world peace will sharply reduce the share of R and D funds allocated to the natural sciences and greatly increase the shares allocated to most other sciences.

Investment in biological, especially medical, research has grown rapidly in recent decades and will continue to grow steadily, as predicted in Chapter XIV, but it will not grow nearly as fast as investment in educational, psychological, and social research during the next five centuries. By 2500 the annual world investment in R and D in each of these last three research fields probably will exceed that in the physical sciences and engineering, which now accounts for over half of total R and D spending.

The recent development of pioneer psychiatric drugs—tranquilizers, energizers, etc.—is but a faint foretaste of the vast range of ever more effective psychiatric drugs which will result from, and induce increasing investment in, the research which produces them. And continuous rapid improvement in methods of education, child care, and adult psychiatric treatment can and will be achieved by expanding relevant R and D.

All common personal problems—choice of vocation, selection and treatment of mate, making friends, sexual behavior, choice of hobbies, physical recreation, etc.—will become and remain major research areas. By 2300, scientists will devote far more time and money to research on such problems than to research on methods of production, for nearly all men will then be economically prosperous and secure.

As predicted in the previous section, religious, moral, and ideological controversies over social policies will gradually be replaced by deliberate scientific experimentation with proposed social reforms. Voting in elections will give way to scientific testing of alternative policies. This will further, and be furthered by, the rise of government by experts predicted in Chapter III. The growth of such social experimentation will be one of the most important trends in scientific research during most of the next 500 years. By 2400 the social sciences will have as broad and firm an experimental basis, as many significant verified conclusions, as physics and chemistry have now.

Social reforms like prohibition and guarantee of bank deposits have often been called social experiments, but in fact they were not so regarded by their chief proponents and opponents, who professed strong moral motives and were often motivated chiefly by personal political or economic interests. When prohibition is eventually treated as a scientific social experiment, different degrees and methods of prohibition will be tested simultaneously in different areas, and each experiment will be designed by social scientists who will carefully observe, record, and interpret the results and terminate the experiment as soon as desired data are secured. There will be no popular agitation by reformers, no voting on the beginning or end of individual social experiments. However, public reaction to each experiment will be noted and treated as part of the experimental data.

Scientists are most contented and most productive when they live and work with colleagues working on the same or similar problems. They aid and stimulate one another when they are closely associated after as well as during work hours. Moreover, scientists working on the same or similar problems need the same equipment and facilities, which are often expensive and can always be provided more cheaply per person for a large than for a small group of researchers. Hence non-teaching scientists will be increasingly segregated in separate research communities like Oak Ridge and Alamogordo, the first such communities. By 2500 over 80 percent of all full-time research workers will live in such separate, highly specialized research communities, and in advanced countries these communities will outnumber those devoted to manufacturing.

Scientific Journals

The first scientific journal was published in London in 1665. Since then growth in the number of scientific (and technical) journals has been exponential, their number doubling every eighteen to twenty years. The number published in 1960 was between 40,000 and 50,000. It will continue to double every twenty years for one or two more periods, but the rate of growth will fall steadily during the twenty-first century. The number will begin to decline before 2200 and will fall steadily thereafter for a century or two. By 2500 it will be less than half the 1960 total. This trend reversal and the succeeding long decline will be due to a continuous fall in the number of languages in which scientific journals are published after perhaps 2100; a steady and indefinite substitution of direct-mail distribution for journal publication of research reports; and the gradual consolidation of competing journals.

While national pride will further increase the number of languages in which scientific journals are published for a few more decades, scientists will publish more and more of their important articles in an ever smaller number of major languages. And as predicted in Chapter XII, the coming world government will eventually require that all scientific articles and books be published in a single language. This reform is inevitable, because it will radically reduce the effort and cost required of scientists to keep up with the literature of their specialty. Most scientists have long been unable to master and keep up with such literature. As a result many ideas and inventions have been repeatedly offered as contributions to science by scientists unfamiliar with earlier presentations of them.

Before 1914, German was used and read by more scientists than was any other language, but since 1914 the use of English has grown much faster, and English has been the chief international language of science since 1945. The number of scientific articles and books published in English is now several times as large as the number in any other language. Foreign demand for

United States scientific publications has been growing much faster than domestic demand. In 1965 about 30 percent of all copies of fundamental American journals of chemistry and physics went abroad and over half of all copies of *Chemical Abstracts*. These percentages will continue to rise for centuries.

Once so well started, such a trend toward growing use of a single international scientific language is self-perpetuating. All scientists wish to be read as widely as possible and can most easily achieve this goal by publishing in the language most widely understood by scientists. Every increase in the use of English for scientific articles and books puts more pressure on non-English-speaking scientists to learn to read and write in English. Hence, if no other language is forced upon scientists by politico-military means, such as would follow a Soviet victory in World War III, English will continue to be used by more and more scientists until it becomes the sole international language of science. This could easily happen before A.D. 2200, and it would result in the publication of all scientific treatises, monographs, and journal articles in English.

Most of the articles now published in scientific journals are read by only a small percentage of subscribers. The resulting waste of printed matter will be markedly reduced by ever-increasing specialization among journals and by growing substitution of direct-mail distribution for journal publication.

It is uneconomic to publish an article of interest to only a few score specialists in a journal having 10,000 subscribers. Publication of such articles makes journals less useful to subscribers, as well as greatly increasing their cost. Hence highly organized, informal publication—mimeographing, lithoprinting, etc.—and direct-mail distribution will gradually replace journal publication of such articles. Each professional association will compile increasingly accurate lists of ever more numerous classes of member specialists and will undertake the informal publication and direct-mail distribution to them of more and more new articles of narrow interest. Governments will increasingly subsidize such distribution to reduce journal publication costs and assure more prompt and adequate distribution of scientific reports. By

2100 most new scientific reports will be mailed to interested specialists rather than published in journals; by 2200, over 80 percent. Professional associations will soon begin to list and acknowledge significant informally published reports in such a way that scientists will receive as much credit for them as for formally published reports. This will greatly reduce the pressure for formal publication and speed up the distribution of all new scientific reports.

In the English-speaking world there are now several competing scientific journals in almost every science. For instance, there are over a dozen different journals to which an economist might send any article of wide interest. This makes it difficult to keep up with the literature on any subject and drastically limits the readership of all articles. Hence rapidly growing specialization among scientific journals is inevitable. By 2500 no journal will publish articles on more than one specialty, the number of specialties in most sciences will be over ten times as large as in 1960, and there will be only one journal in the world for each specialty. Such specialization will greatly reduce the required number of copies of each journal issue.

The results of scientific research are largely useless until they are reproduced and distributed. Moreover, every new research project requires an extensive preliminary review of the available literature. Therefore the case for public subsidization of scientific journals and informal publication is as strong as the case for public support of scientific research. Such support will increase steadily, until by the year 2100 governments in advanced countries will pay over 80 percent of the total costs of publication of all scientific reports and journals, and these total costs will then be twenty to forty times as high as at present. This support will be liberal enough to enable journals both to pay their contributors as well as commercial magazines pay theirs and to sell journal copies at greatly reduced prices or give them away free of charge.

Most scientists must now learn to read two or more foreign languages and should search the journal literature in these and other languages before starting a research project. But such a search is so time-consuming that it is usually done superficially, if at all. As a result much costly research is mere duplication. All advanced governments will spend more and more money to find and translate important foreign scientific books and journal articles. By 2100 over half of all articles published in English-language journals will be translations of foreign articles. Thereafter growing use of a single world language for scientific reports will steadily reduce the proportion of translated articles in journals published in the world language.

In every field of science and in every profession, different teachers and writers use the same terms to denote different referents, or different terms to denote the same referents. This has caused a vast amount of confusion, misunderstanding, and waste of time. More and more professional and scientific associations will establish national and international committees authorized to standardize all terms and symbols used in learned journals, treatises, and texts. And over-all committees will be established to standardize those used in two or more sciences. All these committees will publish dictionaries containing their approved standard definitions. And scientific and professional associations, aided by national governments and the world government, will take more and more effective measures to bring about universal use of standard scientific terms, symbols, and definitions. By 2500 all scientists in all countries will use them.

Statistics

During the past century scientists and executives have become more and more aware of the great value of reliable statistics for business, governmental, and scientific purposes and have steadily increased their relative expenditures on the collection, tabulation, and analysis of statistical data. But such expenditures are still grossly inadequate. For instance, few reliable figures on the growth of these expenditures are available. It has been roughly estimated that such spending by the United States government grew from $38 million in 1953 to $118 million in fiscal year 1965. The continuation of this growth rate would yield spending of about $1,800 million for the year 2000. A twelve-year trend is a poor foundation for a long-run estimate, but there are many other reasons for predicting an indefinite and rapid long-run growth in spending on statistical enumeration, tabulation, and analysis in all countries, especially during the next century or two.

Every increase in the size of a business firm or a political unit increases the supply of and the demand for statistics, and I have already predicted an indefinite and universal growth of such organizations. Every increase in the functions of governments makes necessary the collection and analysis of additional social statistics, and I have predicted that all governments will assume more and more new functions. Social statistics are an essential prerequisite for most social science, and the relative number of social scientists will increase rapidly throughout the next 500 years. Finally the recent invention of electronic computers has greatly simplified statistical record keeping and analysis. The science and technology of statistical enumeration, tabulation, and analysis will continue to improve, and this will steadily increase the demand for statistics.

The range of subjects on which statistics are collected, preserved, and analyzed will broaden steadily. The date, nature, results, and/or amounts of all significant school examinations, intelligence tests, juvenile delinquencies, medical examinations, accidents, fires, crimes, autopsies, marriages, divorces, personal loans, purchases, changes of address, hirings, firings, etc., will eventually be recorded, preserved, and analyzed as statistical data.

American criminal statistics are notoriously inadequate. They fail to report most of the statistical data of interest to a criminologist—parental I.Q.'s, parental income, parental education, parental occupations, parental health, family size, childhood diseases, education of criminal, lie-detector results, etc. By A.D. 2100 criminal statistics will provide ten to one hundred times as much information about each crime and each criminal.

Statistical research on medical and psychiatric problems has barely begun and is certain to expand rapidly. Such research recently disclosed that cigarette smoking causes great increases in the death rate from cancer and heart disease. In this case relatively small expenditures on statistical research revealed vital facts that far larger expenditures on clinical and laboratory research had failed to reveal. Yet many M.D.'s are still strongly biased against such statistical research. This bias will decline steadily, and statistical research will receive a larger and larger share of health-research funds for at least a century or two.

A vast amount of valuable medical data suitable for statistical analysis on electronic computing machines is now preserved for only a few years in medical and hospital offices. By 2100 all case histories and other medical and psychiatric records will be written in standardized terms on standard national forms in duplicate or triplicate. One copy of each such report will be sent to a national medical computing and research center, where it will be used for statistical research on the environmental and hereditary causes of disease, on the efficacy of all treatments for disease, and on the efficiency of individual doctors, clinics, hospitals, and medical district supervisors.

In the United States most statistical data are still collected by cities, counties, states, and private firms, which are semi-independent and therefore still use many different statistical terms, definitions, forms, and methods of collection and tabulation. The gradual integration of government and industry, predicted earlier, will steadily reduce the variation in statistical terms, methods, and coverage. Moreover, national governments will increasingly induce or require semi-independent units of government and private business to use more uniform statistical procedures. By 2100 most significant statistical series will be collected and tabulated by national governments or in accordance with their instructions. They will determine what statistics are to be collected by public agencies, design or review all statistical forms, write all procedural instructions, and check the completeness and accuracy of all statistical enumerations and calculations.

Voluntary international co-operation among national statistical agencies began in the nineteenth century and has grown steadily. It will continue to grow and to reduce international differences in statistical terms and methods until the coming world government supplements it with compulsory standardization. By 2300 nearly all statistics in all countries will be collected in a uniform manner prescribed by the central statistical agency of the world government.

The collection, tabulation, storage, retrieval, and analysis of statistical data will be increasingly mechanized and automated. Ever more elaborate, efficient, and interconnected electronic computers will be used. More and more local, regional, and national computers will be connected with one another and with data suppliers and users. For instance, all local police stations and medical clinics will be connected with such computer complexes before 2200. And by that date scientists in any city will be able to determine any desired new statistical correlation—between age of marriage and I.Q., color of hair and any disease, cigarette smoking and any kind of accident, political attitude and diet, church attendance and any crime, etc.—by directly operating a remote regional, national or world computer complex.

Units of Measurement

Public and expert support for increased standardization of units of measurement has been growing for centuries, and it will continue to grow as international communication, trade, and travel expand. Many standardization proposals have already been adopted, and many more will be, until all units of measurement are the same throughout the world. The coming world government will enforce the last unit standardization measures, including universal use of the metric system, before A.D. 2200. In the meantime voluntary adoption and use of the metric system will continue to spread. Britain will adopt it before the year 2000, the United States before 2100.

The decimal system of measurement will be expanded to include all non-metric units of measurement—monetary, temporal, circular, etc. The British will decimalize the pound sterling before 2000. Centigrade thermometers will replace Fahrenheit in Britain and the United States before 2100. Power will be measured in kilowatts, not horsepower. The circle will be divided into either 100 or 1,000 degrees. A day and night will probably include 20 instead of 24 hours; and a five-day week, 100 hours. By A.D. 2200 the hour will have 50, not 60, minutes, which will yield a day of just 1,000 minutes. A minute will have either 50 or 100 seconds.

The year we would call A.D. 2500 will not be called that. Long before it arrives, our calendar will have been drastically reformed in order to facilitate bookkeeping, statistical work, and date and time determination. The calendar of A.D. 2500 will number the years from some notable event, such as the creation of a world government, considered significant by all peoples, non-Christian as well as Christian. (Christians will make up less than 5 percent of world population.) The year will begin on what is now either June 21 or December 21, because on these days the sun begins to move back toward the equator. December 21 is more likely, because it is so close to January 1.

In the new calendar every year and month will begin on the same day of the week, and, so far as possible, will be equally long. A single printed calendar will be usable year after year, because every year except leap year will be the same, and this minor variation can easily be shown on any perpetual calendar.

The new calendar year will probably be divided into four 91-day quarters (each including three 30-day months and an odd quarter-day), plus an odd year-end day, because this would most facilitate the preparation and use of comparable quarterly and semi-annual accounting and statistical reports. The odd-quarter, year-end, and leap-year days will be the only general holidays in addition to regular weekly holidays. The week will be reduced to 5 days, to fit into a 30-day month divisible by 2 without splitting weeks.

The above predictions concerning details of the new uniform world calendar are of course less certain than the more general prediction that a reformed calendar will be created and universally used. The most likely alternative is a calendar of ten 36-day months, each including six 6-day weeks, with two- or three-day holiday periods in the middle and at the end of the year.

Religious objections to scientific calendar reform are still strong. They will weaken gradually and continuously for centuries, but it is hard to predict when they will weaken enough to permit the adoption of a thoroughly scientific calendar. This goal should, however, be achieved before the year 2300.

The Brain Drain

The flow of highly educated men from less to more developed countries, especially to the United States, has been noted and discussed by numerous writers and is already widely known as the brain drain. It will continue throughout the next 500 years and will grow rapidly during the next two or three centuries.

For 350 years immigration from Europe provided the United States with some highly educated men, but it is only since this immigration was drastically curtailed that the flow of able scientists, professors, writers and other gifted men to the United States has become substantial, thanks chiefly to Hitler and Mussolini. Since World War II the brain drain has continued in a different form and for different reasons. The vast increase in United States spending on R and D—from $4 billion in 1950 to $20 billion in 1964—made it possible for many European scientists and engineers to earn higher salaries and to further their careers by moving to the United States. Moreover, since 1945 the United States has had many thousands of foreign students in its universities, and a large proportion of the most highly educated and gifted scientists among these students have remained in the United States after graduating because employment and promotion opportunities here are far superior to those in their homeland. These conditions will continue for centuries.

Science is international, and a competent scientist can pursue his research in any country. His chief problem usually is to secure financial backing and suitable equipment. He also likes to associate or collaborate with other scientists, especially with the most able men in his field. No backward country and few small advanced countries can provide these advantages. Only the United States, the Soviet Union, and Western Europe can do so now. And these advantages are most attractive to the most able foreign students and scientists.

Scientific geniuses are distributed among countries roughly according to population, but research funds and facilities are and will long remain highly concentrated in a few advanced states with less than one fifth of the world's population. Moreover, the cost of international travel will decline steadily, and restrictions on immigration and emigration of scientists will be loosened. Finally public education, which facilitates the discovery of geniuses, will grow rapidly in backward countries. For these and other reasons the flow of gifted students and scientists from backward to advanced countries will continue to grow. This flow will tend to preserve the relative scientific and economic superiority of the most advanced countries.

The United States will long continue to benefit most from the brain drain because English has become the international language of science and because the United States pays the highest salaries and offers the best research opportunities to foreign scientists. To increase such benefits, it will soon abolish all immigration restrictions on the entry of foreign scientists and engineers with university degrees. By the year 2100 over 50 percent of top United States scientists—for instance, Nobel Prize holders—will be foreign-born. And the proportion of such scientists born in Asia and Latin America will rise much faster than the proportion born in Europe.

The Soviet Union does not now encourage foreign scientists to settle or work there, but it will soon begin to do so, and will adopt more and more policies designed to increase such immigration. By 2100 over 20 percent of top Soviet scientists and engineers will be foreign-born; by 2200, over 30 percent. If the Soviet Union wins World War III, these rates will be much higher.

CHAPTER XIX

Conclusion

HERE I shall discuss the probable effects of one or more devastating nuclear wars upon the social trends predicted in preceding chapters; describe a typical American family and its routine life in the year 2500; explain which of the major social trends predicted for the next 500 years will probably continue throughout most or all of the following 500 years; and criticize one recent example of historical pessimism.

The Effects of Nuclear War

As explained in Chapter I, a devastating nuclear war is highly probable, and such a war will affect most future social trends. To simplify the problem of predicting how fast these trends will develop, I have based nearly all my predictions on the assumption that there will be no major nuclear war. I tried to justify this assumption by arguing that a major nuclear war would result in the creation of a world government which would prevent the recurrence of such a war and that one such war would merely slow down or accelerate inevitable social trends by a few decades, effects which would only slightly alter the cumulative results of social trends continuing throughout most or all of the next 500 years.

It is now appropriate to consider in more detail how a major nuclear war would affect individual social trends during the immediately following decades. I shall discuss effects on certain major trends only, but my analysis should suggest the effects on many other trends.

For the purpose of this discussion let us assume a single brief nuclear war which would, before the year 2100, destroy half the population and two thirds of the industrial capacity of the United States, the Soviet Union, and the rest of Europe, but would leave the victor strong enough to establish a world government and ensure world peace, or at least freedom from major nuclear wars.

On first consideration it may seem that such a devastating war would seriously slow down or reverse most major social trends. This was my first conclusion. On reconsideration, however, I realized that such a war would probably speed up more social trends than it would slow down.

First, as noted in Chapter II, it would accelerate the trend toward unification of all nations into a single world state. The terrible suffering due to a nuclear world war would greatly increase the demand for a world government, and victory would enable the winner to create such a state by force, or would induce surviving military powers to do so voluntarily.

Second, a major nuclear war would hasten most if not all of the other political trends predicted in Chapter III. The enormous devastation would greatly increase both the need and the public support for rationalization of government, that is, for all reforms which would enable governments to act more quickly and efficiently to assure a rapid postwar national recovery. In particular the problems of recovery would be so complex and extensive that they would require a marked temporary centralization of governmental authority in countries like the United States, where such authority is now highly decentralized. It would be impossible for fifty American states and hundreds of cities acting independently to restore communications, transportation, food supply, etc., in the way most beneficial to the nation as a whole. One-house legislatures could act much more quickly than two-house legislatures and would therefore become much more popular. All legislatures would have to delegate most of the direction of national recovery to administrative agencies, including many new agencies with new powers. And once such measures had proven their advantages in the recovery period, they would be much more popular in the post-recovery period.

Third, a nuclear war would speed up some eugenic trends.

It would result in the birth of many more deformed or feeble-minded children, which would increase the demand for infanticide, both to achieve eugenic ends and to reduce the burden on an impoverished nation of supporting and educating such children. Furthermore, the long-run dysgenic effects of a major nuclear war would increase interest in and demand for long-run eugenic measures to offset such effects.

Fourth, in capitalist countries the devastation due to such a war would hasten the growth of government control over private business firms. During World Wars I and II all capitalist participants greatly expanded public control over private business in order to mobilize their economic resources more rapidly and efficiently. World War III will be too short to permit such a wartime development, but the post-war recovery will see a similar and much more drastic extension of government control over private business. It will be more comprehensive both because the need for such control will be much greater and will last longer and because economists are constantly learning how to plan and carry out more radical and effective control measures.

For instance, a postwar capitalist country which had lost most of its industrial capacity would almost certainly assume virtually complete control over the investment and reinvestment of all private capital funds in order to assure priority for the most needed reconstruction projects. And it would adopt prompt and vigorous measures to radically reduce the variety of manufactured products, limit advertising, curtail cross-hauling of like products, unify and rationalize the transport system, etc. In general, a post-nuclear-war government would use its powers to speed up all old economic trends which obviously increase the productivity of capital and labor.

Fifth, a post-nuclear-war capitalist government which had lost half its labor force and capital would radically speed up many well-established agricultural trends. It would force the abandonment or merger of most small farms into much larger units, thus reducing the number of farms by 50 to 90 percent within a few years. It would require the co-operative use by two or more adjacent farms of most tractors, combines, and other expensive durable farm machinery, which would permit a sharp cut in the share of labor and plant capacity used to produce such machinery. It would require many less competent farmers to improve their farming methods. It would abolish nearly all limitations on the production and importation of essential farm products. To facilitate the rapid achievement of such reforms, it would nationalize much, perhaps most, farm land.

Sixth, a capitalist country which had lost over half its labor force would accelerate the growth in the proportion of married women in the national labor force. To promote this growth, it would rapidly increase the number of institutions providing preschool and after-school care for children. It would also postpone the retirement of older male and female workers and would recall many retired workers into the national labor force.

Seventh, such a government would integrate all private employment agencies and activities into a single national system, both to save the time of workers seeking employment and to ensure the best possible allocation of professional and skilled workers in short supply.

Eighth, a major nuclear war would speed up several educational trends. It would induce more secondary and higher schools to require their students to work part of each day, week, or year—probably half of each day. It would persuade many educators to use their remaining facilities several hours longer each day, more days a week, and more months a year. It would increase emphasis on vocational studies. It would stimulate efforts to reduce the time required by the more able students to complete their education, including segregation of such students in special classes which advance more rapidly than other classes.

Ninth, a major nuclear war would almost certainly hasten the growth of comprehensive city planning. The destruction of most urban buildings would clear the ground for such planning, and increased government control over reconstruction would facilitate such planning. Public and expert appreciation of the benefits of city planning has grown steadily since 1945, so reconstruction after World War III should be much better planned than reconstruction after World War II, which itself stimulated city planning.

The destruction of most motor vehicles, oil refineries, auto factories, and garages would favor the substitution of mass rapid transit for private-car use in transporting workers to and from their jobs, and shoppers to and from stores. The sharp reduction in real wage rates would intensify and prolong this effect. City planners would therefore be more likely to plan new and reconstructed cities so as to reduce the distance between homes and places of employment. Moreover, those who ration and allocate the remaining urban housing would require many workers to live nearer their places of employment.

Finally, a major nuclear war would markedly accelerate all trends which are gradually rationalizing the provision of medical, dental, and psychiatric care. It would suddenly destroy most health-care facilities and equipment and greatly increase the proportion of the population requiring such care. These effects would prompt health officials to hasten the growth of professional specialization, the construction of larger hospitals, specialization among hospitals, group medical practice, public financing of health services, and other trends which enable doctors to care for more patients with less equipment. Once these rationalization measures had been temporarily adopted, it would be difficult to abandon most of them later.

Nearly all of the post-nuclear-war recovery measures predicted above would be initially adopted as temporary emergency policies. But the recovery period after a major nuclear war would be much longer than the emergency periods during and after World Wars I and II. And many temporary measures adopted during and after these wars became permanent. A much larger proportion of temporary post-World-War III recovery measures will outlast the recovery period.

While a major nuclear war would probably speed up most of the long-run social trends discussed in this book—especially those which would quickly make government, business, and labor more productive—it would slow down or set back some of them, especially those which result chiefly from the growth of average family income, of education, of eugenic reform, and scientific research.

The most significant immediate effect, of course, would be a sharp reduction in average real personal income. It might take several decades to restore this income to the prewar level and resume the long-run advance to ever higher income. During most of this interval the proportion of world income spent on secondary and higher education, public libraries and museums, research and development, parks and playgrounds, air and water purification, language reform, and other such less immediately essential free goods and services would remain well below prewar levels.

A war which reduced the population by 50 percent would also stop or slow down the growth of government efforts to promote birth control. The sharp decline in real family incomes would, however, prompt most individuals to increase their private efforts at birth control, especially in defeated countries.

Since a nuclear war would cause an immense amount of suffering and would make most people in devastated countries more anxious about their future, it would probably bring about a temporary religious revival, especially in defeated countries. World War II produced such a revival, even in Soviet Russia.

Life in A.D. 2500

I have been discussing the short-run effects of a major nuclear war upon some of the most important social trends predicted earlier. I now wish to summarize briefly the long-run effects of such trends. To do this, I shall describe the world of A.D. 2500, with special attention to the life of an average American family.

In the year 2500 the entire world will be governed by a single, stable world government. The leaders and middle executives of this government will be professionally trained social scientists and public administrators responsible only to their superiors or to their own professional association. Elections will have been completely replaced by public-opinion polls, and public opinion will be molded by education, publications, and broadcasts planned by the government to promote sound scientific thinking about all current socio-political problems.

The world government will be highly centralized. It will have about a dozen major regional administrative subdivisions, of which North America will be one. Each major industry—transportation, retailing, local public utilities, etc.—will be organized as a single publicly owned worldwide monopoly. The production of nearly all tangible goods will be guided by marginal profits and losses, not by economic plans. Most services—education, research, health care, child care, etc.—will be provided free of charge. Their total cost will exceed half the world GNP, and their outputs (but not their methods of operation) will be controlled by economic plans. Military defense, which now costs 8 percent of world income, will cost less than 0.1 percent, because nearly all military forces will have been disbanded.

Free trade will be universal, and the entire world output of many small goods will be produced in a single plant or local complex of plants. Specialization among factories and farms will have vastly increased. As a result the average tangible good will move several times as far as in 1960 to reach its consumer, in spite of the elimination of all cross-hauling of like goods.

Less than 5 percent of the world's labor force will be engaged in agriculture, and nearly all of them will live in towns which offer most of the advantages of city life. Over 80 percent of the world's population will live in planned garden cities having more than 100,000, but fewer than 1,000,000, inhabitants.

The world of A.D. 2500 will have a single near universal culture. The vast majority of people in each occupation will speak the same language, read the same books, attend similar schools, and listen to the same TV and radio broadcasts. They will eat similar food, wear similar clothes, and drink the same drinks in all countries with similar climates. They will live in similar housing built in communities and cities planned by the same international architectural organization. They will work in similar factories, offices, and farms and travel on similar ships, planes, and buses. Their incomes will all be determined in the same way, largely according to a single world wage policy. They will all use the same methods of birth control and eugenics and have the same average number of children per family. Remaining cultural differences will be largely interoccupational, not international.

The great majority of the world's adults will be non-religious and amoral (without religious or moral beliefs). No church will receive any government financial support or tax exemption. Less than 20 percent of the world population will attend religious ceremonies or pray at home. No religious oaths will be required of witnesses or government officials. No country will have a religious sect which includes more than 10 percent of its population. And no laws or court decisions will be based upon natural rights or unverifiable moral principles. All governments and courts will strive to increase measurable welfare rather than to promote religion, justice, or morality.

In the year 2500 the typical American family will consist of two working adults and two children. They will have a real family income (including free goods and compulsory saving) well over 20 times the United States 1960 average and over twice the world average in 2500. They will live in a spacious six- to ten-room apartment in a large tall building with fine views from most rooms. The apartment building will be part of a carefully planned satellite community, built as a single construction project, in a region with a superior climate. Each apartment will be equipped with numerous labor-saving and recreational conveniences—built-in color television sets, air-conditioning and air-sterilization systems, dust precipitators, dumbwaiters or delivery tubes, built-in vacuum cleaner pipes in each room, television telephones, etc. It will also contain a library of over 10,000 microfilmed books, musical tapes, and movie films, which will occupy less than twenty cubic feet.

Most retail buying of convenience goods—drugs, groceries, standardized clothing, etc.—will be done by dialing catalogue numbers on a home retail-order taker, and purchases will be delivered to most homes by an automatic package-delivery system. All shopping goods will be displayed and sold in a single department store in each satellite city. Every home will have a set of catalogues which describe and picture in color all retail goods. The variety of United States retail goods will be much smaller than in 1960, due to simplification and standardization.

Color television sets will be built in one or more rooms of all homes. They will receive throughout the day and evening over one hundred different channels, no two of which will offer the same program at the same time. All TV programs in each region will be planned and co-ordinated by a single office so as to assure an optimum variety of programs at every hour of the day and night. All new plays, concerts, operas, major sporting events, and other popular entertainments will be broadcast repeatedly by television. And a wide variety of fine educational lectures, laboratory experiments, travel pictures, and historical films will also be constantly on the air. There will be no advertising before or during any TV broadcast, except during those few which consist entirely of informational commercials.

Both adults will work full time (three to four hours a day for about 200 days a year) and together they will earn far more than $200,000 (1960 dollars) a year. Taxes will take over half of this gross income and will pay for free medical, dental, psychiatric, and hospital care; child care and education for all children under twenty; scientific research (which will consume over 10 percent of world income), TV and radio broadcasting, etc.

Both children will live in public boarding nurseries, kindergartens, or schools for sixteen to twenty-two hours a day. All school systems will offer at least five separate educational channels, with different teachers, texts, and courses for each channel. Students in the highest channel will learn to read by age four or five and will obtain the equivalent of a good 1960 university degree by age sixteen; those in the next highest, by age eighteen. Both graduates and drop-outs will be assured a wide choice of jobs on leaving school and will always be able to find suitable employment, usually near home. As a result of this and other reforms, crime rates will be 80 percent below the 1960 American level. Alcoholism, tobacco use, narcotic addiction, and gambling for high stakes will be equally reduced.

Adults will spend two to ten hours a week in formal education throughout their lives. Physical recreational facilities will be relatively twenty to fifty times as abundant as they now are in the United States, and most adults will devote at least an hour each day, from age twenty to age eighty, to participation in some active physical sport.

By 2500 eugenic and education reforms will have raised the average American I.Q. above 140 (measured by 1960 tests). Males with an I.Q. below 130 will be subject to compulsory sterilization, before they have any children. The great majority of children will be the product of artificial insemination with sperm from superior men. The average strength, health, beauty, grace, and I.Q. of the United States population in 2500 will be superior to those of the best 0.1 percent in 1960.

Personal incomes will differ little. The richest American family of four will have an income less than double that of the poorest similar family. Most families will have incomes less than 20 percent above or below the average for similar families. Hence my description of the life of the average American family will apply to nearly all such families in 2500.

Average personal income will be almost the same in every occupation. The chief remaining income differences will be due to measurable differences in individual output, not to differences in education. Bonuses will be paid for doing unpopular work and for working in unpleasant climates.

Daily life in American cities will be far less complicated in 2500 than it is today. No one will have to make any effort to find a suitable job. This will be as easy as finding a retail store today. Few families will own private cars or homes and have to worry about the purchase, insurance, maintenance, repair, and resale of such property. The trusts which own and rent housing and pleasure cars will handle all such chores. Personal shopping will be largely replaced by mail and phone buying. And when people plan retail purchases, they will have full and honest information on all goods. They will not need to worry about deceptive advertising, shoddy merchandise, overselling, overcharging, etc.

Insurance against all risks will be provided all citizens without any effort or request on their part. No separate insurance premiums will be charged. All monthly bills will be deducted from personal bank accounts and reported on monthly bank statements, so no individual will have to make any effort to pay his bills. Personal loans will be freely granted to all persons with legitimate needs, without any special credit investigation, and loan collection will be as simple and effortless as the collection of other bills.

All housing will be in communities carefully planned so that nearly all residents live near shopping centers and their places of employment. To reach these places, they will walk, or ride slow quiet buses, along streets free of private cars and fast noisy commercial vehicles. As a result of these and other reforms street-accident rates will be more than 90 percent below 1960 United States levels.

The comprehensive simplification and tranquilization of urban life predicted above will help to reduce mental illness. Eugenic advances and the provision of ever more free psychiatric care will have the same effect. By the year 2500, United States mental illness rates will be more than 90 percent below 1960 levels.

It may be objected that urban life with so few remaining pressures and problems will be dull. However, elimination of job-finding, housekeeping, child-tending, and property-management chores will free men and women for more important and more stimulating problems and activities—adult education, travel, child training, social activities, wholesome sports, hobbies, reading. Instead of worrying about trivial problems and serious but unnecessary risks, people will worry about significant problems and necessary risks.

The language spoken by Americans and by most other people in 2500 will be a new artificial language designed by linguistic scientists to help men learn, think, speak, and write more rapidly and clearly. Its use will enable children to learn more easily and rapidly how to read, write, and reason correctly and will reduce by over 50 percent the size of old books translated into the new language.

Each major province of the world government will contain

one or more libraries with copies of all extant manuscripts and publications. These libraries will provide free or very cheap microfilm copies of any such item to any person upon request, usually within twenty-four hours. All private studies and homes will have microfilm projectors.

Most Americans will be employed in performing professional services in nurseries, schools, universities, research laboratories, design institutes, experimental stations, museums, medical clinics, hospitals, theaters, government offices, etc. Less than 10 percent will be employed in producing tangible farm or factory products. Nearly all factories will be highly automated and will operate continuously 365 days a year.

When stated in this summary form, my predictions of American life in the year 2500 may seem utopian. But nearly all have been based upon trends in American thought and behavior already obvious and well established in 1960. I am convinced that they are realistic, that future history will roughly verify the great majority of them. The results will be utopian. But, then, a medieval European peasant would look upon a modern American town as a utopia.

I have been describing how the typical American family will live in A.D. 2500. The life of people in other countries will be less luxurious but otherwise little different. After 500 more years of steady cultural homogenization, all the people of the world will live similar lives. Average family income in backward countries will still be much less than half that in America, but the difference in style of life between a family with $50,000 annual income and one with $200,000 is minor now and will be minor then. The big cultural differences today are between families with a $400 annual income (China and India) and those with $12,000 (the United States), or between the very rich and the very poor within any country.

The Years A.D. 2500 to 3000

I have argued that major social trends are predictable because, once started, they usually continue for centuries. If this thesis is sound, it should now be possible to project many of the social trends predicted for the next 500 years well into or throughout the second 500 years. This section will be devoted to such projections.

Of the thirty-one major general social trends predicted in Chapter II, twenty-three are likely to continue well into, and most of them throughout, the period A.D. 2500 to 3000. Hence it is easier to explain why eight of the thirty-one may not or will not continue than why the others will. These eight are population growth, birth control, urbanization, industrialization, monopoly, collectivization, feminism, and decline in income differences. All but the first have absolute limits.

The entire world probably will be highly industrialized and urbanized and nearly all industries organized as monopolies well before 2500. Birth control should also become universal and near optimum before then, and this might end population growth. Women will almost have achieved an ideal share in all socio-economic activities. Unjustifiable differences in personal real income will have become negligible. And all property which ought to be collectively owned will probably be socialized before 2500.

On the other hand, nearly all the other twenty-three major general trends are likely to continue throughout most or all of the period 2500 to 3000, for much the same reasons that they are likely to continue from 1960 to 2500. And each continuing trend will reinforce one or more other major social trends. For instance, the inevitable continuation of large-scale scientific research will steadily increase the stock of human knowledge, which will tend to prolong the average period of education, require ever greater specialization among professional men, facilitate automation, and increase real wages and leisure. Similarly, continuing eugenic reform will create men ever more interested and productive in scientific research, as well as ever more efficient in all other economic activities, which in turn will help to raise real wages, increase leisure, make men less religious, and promote education and meritocracy. Furthermore, every increase in real wages will favor more automation and more specialized large-scale production. But it is unnecessary to repeat here all the arguments presented earlier in this book.

The number of less general and less significant social trends predicted for the next 500 years which will probably continue well into or throughout the period 2500 to 3000 is much larger. It includes:

1. Increasing relative study and prediction of social trends.
2. Increasing scientific social experimentation.
3. The decline of racialism, provincialism, and nationalism.
4. More artificial insemination.
5. More sterilization.
6. More use of psychological testing.
7. A steady rise in average I.Q.
8. Continued migration to more pleasant climatic areas.
9. Continued miscegenation.
10. A decline in international wage-rate differences.
11. A decline in average hours of labor.
12. Relative expansion of mail-order and phone-order buying.
13. More government control over consumption of harmful goods.
14. More standardization of goods.
15. More regional specialization in agriculture and manufacturing.
16. Relative increase in spending on continental landscaping.
17. Relative increase in spending on public gardens, parks, forests, etc.
18. Relative increase in spending on entertainment and recreation.
19. Centralization of accounting operations.
20. Ever-growing relative use of desalted water.
21. Domestication of more sea animals.
22. Growth of ocean agriculture.
23. Substitution of synthetic for natural foods.
24. Growth of interregional and intercontinental traffic.
25. Increase in proportion of planned one-project communities.
26. A decline in the number and use of minor languages.
27. Constant improvement of major surviving languages.
28. Ever greater relative investment in organizing and preserving knowledge.
29. More supervision of parental care of children.
30. Relative expansion of public pre-school child care.
31. Prolongation of pre-school and university full-time education.
32. Relative growth of adult education.
33. More individualization of all education.
34. More use of teaching machines.

35. More use of boarding schools.
36. Relative expansion of health care.
37. More professional aid in selecting mates.
38. More sexual intercourse from age fourteen to age eighty.
39. More government effort to promote personal friendship.
40. A decline in faith in ideologies.
41. Better exploitation of gifted persons.
42. A continued lengthening of average life and work spans.

The above list is meant to be illustrative. Any reader should be able to add to it. But it should suffice both to suggest many important social trends which will continue during this second 500 years and to support my basic argument that future social trends can be predicted. If so many trends can safely be predicted for this second period, my predictions for the first 500 years should seem more plausible.

Most of the major general social trends predicted for both halves of the third millennium A.D. will probably continue throughout all of the fourth millennium. These include the relative growth of research and education, the decline of religion, eugenic progress, the rise in real wage rates, the growth of leisure, automation, specialization, increase in the scale of production, growth of free distribution, cultural homogenization, and growth of personal freedom. The inevitable continued accumulation of knowledge will alone suffice to prolong many such trends indefinitely. Moreover, most of them are mutually reinforcing.

Further progress in social science will eventually enable social scientists to state trends which describe social change both over several thousand past years and over several thousand future years, perhaps over far longer periods. I believe that some of the trends stated in this book will gradually be revised so that they describe social change over such long periods. But this task is too difficult to be undertaken here.

Suicide of the West?

In this book I have made over a thousand verifiable predictions, nearly all of them optimistic. These include an indefinite increase in real wages, a radical decline in disease rates, the Europeanization of Asia and Africa, and the creation of a strong world government dominated by Western nations. Hence my book might well have been named "The Victory of the West." I note this implication because I wish to compare my book with James Burnham's *Suicide of the West* (1964).

In this book Professor Burnham indicts liberals for being perennial and dogmatic optimists, for accepting "historical optimism," for believing in "progress." He also asserts that liberalism is an ideology, that is, a more or less systematic set of ideas none of which is verifiable. (This is also the definition of ideology used in Chapter XVII above.) If this definition is correct, not one of the many verifiable predictions made in my book is liberal. But most are in fact widely accepted by liberals. And they certainly support the claim that liberals are optimistic.

The most remarkable fact about *Suicide of the West* is that although it indicts liberals for accepting ideological and therefore unverifiable doctrines, it offers no verifiable alternative. The author seems unaware that if the basic principles on which most liberals agree—he lists nineteen of them and their conservative opposites in one chapter—are unverifiable, all denials of these principles are equally unverifiable. For instance, if historical optimism is unverifiable, and therefore senseless (as logical positivists would conclude), historical pessimism is equally senselesss. It is hard to believe that a professional philosopher and logician is unaware of this, but Professor Burnham nevertheless rejects only liberal doctrines, like optimism, as unverifiable.

Furthermore, the phrase "suicide of the West" also seems to be senseless. The author does not explain how a prediction of such suicide could be verified. I suspect that even if all the optimistic predictions I have made were fully realized, Professor Burnham would still claim that the West was declining or had committed suicide. Certainly he carefully refrains from making any specific verifiable pessimistic predictions. And the reason for this is obvious. Almost any such prediction would sooner or later be proven false, and this would reduce support for his social doctrine. Those Christians who predicted specific dates for the end of the world were repeatedly made to look ridiculous by the failure of their prophecies. James Burnham wants to avoid this fate. Hence he discusses the future suicide of the West without explaining what such a suicide would be and without making a single verifiable pessimistic prediction. And if all observable historical trends continue to be materially beneficial, he, or some of his successors, might explain that he had been talking about an unobservable spiritual suicide.

To support his thesis that the West probably will continue to decline and will eventually commit suicide, Professor Burnham argues that the West has been declining since 1914. His chief evidence for this is the great contraction of Western colonial empires during the years 1914 to 1964. He assumes without much discussion that westernization requires colonialism. He ignores the vital facts that westernization proceeded much faster in Japan than in any European colony and that all former colonies are striving to westernize themselves. His failure to realize that continued westernization of Africa and Asia is inevitable suggests both ignorance of modern social trends and a gross undervaluation of Western culture. A culture as obviously superior as that of the West does not have to be imposed by force: it will be voluntarily adopted by all who become familiar with it.

As further evidence for his claim that the West has been declining since 1914 and will continue to do so, James Burnham refers with alarm to the rise of the Soviet Union. He asserts that the Soviets have transformed Russia from a Western into a non-Western nation. But surely it is naive to believe that any government can quickly achieve such a transformation. Moreover, the Soviets have actually devoted most of their efforts to westernizing Russia by promoting industrialization, universal education, Western medical care, and scientific research. One major result is that the Russian birth rate has fallen to the West European level. Thus Russian culture is more Western today than ever before. The cold war is a civil war within the West, not a contest between the West and the East.

It is true, of course, that the development of nuclear weapons has made possible the annihilation of mankind. This is the sole plausible reason for fearing and discussing the "suicide of the

West." But James Burnham does not emphasize this reason. He thinks the decline of colonialism and the rise of the Soviet Union are more significant. And the policies he advocates, including an intensification of the cold war, are precisely those most likely to bring about a nuclear war which would certainly weaken the relative military and economic power of the West.

SELECTED BIBLIOGRAPHY

AND

INDEX

Selected Bibliography

(*designates most significant)

Books on Social Trends

*Allen, F. R., H. Hart, D. C. Miller, W. F. Ogburn, and M. F. Nimkoff. *Technology and Social Change.* New York: Appleton-Century-Crofts, 1957. A collection of essays on social change by those U.S. sociologists who have contributed most to the theory of social change.

Baade, Fritz. *The Race to the Year 2000—Our Future: a Paradise, or the Suicide of Mankind.* Garden City, N.Y.: Doubleday, 1962. A German agricultural economist predicts that food shortages will not limit population growth and that backward nations will be rapidly industrialized. By A.D. 2000, Chinese urban workers will be five times as numerous as U.S. workers and almost as well provided with energy and capital goods. This seems highly unrealistic!

Beckwith, Burnham P. *The Economic Theory of a Socialist Economy.* Stanford, Cal.: Stanford University Press, 1949. This treatise on welfare economics prescribes the ideal solution for a wide variety of politico-economic problems. If governments tend inevitably to adopt ever more rational solutions of all social problems, any sound welfare economic theory should help men to predict the future.

*Bellamy, Edward. *Looking Backward.* New York, 1887. Often reprinted and translated, this is the most influential and plausible of modern utopias. His *Equality* (1897) also suggests many future trends.

Botein, B., and M. A. Gordon. *The Trial of the Future: Challenge *to the Law.* New York: Simon & Schuster, 1963. Two lawyers discuss current legal problems and trends.

Boulding, Kenneth E. *The Meaning of the Twentieth Century.* New York, 1964. A religious economist discusses and projects "the great transition . . . from civilization to postcivilization," with emphasis on economic development. This book is one of a series intended "to point the way to a reality of which scientific theory has revealed only one aspect" (p. x).

Bryson, Lyman, ed. *Facing the Future's Risks.* New York: Harper & Bros., 1953. The future in physics, chemistry, biology, economics, politics, crime, population, etc., is predicted by thirteen experts.

——. *The Next America. New York:* Harper & Bros., 1952. Contains predictions in a wide variety of fields, with special attention to art and local government.

*Burnham, James W. *The Managerial Revolution.* New York: Day, 1941. An able pioneer discussion of the trend toward meritocracy, written by a former Trotskyite professor of philosophy. He thought that the 1940 U.S. election was "the last" or "next to last regular presidential election" (p. 261).

——. *The Coming Victory of the West.* New York: Harper & Row, 1965. Discussed in text.

*Carr, Edward H. *The New Society.* London: Macmillan, 1960. A brilliant historian explains why "modern history begins when history becomes concerned with the future as well as with the past." He expects the social trends advanced by the French, American, Russian, and industrial revolutions to continue for centuries.

*Condorcet, Marquis de. *Sketch for a Historical Picture of the Human Mind.* Paris, 1794; London: Weidenfeld and Nicholson, 1955. The most successful of all pre-1940 efforts to predict many future social trends.

Darwin, Charles Dalton. *The Next Million Years.* New York: Doubleday, 1953. Contains pessimistic conclusions derived from basic prediction that men will not limit population growth sufficiently to achieve a good life.

Drucker, Peter F. *Landmarks of Tomorrow.* New York: Harper &

Row, 1959. "This book is a report on . . . today . . . not . . . the future" (p. x). It covers "the philosophical shift from the Cartesian universe . . . to the new universe"; the rise of education, industry, etc.; and "the new spiritual—or . . . metaphysical—reality." "What we need is a return to . . . religion" (p. 264).

Eldridge, H. Wentworth. *The Second American Revolution.* New York: Morrow, 1964. A liberal political scientist recommends more political centralization, creation of a meritocracy, unicameral legislatures, etc.

Ellul, Jacques. *The Technological Society.* New York: Knopf, 1965. A Christian French sociologist laments the growing reliance upon utilitarian techniques—rather than prayer, moral decisions, mystic intuition, etc.— to solve personal and social problems. He predicts that this trend will lead to more and more economic planning, government by experts, economic and political centralization, world government, collectivism, etc.

Ernst, Morris L. *Utopia 1976.* New York: Rinehart, 1955. Includes a wide variety of short-run, unstudied, overoptimistic predictions by a liberal lawyer.

Furnas, C. C. *America's Tomorrow: An Informal Excursion into the Era of the Two-Hour Working Day.* New York: Funk & Wagnalls, 1932. A Yale professor of chemical engineering overdoes the informality act and buries some vague predictions in a mass of chatter. He predicted television, but not the New Deal, Medicare, computors, or the advent of nuclear power.

Gabor, Denis. *Inventing the Future.* New York: Knopf, 1964. This exile Hungarian physicist claims that "the future cannot be predicted," but he offers invented solutions for three "great" problems: nuclear war, overpopulation, and leisure. He fears that automation will cause heavy unemployment.

Gallup, George. *The Miracle Ahead.* New York: Harper & Row, 1964. This book does not predict any miracle ahead but suggests some methods of achieving great social progress: more effective use of our mental powers; more effective use of the talents of ordinary individuals, to be achieved by organization of unpaid discussion groups; the wider use of new methods of scientific research, especially statistical research which uses electronic computers; and inducing our schools to teach the necessity and advantages of continuous social change.

*Heilbroner, Robert L. *The Future as History*. New York: Harper & Row, 1960. This is not a systematic history of the future. The author merely tries to reconcile Americans to a few major but unpopular social trends, such as the growth of bureaucracy, government control, and socialism, especially in undeveloped states.

———. *The Limits of American Capitalism*. New York: Harper & Row, 1966. A study of how capitalism is changing and will change during the next 100 years. Emphasizes rising numbers and influence of new non-business elites. Predicts that growth of science and rational attitudes will result in radical but peaceful change in U.S. social system.

Kerr, C., J. T. Dunlop, F. H. Harbison, and C. A. Meyers. *Industrialism and Industrial Man*. Cambridge, Mass.: Harvard University Press, 1960. Four labor economists predict universal industrialization and cultural homogenization of mankind.

*Lundberg, Ferdinand. *The Coming World Transformation*. New York: Doubleday, 1963. A sociologist predicts a wide variety of social trends during next 150 years. This is the only such book by a contemporary social scientist.

Manuel, Frank E. *The Prophets of Paris*. Cambridge, Mass.: Harvard University Press, 1962. An excellent review of the brilliant predictions made by Turgot, Condorcet, Saint-Simon, Fourier, and Comte.

Mercier, Louis Sebastian. *L'An 2440*. Paris, 1771. This pioneer science-fiction author suggested inextinguishable lamps, motion pictures, and worship of science.

Michael, Donald L. *The Next Generation*. New York: Vintage Books, 1965. This is based on a report to the U.S. government on those predictable 1964-84 trends most likely to affect youth-development programs. It predicts economic, technological, sexual, family, educational, and other trends.

*Ogburn, William F. *Social Change.* New York: Viking, 1922, 1950. A classic work by a sociologist on the causes and process of social change.

Platt, John R. *The Step to Man.* New York: Wiley, 1966. A biophysicist predicts a notable increase in human intelligence and a world without wars, poverty, overcrowding, and disease.

*Schumpeter, J. A. *Capitalism, Socialism, and Democracy.* New York: Harper & Brothers, 1942. An able conservative Austrian economist regretfully predicts the continued rise of democratic socialism in advanced nations.

Seidenberg, Roderick. *Anatomy of the Future.* Chapel Hill, N.C.: University of North Carolina Press, 1961. This is another lament that society is being ever more rationally organized and managed. The author deplores the apparently inevitable victory of "triumphant rationalism" and calls for a return to an emotional, intuitive, spiritual life.

*Skinner, B. F. *Walden II.* New York: Macmillan, 1948. A stimulating recent utopia by a famous Harvard psychologist.

Sorokin, Pitirim A. *The Basic Trends of Our Times.* New Haven, Conn.: College and University Press, 1964. Another lament! The three basic trends are a shift of creative leadership from the West to Asia and Africa, disintegration of materialistic cultures, and the rise of an "integral" religious culture. This contradicts Ellul and Seidenberg.

Teilhard de Chardin, P. *The Future of Man.* New York: Harper & Row, 1965. A Jesuit biologist predicts a universal community of men without individual minds but rather "an envelope of thinking substance." He foresees "the collectivization of mankind."

Wagar, W. W. *The City of Man.* New York: Houghton, Mifflin, 1963. A review of "prophecies of a world civilization" by Wells, Spengler, Toynbee, the Huxleys, and others.

*Wells, H. G. *A Modern Utopia.* London, 1905. Predicts a global community, rationally organized, without war, poverty, and disease.

——. *The Shape of Things to Come.* London, 1935. Pessimistic science fiction foretelling totalitarian dictatorship, constant warfare, and economic decline.

*Young, Michael. *The Rise of the Meritocracy, 1870–2033.* London: Thames & Hudson, 1958. Able explanation of a major social trend he dislikes.

Books on Technological Progress

Adabashev, Igor. *Global Engineering.* Not read.

Barach, Arnold A., and the Kiplinger Washington editors. *1975 and the Changes to Come.* New York: Harper & Row, 1962. This book emphasizes "physical and material," not social, trends, and offers possibilities, not predictions. "No man is wise enough to foresee accurately . . . great social changes" (p. vii). Use of the term *accurately* begs the question, but the authors apparently feel the same about useful prediction of social change.

*Brown, Harrison. *The Challenge of Man's Future.* New York: Viking, 1954. An excellent study of possible future shortages of food and raw materials and possible techniques for overcoming them.

Clarke, Arthur C. *Profiles of the Future.* New York: Harper & Row, 1962. A brief, readable, and visionary forecast of technological advances, with emphasis on the conquest of space, by a popular science-fiction writer.

Gordon. T. J. *The Future.* New York: St. Martin's Press, 1965. A rocket engineer features predictions about space exploits and other technological advances. He also discusses solutions to the problems of nuclear war, automation, and population growth. His book is based on a Rand Corporation questionnaire survey of the opinions of 150 experts.

Gouschev, S., and M. Vassiliev, eds. *Russian Science in the 21st Century.* New York: McGraw-Hill, 1960. Two Russian journalists interviewed 27 eminent Soviet scientists and engineers on technological trends in a wide variety of fields during years 1957-2007. Stimulating but superficial and overoptimistic.

*Jarrett, Henry, ed. *Science and Resources: Prospects and Implications of Technological Advance.* Baltimore: Johns Hopkins Press, 1959. Eighteen brief comments by able experts on genetics, weather, mining, chemistry, nuclear energy, and space. Includes plausible argument that economic progress will not be significantly slowed by mineral shortages, because mining and processing now cost only 2 percent of world GNP, less than annual increment.

Leach, Gerald. *Science Shapes Tomorrow.* New York: Day, 1963. The scientific theory behind, as well as the future applications of, recent scientific advances in physics, chemistry, biology, etc., are well discussed, with special attention to new methods of producing power and food.

Thomson, George. *The Foreseeable Future* (rev. ed.). Cambridge University Press, 1960. Academic in style and conservative in conclusions, this brief study deals largely with energy, materials, transport, communication, weather, food, and biology.

Index